D1272711

Black Political Thought in the Making
of South African Democracy

Black Political Thought in the Making of South African Democracy

C. R. D. Halisi

INDIANA UNIVERSITY PRESS
BLOOMINGTON AND INDIANAPOLIS

FINKELSTEIN
MEMORIAL LIBRARY
SPRING VALLEY, NY

3 2191 00974 5117

This book is a publication of

Indiana University Press
601 North Morton Street
Bloomington, IN 47404-3797 USA

http //www indiana edu/~iupress

Telephone orders 800-842-6796

Fax orders 812-855-7931

Orders by e-mail iuporder@indiana edu

© 1999 by C R D Halisi

All rights reserved

No part of this book may be reproduced or utilized in any form or by any
means, electronic or mechanical, including photocopying and recording, or
by any information storage and retrieval system, without permission in writing
from the publisher The Association of American University Presses' Resolution on Permissions constitutes the only exception to this prohibition

The paper used in this publication meets the minimum requirements of
American National Standard for Information Sciences–Permanence of Paper
for Printed Library Materials, ANSI Z39 48-1984

Manufactured in the United States of America

Library of Congress Cataloging-in-Publication Data

Halisi, C R D , date
    Black political thought in the making of South African democracy /
C R D Halisi
        p   cm.
    Includes bibliographical references (p   ) and index
    ISBN 0-253-33589-2
    1 South Africa—Politics and government—20th century 2 Blacks—
Race identity 3 Blacks—Intellectual life 4 Nationalism—South Africa—
History—20th century 5 South Africa—History—Autonomy and inde-
pendence movements 6 South Africa—Race relations I Title
DT1928 H35   1999
320 54'089'96—dc21   99-38817

1   2   3   4   5   04   03   02   01   00   99

To my mother, the memory of my father, my children, grandchildren, and extended family, and to three Africanists who helped me to better appreciate the continent–Bert Hammond, Richard Sklar, and Sam Nolutshungu

CONTENTS

Foreword

In July 1976, scarcely more than a month after the deadly suppression of protests by black secondary school students in the township of Soweto, C. R. D. Halisi arrived in South Africa to begin his study of black political thought under the auspices of the Social Science Research Council of the United States. He became a resident of Soweto and experienced the daily life of a black person in an urban area of the apartheid state. During the course of his year-long research, he traveled widely within the country and met many influential resisters, among them the venerated Robert Sobukwe, in the twilight of his life, and the late Steve Biko, a kindred spirit, whose legacy will be enhanced by the publication of this book.

African resistance to white rule in South Africa is centuries old. On both sides, political thinkers have been compelled to choose between the values of interracial cooperation and racial domination. As a result of the Anglo-Boer War of 1899–1902, Great Britain unified several territories into a single state under white rule. The subject races—indigenous Africans, Indians, and Coloreds (persons of mixed racial descent)—could choose between two alternative pathways to freedom. On the one hand, they could seek to attain full democratic rights within a multiracial polity in association with those members of the white ruling minority who would be willing to support the democratic cause as a matter of principle. On the other hand, indigenous African people, constituting a vast majority of the oppressed racial groups, could aim to recover their ancestral land and then determine the extent to which legal rights would be vouchsafed to the descendants of non-African conquerors and settlers. These opposing choices demarcated the main dividing line between rival black thinkers and their political organizations throughout the twentieth century.

Ever since its founding in 1912, the African National Congress has been dedicated to the ideal of racial equality. The present-day rendition of that principle as nonracial democracy signifies a political order based on equal rights for all citizens regardless of their racial origins. However, there has always been an underlying cross-current of black nationalist thought based on a medley of related sentiments, including racial grievances, traditional political values, and patrimonial claims to land. During the late 1960s and early 1970s, while both the African National Congress and its racially separatist rival, the Pan-Africanist Congress, were outlawed and effectively suppressed within the country, Biko and his associates resuscitated racial nationalism in a new form, which they called "black consciousness." Meant to embrace the aspirations of all nonwhites, black consciousness captured the imagination of many youths, who were aware of black power and "new left" political movements in other countries but deprived of normal relationships with the outside world by severe restrictions on their freedom of movement and political activities, including speech. Eventually, black consciousness organizations, which had sprung into being spontaneously, in all walks of life—political, economic, social, artistic, and professional—were outlawed by the regime. Thereafter, the initiative for resumption of the internal struggle against apartheid was assumed by leaders of mass organizations affiliated, for the most part, with the African National Congress, which had an unrivaled capacity to generate multiple pressures, including military operations, for democratic change. Thus did the ANC's principle of nonracial democracy prevail as the predominant political ethos of the new South Africa. Yet racial nationalism, and certain forms of ethnic nationalism, white as well as black, persist as powerful undercurrents of South African political thought.

The philosophy of black racial nationalism was promoted during the early to mid-twentieth century by various pioneers of Pan-African thought, among them Edward Wilmot Blyden and Joseph E. Casely-Hayford in West Africa, John L. Dube in South Africa, and the Jamaican, Marcus Garvey, whose followers were influential throughout Africa. Its popular appeal is undeniable. Still, the goal of black empowerment implies success in business enterprise, which is inseparable from forms of social elitism and class privilege. Therefore, ideologies of racial nationalism have always combined the contradictory tendencies of popular power and oligarchic power. In South Africa, as elsewhere, demands for racial justice have been utilized by populists to challenge liberal justifications for property rights and by elitists to justify black empowerment regardless of the degree to which power may be concentrated in the hands of a few. As Halisi shows, however, racial nationalists in South Africa have been highly susceptible to the appeal of nonracial arguments: Thus racial populists appreciate the virtues of nonracial social democracy while their elitist counterparts value the limitations on popular power which characterize constitutional forms of government. In practice, therefore, the difference between "black republican" thought and the philosophy of "multiracial union," as these opposing viewpoints are explained by Halisi, is one of degree and disposition rather than life and death in the arena of politics.

In this work, the concept "republican," derived from recent contributions to the theory of citizenship, is used to clarify the challenge posed by racial nationalism, both black and white, to the political stability of multiracial South Africa. The concept of racial republicanism connotes a form of collective political identity, a sense of peoplehood, based on racial sentiments that are difficult to reconcile with the precepts of South Africa's nonracial constitution. However, republicanism, unlike nationalism, is an idea about the form and nature of government rather than the liberation of a people from alien rule or the exercise of national power. Properly understood, the ideals of racial republican movements in South Africa might be harnessed by prudent national leaders to reinforce the principle of racial equality upon which the post-apartheid political order is founded. Halisi's analysis of black republican thought may prove to have profoundly practical implications.

To be sure, the widespread dissemination of republican thought, black and white, implies ambivalence in the minds of a majority of South Africans about the legitimacy of their country's nonracial constitution. Since the South African polity has a dual (liberal and republican) intellectual origin, many citizens experience a sense of reluctance to share a single national identity with all of those who are defined by law to be their compatriots. This problem can be explained and surmounted, but it cannot be evaded by those who aspire to build a stable democracy in South Africa.

RICHARD L. SKLAR

Acknowledgments

The publication of this book provides me with an opportunity to acknowledge the individuals, organizations, and foundations that have made possible my more than two decades of scholarly involvement with South African society. Richard L. Sklar must be credited with pointing me in the direction of South African studies. His excellent graduate seminar on South Africa at UCLA was my first experience with the academic literature on the subject. Although I came to graduate school in the early 1970s from a black movement background and with an interest in studying theories of race, class, and revolution, Dick Sklar asked me a question that led me to South Africa. He inquired as to why I "wanted to study *theories* of race, class, and revolution when there was a struggle going on in South Africa that involved these very social forces?" Dick and his wife Eve never lost faith in me or this project—whether as field research, dissertation, or manuscript—and proved an inexhaustible source of inspiration, encouragement, and editorial advice. Although he does not particularly care for the term, one could not hope for a better academic mentor or a more supportive friend than Dick Sklar. I would also like to thank my good friend Gerald Bender and his wife Tammy, whose generosity and support took countless forms and, like that of the Sklars, covered the entire period from field research to publication. Jerry is the most proactive friend imaginable and was always prepared to join with me to directly confront any obstacle that hindered my career or personal development. Moreover, Jerry was gracious enough to lend his considerable computer and photographic expertise to our collaborative design of the book's cover.

Support from the Social Science Research Council: Foreign Area Fellowship for Africa and the Near East allowed me to live in Southern Africa during the watershed years of 1976–78. In preparation for field research or making sense of what I experienced upon my return, several individuals were especially helpful. These include Leo Kuper, Thomas Karis, Thami Mhlambiso, Nana Mahomo, Mazizi Kunene, Tim Ngubane, Ann Bernstein, Madodu Hlatshwayu, Gloria Waite, Ntongela Masilela, Peg Nixon, Leta Mbula, Caiphus Semanya, David Sibeko, Hans Ries, and Bobby Hill.

I would like especially to thank Gail Palma, who worked for the Social Science Research Council, for her assistance while I was in New York making arrangements to depart for the field. Several years later, Gail moved to Los Angeles, where she again assisted me with the preparation of my manuscript for publication. My good friend and comrade, the late Paul Nakawa, made his home in East Orange, New Jersey, available to me the entire time that I was in New York making final preparations.

Sam Nolutshungu, whom I met in Los Angeles when I returned to the United States, had a tremendous impact on my understanding of the Black Consciousness Movement. Sam's wisdom and insight on matters pertaining to South Africa has greatly influenced my thinking and, owing to his untimely death, he will be sorely missed. Along with Richard Sklar and Bert Hammond, I have dedicated this book to Sam.

Before arriving in Johannesburg, I spent several months in Dar es Salaam, Tanzania, talking with South Africans forced into exile and scholars at the university. After leaving Tanzania, I spent brief periods in Botswana and Zambia. In the course of my travels in these four African countries, I incurred debts of kindness and hospitality that I will never be able to fully repay. I am especially indebted to Hasan and Santar Jambo, Fred Umoja, Babatunde and Akiba Folayemi, Sandra Nelson, Kaijuka, Pat Miller, Alwiya and Ahmed Heshim, Kleist Sykes, and Sensei Bomani for their generous assistance. In his/her own way, each of these kind souls helped to make my stay in Tanzania enjoyable and comfortable. In addition, several other individuals shared their time and insights with me. These include Willie Kgositsile, Karrim Essack, Nathan Shamuyarira, Esi Bullocks, Geri Stark, Sandra Hill, Janki Tschanneil, Nathaniel Honono, Wycliffe Tsotsi, Elias Ntloedibe, and Pearce Gqobose. I also had the good fortune to spend time in Zambia talking with I. B. Tabata and Janub Gool. Through conversations with South Africans forced into exile, I gained a greater appreciation of the theoretical contributions of the smaller Non-European Unity Movement, as well as a deeper understanding of the better-known African National Congress and Pan Africanist Congress.

During a short stay in Botswana before I entered South Africa, Gail and John Gerhart were kind enough to let me stay at their home for several days. Gail was most generous with her counsel and source materials on black movements in South Africa. In addition, Harry Nengwekhulu, Sipho Buthelezi, and Joe Matthews and his family all proved to be wonderful hosts and priceless sources of insight into the complex situation that I was on my way to research.

I entered South Africa on August 24, 1976, the day of a massive worker stayaway, and departed more than a year later. During the course of my stay in that country, I was the beneficiary of so much support from such a wide array of individuals that it is not possible to acknowledge all those who reached out. However, the kindness and concern of all who befriended me contributed to my overwhelmingly positive experience at a time when the nation was poised for a decade of worsening civil war. While I will surely forget to mention some individuals who were helpful to me, these acknowledgments are intended to convey my admiration for the strength, dignity, humanity, and generosity of spirit with which black South Africans negotiated the massive violation of their civil and human rights by the apartheid state. Post-apartheid generations will have to strive mightily to match this standard of civic virtue and collective sacrifice. In this respect, my field experience and subsequent visits to South Africa have made clear to me that the qualities the world has come to so admire in Nelson Mandela reflect traits common to black South Africans as a whole.

I would like to thank Alosi Moloi—a friend from UCLA who returned home several months before I arrived—for allowing me to stay with him and his mother in Mofolo township until I secured accommodations at Glyn Thomas House on the premises of Soweto's Baragwanath Hospital complex. Glyn Thomas House served as a segregated dormitory for approximately thirty-five black (African, Indian, and Coloured) students attending the University of the Witwatersrand with so-called ministerial consent. Because of apartheid restrictions, these students were not allowed to reside on the Wits campus. While at Glyn Thomas House, I developed many friendships and acquaintances, including Peter Mabe, Marcia Thloane, Snowey Msengane, Martin Sebesho, Mduduzi Kunene, Ratha Mokgoatlheng, Rubin "the Cook" Mosela, the Jadwat family, and G. K. Enkara. All of them in some way taught me something unique about South Africa.

As I came to better know Soweto, I developed friends in the

various townships. "My main man," Don Mphahlele, was instrumental in introducing me to many aspects of township life in Alexander as well as Soweto. Through him I met other friends, including Steve Marite, Farouk "Boy" Meta, Fanny Maringa, Given Sabelo, and many others. Moreover, I quickly learned to appreciate the social and political role of shebeens and clubs like the Pelican in Soweto. In addition to the fun they provide, shebeens allowed me to hear and have frank discussions with a cross-section of people with whom I might not otherwise have had the opportunity to interact. Don and I also spent time in Swaziland, Lesotho, and he was kind enough to drive me to Botswana at the end of my stay in South Africa.

Although I traveled around the country, my base was Soweto-Johannesburg, where I developed many lasting friendships and contacts. Allie Dubb, who was then Acting Director of the African Studies Institute at the University of the Witwatersrand, allowed me access to many of the institute's resources. In addition, several people associated with the University of the Witwatersrand were especially helpful. Most notably, Phil and Chris Bonner, who became my close friends, were always a source of assistance and insight. Through them I met several important academics and trade unionists, which allowed me to gain an appreciation of the black trade union movement, then in its embryonic stages. Through either the Bonners, Wits, or the South African Institute of Race Relations, I was exposed to a number of scholars and experts. These include Tim Couzens, John Kane-Berman, Belinda Bozzoli, Charles van Onselen, Eddie Webster, Morris Kagan, Peter Delius, Taffy Adler, Jon Lewis, Patrick Laurence, Jean Marquard, Phyllis Lewsen, John Barratt, Fanny Klenerman, Bruce Murray, Ellen Hellmann, Francine Godfrey, and Steven Friedman.

On one or more occasions, the following individuals, primarily in Soweto, shared their time with me. Therefore, I would like to thank Drake Koka, Kenneth Rachidi, Shimani Kumalo, Madikolo Motumi (and other members of the Johannesburg Black Social Workers Association), Mandla and Nomsisi Kuzwayo, Emma and Tom Mashinini, Nthato Motlana, Dumasini Kumalo, Christopher Mageza, the late Aubrey Mageza and his wife Molly, Joyce Poo and her friend Zora, Gibson Thula, Quedusizi Buthelezi, Tanjiwe Mtintso, Sam Motsuenyane, Leonard Mosala, Lucy Mbuvelo, Force Khashane, and Don Mattera.

Through a common friend at Glyn Thomas, I was fortunate

enough to meet Maya Koboka, who agreed to accompany me on a drive to Natal and the Cape and to introduce me to some of the black activists she knew. Through her contacts Maya was, either directly or indirectly, responsible for my having the opportunity to meet Steve Biko, Barney Pityana, Robert Sobukwe, Mamphela Ramphele, Father Patrick Mkhatshwa, and Peter Jones. For example, in Kimberly, Daniel "School Boy" Sekgoro, one of Maya's friends, arranged for me to spend an unforgettable afternoon with Robert Sobukwe. After leaving Kimberley in early May of 1977, I spent a few days in Durban, where I had a memorable evening of discussion with Fatima and Shehnaz Meer. From there I drove to King Williams Town, where I spent a weekend with Steve Biko and some of his associates at Zanemphilo Community Health Centre. It turned out to be an extraordinary weekend for several reasons. This stimulating encounter with Biko took place only four months before his brutal murder by South African police. Not only did I meet Steve and Mamphela, but their son Hlumelo and my daughter with Maya, Luyanda, were born on the same day nine months later.

After leaving King Williams Town, I stopped in Port Elizabeth, where I was able to spend time talking with Barney Pityana, who, like Steve and Mamphela, was under a government banning order. Shortly after I met with him, Barney went into exile, later emerging as head of the World Council of Churches' Committee to Combat Racism. In 1990, Barney was kind enough to include me in a major conference on the legacy of Steve Biko and Black Consciousness held in Harare, Zimbabwe.

In the Capetown area, I had very useful conversations with Francis Wilson of Capetown University, R. E. Van der Ross of the University of the Western Cape, Sonny Leon of the Labour Party, and John Gomas, a former member of the South African Communist Party. Howard Lawerence was kind enough to help me arrange the latter two meetings. On a separate trip to the Transkei, Professor Mlahleni Njisani, whom I knew for many years in California, was especially hospitable.

Upon my return to the United States, I lived for a few years in Los Angeles and then took a faculty position at Indiana University. Since I did not return to South Africa for more than a decade, Indiana University proved to be a Mecca of contact with South Africa and South Africans. Patrick O'Meara, who was then Director of African Studies, hailed from South Africa, and he, along with Brian Winchester, the Assistant Director, were, like me, committed students of Southern African politics. I would like to thank Patrick for his unceasing support of my research as well as my overall career. As a result of his efforts and those of many others, IU proved to be a fertile place to continue my work on South Africa. Before she left IU for the University of Florida, Gwendolen Carter was, likewise, supportive of my research; she invited me to Gainesville for one of the lecture series established by the university in her name.

Fortunately for me, Indiana University had a number of exchange programs that brought several South Africans to the campus. Therefore, over the years, I was able to develop a large circle of friends who were either from South Africa or concerned with the abolition of apartheid. This allowed me to remain involved with South African affairs, and after 1988, with the help of various grants from International Programs, I began to travel to South Africa on a regular basis. Many of the South Africans who studied at IU or who visited the campus became an important network of friends and contacts inside the country.

I would like to thank Seboko (Oupa), Barbara, Nkidi, Katlego, and Lesedi Monamodi, who were like my family away from home. My discussions with Oupa about various aspects of South African politics were an important part of my life in Bloomington for more than a decade and were always informative and enjoyable, if occasionally heated. Although Oupa did not return home for many years, Muntu, William, and Mimi, his mother, father, and sister, as well as several of his close friends, especially Sydney Machele and Lakzin Legwale, were always gracious hosts whenever I visited South Africa.

During his studies at IU, Christopher Thomas, another close friend, was a major resource on new scholarship on South Africa and was the first person to call my attention to the writings of Bennie Kies. After he returned to South Africa, Chris, who teaches at the University of South Africa, allowed me to stay with him on several trips to Johannesburg. I would also like to thank Rehebohile Moletsane of the University of Natal for her generous and steadfast assistance and important insights on black education during the period when she was completing her Ph.D. in education at IU.

Helen Suzman, who was a frequent visitor to IU, became a good friend. Helen always went out of her way to make sure that, when I was in South Africa, I met interesting people and attended events that enhanced my understanding of changes taking place in the country.

While I will not be able to recall everyone, I would like to acknowledge some of the South Africans (and a few non–South Africans who were, nonetheless, deeply involved with South African affairs) who shared their time and insights while they were either students or visitors at IU. These include Maria Ntsala, Nono Maja, Anne Mouton (and their colleague Eric), Ahmed Essop, Xoliswa Mantanzima, Gibson Sirayi, Neville Alexander, Bernadette Hadden, Allim Milazi, Faud Kassim, Tom Lodge, Wilmot James, John Samuel, Ashly Ward, Johnny Mekoa, Phirosaw Camay, Lyban Mabasa, Allister Sparks, Erla Heyns, Angela Impey, Suren Moodliar, James Thindwa, Bongi Busika, Tendai Manzvanzvike, Bill Nasson, Peter Walshe, Poobie Naicker, E. C. Zingu, William Shisana, Dumsini Kumalo, Randall Robinson, Mala Singh, Bobby Mouane, Anil Sookdeao, Goloom Vahed, Vuyo Wagi, Dudu Maseko, and a number of informative visitors from the South African Committee on Higher Education.

At IU, several staff members helped me to produce the final draft of my thesis and/or assisted me with early versions of book chapters. I would like to thank Barbara Hopkins, who typed my thesis and later helped with the manuscript. Patricia Withered helped me transfer my chapters from the Political Science Department's old mainframe to my first personal computer. Nancy Lorey's assistance with the bibliography of my thesis proved invaluable. I would also like to thank Jude Wilkerson and Sue Hanson for their constant help with the little emergencies that often cropped up in the course of my working on various phases of this project. Nancy Schmidt, the Africana Librarian at IU, was a blessing for anyone conducting research on Africa. Largely through her efforts, IU's holdings on South Africa, and Africa, were superb. Nancy went out of her way to acquire materials that I needed for my research, and her knowledge of sources of information on African subject matter was truly humbling.

Freddie Diamant, Bernard Morris, Charles Bird, Bonnie Kendall, Drew Smith, Jack Bloom, and Gail Rosecrance commented on all or parts of this manuscript. Avi Davidi, a graduate student at USC, helped with the bibliography accompanying this book. After moving to Bloomington, I stayed in contact with Wendy Sarvasy, a friend from graduate school, who constantly encouraged me to think about my work on South Africa in light of citizenship theory. In addition, Wendy gave my dissertation an intensely critical reading that was helpful in the transition from thesis to book. Russell Hanson and Kevin Middlebrook provided me with helpful advice and insights at different stages in my writing, and their support is especially appreciated. I would like to acknowledge several other IU colleagues who were important to the intellectual environment that helped to make this book possible—the late J. Gus Liebenow, Richard Stryker, Jeff Isaac, Jean Robinson, Jack Bielasiak, Norm Furniss, Tim Tilton, and Takyiwaa Manuh. In addition, the students in my graduate seminars on South Africa at IU were important sounding boards for my ideas and often taught me as much or more than they learned.

In addition to the Social Science Research Council, several foundations, programs, libraries, and individuals associated with these organizations helped to fund this research, allowed me time away from teaching to write, or assisted with publication. Therefore, I would like to thank Hazel Love and UCLA's Graduate Advancement Program, the Stern Memorial Fellowship sponsored by the Political Science Department at UCLA, the International Division of the Ford Foundation, Henry Remak and IU's Institute of Advanced Studies, Leonard Thompson and the Southern African Research Program at Yale University, the World Council of Churches, the National Fellowship Council, Karen Fung of the Hoover Institution Library, Sylvester Whitaker, Mike Preston and Clare Walker of USC's Center for Multiethnic and Transnational Studies, Barney Pityana and the World Council of Churches, the World University Service, IU's President's Council on International Programs, as well as John Gallman of Indiana University Press.

I have been blessed with a family and several close friends who supported my work. My four children—Taifa, Libalele, Osiris, and Luyanda—are all, in one way or another, victims of this book, and I thank them for their continuous patience and support. Likewise, my mother, Gladys Daniels-Wilson, my oldest brother and his wife, Frederick Daniels, Jr. and Cecile, and my other older brother, Reginald Daniels-Endesha, have supported my efforts in numerous ways.

Since I returned to Los Angeles over four years ago, several close friends have been particularly helpful. Just as my nephew Askari Daniels-Endesha helped me drive to Bloomington, my friend Gilbert Blades helped me to drive back to the Los Angeles area. Debra Jackson, my oldest daughter's best friend, assisted me in the reorganization of my books and research materials, and was a constant source of support and encouragement. Tamanika Ivie gave me invaluable computer support when I was in the process of completing the final chapters of this book. Moreover, she, Philip Warlick, Peter Nkwe, and Courtney Hunter read over (or listened to me read and reread) these chapters on what must have seemed like hundreds of occasions.

Finally, the individuals I have acknowledged are in no way responsible for what is contained in this book. For that, I accept full responsibility.

Black Political Thought in the Making
of South African Democracy

1. ❀ Nationality and Race

In colonial Africa, racial nationalism was transformed into a multitude of territorial nationalisms by the boundaries of colonial governments. In South Africa, however, racial nationalism persisted as a potent political force throughout the colonial, postcolonial, and apartheid eras of racial domination. Although racial nationalism has been eclipsed in post-apartheid South Africa by liberalism, favored by the ruling African National Congress (ANC), realists continue to reckon with its continuing popular appeal. This study examines the imprint of black racial nationalism on political thought in South Africa with particular reference to rival conceptions of citizenship.

Recent analyses of citizenship have distinguished between liberal and republican traditions of thought.[1] The liberal tradition is individualistic and libertarian; the republican prototype is communitarian and popular. In this study, devoted to black political thought, the two traditions shall be denominated multiracial unionism and black republicanism respectively. The former signifies the quest for a single national identity in a multiracial state: the latter connotes racial exclusivity. Thinkers associated with each of these perspectives have made seminal contributions to the emergence of a broadly based democratic movement in South Africa, one that encompasses the working poor as well as the politically active intelligentsia.

Forged in the crucible of racial oppression, black political thought fluctuates incessantly between the values of racial autonomy and interracial social incorporation. Consequently, the pairing of black republican identity and multiracial union has become a core antinomy of political thought for black South Africans. Translated into race relations, the multiracial unionist conception of citizenship fosters racial integration and equality before the law, while black republican thought promotes community-based political consciousness. All too often, however, commentators treat these abstract ideas as if they were social facts. Conventionally, they suggest that multiracialists have risen above racial consciousness while black republicans have succumbed to reverse racism. The present writer is wary of that pitfall and shall not champion either position against the other.

In this work, the familiar distinction between liberal and republican citizenship will be applied to black South African political thought in two innovative ways. First, I will examine the use of Western political concepts—specifically, democracy, liberalism, socialism, and populism—by black political thinkers who have grappled with the problems of prospective citizenship in a multiracial state. Second, I will attempt to elucidate the interdependence of racially conscious and nonracial discourse in the political thought of black South Africans.

DUAL CITIZENSHIP

The concept of citizenship is basic to social organization because it identifies "those who are and who are not members of a common society." It is a moral, as well as a legal concept, properly understood as being "part of an educational program and of an inspiring moral tradition in which each generation acknowledges a connection to all others and a responsibility to them all for maintenance of the community and the traditions."[2] The very word "citizen" denotes an identity that "traces the development of the 'self' in relationship to the state as a critical part of citizenship, especially the development of self- or community-oriented attitudes and behaviors."[3]

With respect to relations of power, citizenship is an idea about government, specifically participation in the highest, or sovereign, authority. Originally, modern citizenship was synonymous with exclusivity and oligarchy. By the mid-nineteenth century, however, it had become the foundation for civil, political, and social rights which tend to undermine oligarchic privilege. While T. H. Marshall is often credited with having developed the first sociological theory of citizenship, the Tocqueville/Durkheimian approach to civic culture and the Gramsci/Marxist theory of civil society have also contributed to our understanding of the political implications of citizenship.[4] A central concern of any general theory of citizenship would have to be the relationship between rights and obligations.

In a seminal essay on citizenship, conceived as an ideology of state legitimation in Africa, Peter Ekeh astutely recognized that colonial rule had bisected attitudes of Africans toward their rights and obligations.[5] Colonialism and segregation had created a sense of "dual citizenship," with the result that ordinary people felt little, if any, moral attachment to the legal order while they continued to respect the norms of traditional society. Although the term "dual citizenship" usually refers to a legal status involving two or more nations, the concept has also been applied to other nonlegal circumstances thus: (1) situations where participation within a single nation-state is characterized by systematic exclusion of certain persons from the community; (2) situations involving membership in ancestral or primordial communities which make up a modern state.

The first of these instances corresponds to the kind of segregation experienced by blacks in the American South and apartheid South Africa. The second, as Ekeh and others have perceived, is the normal condition in the vast majority of African countries. In any given country, the nature of dual citizenship, as a moral concept, depends upon its distinctive mix of liberal (individualistic) and republican (exclusivist) traditions of citizenship. With respect to sub-Saharan Africa, the duality of the liberal-republican tension has been distinctively formulated as dual publics (Ekeh), dual authority (C. S. Whitaker; Sklar), dual citizenship (Halisi; Ndegwa), and the bifurcated state (Mamdani).[6]

Its history of racial domination and the related exploitation of the black majority have shaped South African thought on the question of citizenship. In this work, the term "racial proletarianization" refers to the impact of racial domination on the black working class.[7] By defining a field of events within the boundary categories of race and class, racial proletarianization will serve as a conceptual background for delineation of themes in black political thought, particularly race consciousness, citizenship, and populism. I will argue that the triangulation of these three concepts is an especially fertile arena of social thought in post-apartheid South Africa. Indeed, the concluding chapter of this book will discuss dual citizenship and populism in the New South Africa.

In South Africa, as in the United States, racial stratification influenced the gestation of the working class. Among black South Africans race is mediated, to some extent, by ethnicity. In contrast, among African-Americans, slaves of diverse ethnic backgrounds were forced into a single racial identity. In both societies, free and forced labor coexisted, primarily defined by the relation of race and rights. As Sam C. Nolutshungu makes evident with reference to South Africa, race functioned as a social marker that helped the state to define the boundaries of citizenship.

> The ideological category of "race" has been the primary line of political differentiation: indicating whose consent or acquiescence is to be sought and who is to be primarily coerced. Race performed

a double function—legitimation, and of providing a practical principle of political organization. . . . The first and most evident effect
of racializing politics has been to create a winning combination of
coercion and consent, a distinctive technology of domination suited
to the heritage of colonialism and its continuing economic processes (i.e., forcible proletarianization and territorial dispossession,
and the collective anxieties and hostilities integral to conquest).[8]

Segregation made racial identity central to the struggle for democratic citizenship. In turn, racialized citizenship meant that black civic
and national identities were given their most meaningful expressions
in the drive for liberation, viewed either as black majority rule or
African statehood. Although "liberation" was the primary aspiration
of most black South Africans, the attainment of citizenship rights, a
demand which often seemed far too moderate, was central to democratic transformation. In a very fundamental sense, the struggle for
liberation required black activists to confront nascent questions of
citizenship and national identity—how the "people" are to be defined,
who belongs to the political community, and what are the criteria of
inclusion and exclusion. In brief, differences between multiracialists
and black nationalists over the social character of the liberation
struggle were often predicated on rival conceptions of citizenship.
Ideological debates within the movement over black republican identity or multiracial union as strategies of struggle accentuated race or
class perspectives in ways that revealed support for either of the two
competing approaches to political community and, therefore, coali-
tion-building, in black South African liberation thought. For the most
part, liberal and Marxist scholars, despite their substantive disagreements, have advocated multiracial union defined as the call for class
alliances across the racial divide. In opposition to that viewpoint,
proponents of black republican identity have insisted that class alliances be exclusive to African or black (including Indian and mixed-
race Coloured) South Africans.[9]

Polarities such as black republican identity and multiracial union
have influenced the meaning of citizenship and political participation in various racially stratified societies. Everywhere segregation
produced a system of ascriptive citizenship, often a kind of white
republicanism, to which blacks responded with their own racially
embedded civic ideals. For that reason, designations such as "race-
man" or "racewoman" (a man or woman primarily devoted to the
moral, political, and social uplift of the black race) are comprehen-

sible as expressions of civic republicanism.[10] Racial nationalism, like other forms of nationalism, usually expresses a deeper sense of people- or nation-hood whose emotional content is inspired by an imagined community—a black community conceived either, or at times both, in national and pan-national terms.

Historical accounts of segregation in South Africa and the United States have tended to stress the violent curtailment of rights and the role of that process in class exploitation. However, few studies theorize the interaction of black republican identity and multiracial union as citizenship-inspired responses to segregation. In a recent comparison of ideologies of black liberation in South Africa and the United States, George Fredrickson provides an intellectual history that explores the theoretical interaction of black republicanism and multiracial liberalism. Fredrickson's characterization of the relationship between these two perspectives is cogent:

> [T]he emphasis on race pride that often accompanied universalistic demands for individual equality and assimilation, as well as the recurring endorsement of separate action and group solidarity as a means to the attainment of equality and political incorporation, reveal the persistent tension between cosmopolitan, genuinely color-blind perspectives and those which viewed blackness as existentially inescapable and culturally invigorating. It was not so much a matter of choosing between integrationist cosmopolitanism and racially pluralistic ethnocentrism as a basis of political action, as finding a way to reconcile them so that blacks could find fulfillment in two ways at once—as the generic human beings of liberal theory and as a special people whose unique historical experience could be represented or symbolized by reference to color.[11]

With respect to the African-American context, W. E. B. DuBois's *Souls of Black Folk* remains the classic statement on double consciousness (regarding his identity as an American and a Negro) produced by bifurcated citizenship in a racially stratified society.[12] The power of DuBois's portrayal of double consciousness comes from his refusal to reject either the black republican or multiracial sides of his political self, a stance that brought him into conflict with the most influential black republican thinkers of his day. During his early political career, DuBois confronted both the conservative black republicanism of Booker T. Washington and the radical, populist black nationalism of Marcus Garvey. With the coming of the African-American civil rights struggle, the race-conscious–nonracial polarity was personified by the lives of Martin Luther King and Malcolm X. As the most articulate spokesmen for multiracial union and black republican identity, both came to realize the degree to which their respective positions were intertwined. Malcolm X claimed that he often (purposely) took hypernationalistic stands in order to encourage political concessions by the white establishment to King and other integrationists. On the other hand, King warned Americans of the threat black power posed to multiracial unity should white hostility to racial equality persist.[13]

In South Africa, similar tensions exist between multiracial unionists and black republicans; the problem surfaced dramatically in 1959, when the Pan Africanist Congress (PAC), a black nationalist movement, broke with the African National Congress (ANC). Ever since, the ANC-PAC split has complicated the relationship between multiracial union and black republican identity, with each faction accusing the other of heresy. If any one black republican ever approximated the stature of Nelson Mandela, that person was his former ANC Youth League (ANCYL or Youth League) colleague, the late Robert Sobukwe (1924–1978) of the PAC. In 1977, this writer spent a few hours with Sobukwe at his home in Kimberley, where he lived out the last days of his life under government restriction. In a quiet yet powerful voice, he spoke about the ways his political outlook had changed over the years, especially his earlier anti-Indian sentiments. Sobukwe confessed that, as an exile movement, the PAC had proven no match for the ANC and its allies. He, nonetheless, held firm to the belief that the nationalist consciousness of the African people, better represented by the PAC than the ANC, would triumph if a plebiscite were held on the meaning and direction of the liberation struggle. Although Sobukwe, unlike Mandela, remained a black republican, both men's lives are powerful testaments to the complex relationship between race consciousness and nonracialism that this work seeks to convey.

As argued above, multiracial union and black republican identity reflect, for South African citizenship, a prime polarity in black political thought. In other situations affected by racial domination, this kind of polarity may be alluded to as separation-integration; race-conscious–nonracial; Afrocentrism-Eurocentrism (in Africa); and black power–civil rights (in the United States). The argument contained herein regarding black political thought rests on the following assumptions: (1) The tension between race-conscious and nonracial perspectives offers a useful theoretical vantage point from which to interpret black politics; (2) when these polarities are overlooked or minimized by analysts, an important dimension of black political thought is thereby neglected; (3) since these polarities reflect social tensions in the lives of black people, they will find expression in individual thought and action; (4) given that the tension between nonracial and race-conscious populist discourse bisects every other ideological confrontation, this polarity can be thought of as being "indigenous" to black political thought.

BLACK CONSCIOUSNESS

Soweto is the name given to the more than two dozen sprawling townships built to house Johannesburg's large black working class and its small but growing middle class. In 1976, on the evening of my first day as an independent scholar living in Soweto, I was taken to a shebeen (a home used as a speakeasy). There, an intense discussion was in progress prompted by ANC leaflets that had been distributed in the township the previous night. Some shebeen customers felt that the ANC was only trying to co-opt the mobilization achieved by the youth of the community-based Black Consciousness Movement (BCM). Others were equally adamant in their view that the ANC had legitimate pride-of-place as South Africa's senior liberation organization, and that whatever the BCM had accomplished was, at least in part, attributable to the efforts of the veteran liberation movements. What was apparent to me from this discussion, and many others to follow, was how clearly black South Africans comprehend the relationship between race-conscious and multiracial strategies of struggle. Moreover, the controversy of my first night in the shebeen was by no means an isolated incident; similar debates were more prevalent on university campuses.

The decade prior to the Soweto Rebellion of June 16, 1976, was one of political renewal culminating in the intellectual and artistic ferment associated with the BCM. It was also a time of catalytic debates over the meanings of liberation, democracy, and, by extension, citizenship. I soon came to see that among black South Africans, similar to African-Americans, there was a popular, deeply entrenched tradition of black political thought characterized by great vitality, gravity, and urgency. Specifically, I concluded that liberation ideology could assume either a multiracial or black republican form and, yet, remain within the broadly accepted boundaries of common political discourse. In the 1970s, the ANC, the PAC, and the South African Communist Party (SACP) were outlawed while groups associated with the BCM were targeted for suppression by the government. Still, advocates of multiracial union and black republican identity could be readily distinguished by the core assumptions of their political stances. Later, similar differences would impact the burgeoning trade union movement that was beginning to challenge apartheid in the workplace.

Residing, at first, with a friend in Mofolo township and, then, in a segregated student dormitory inside Baragwanath Hospital, a facility for Africans in Soweto, I pondered the relationship between academic and grassroots political discourse. Soweto and other townships were in a state of constant turmoil, as were black campuses, both university and high school. Founded in 1968 during a period when veteran liberation movements had been forced to operate in exile or underground, the BCM and its student leadership had been at the center of renewed internal opposition to apartheid for nearly a decade. However, scholars and activists sympathetic to the ANC, SACP, trade unions, or the multiracial union idea in general, frequently criticized the BCM for its elitism and weak links to the working masses.

Over the following decade, a virtually hegemonic intellectual orientation, based on the idea of class struggle, was embraced by movement activists and intellectuals, due largely to the successes of the ANC-SACP underground and the growing influence of its internal allies.[14] Within the BCM, members driven into exile after the Soweto Rebellion were largely responsible for the internal wing's sea change from an emphasis on Black Consciousness Philosophy to Marxist class analysis. As a consequence of this ideological shift, the BCM's own distinctive contributions to the revitalization of internal opposition was, for a time, overlooked or minimized by political rivals as well as many scholars. Today, however, as former members of the BCM have assumed positions of power and influence in post-apartheid South Africa, the intellectual winds have shifted in favor of a more generous interpretation of the movement's legacy. Journalists and scholars nowadays assert what once sparked controversy—that the BCM was central to the revitalization of internal protest in the 1970s.

Most of the strains between the BCM and ANC were based on political, ideological, and tactical disagreements, yet some were also clearly the result of generational differences between a new and old

left. As I will discuss in chapter 4, South Africa during the 1960s produced its own indigenous New Left. The leaderships of various South
African student groups had connections to, and attitudes reflective
of, the international New Left. Within the confines of this indigenous
New Left, black and white student activists had complex political relations. Nevertheless, New Leftists held ideas about nationalism, internationalism, race relations, and citizenship that revealed a distinct
generational identity.

During periods of intense anti-apartheid ferment, the boundary
between scholarship and politics was often blurred or entirely invis-
ible. Since many scholars were activists simultaneously participating
in struggles on black or white campuses, in trade unions, and in
community organizations, their writings and research often revealed
the growth pangs of the struggle for a democratic South Africa. From
the late 1970s through the 1980s, liberal and Marxist academics were
engaged in debates over the primacy of race or class as the core
identity of the liberation struggle. While historians and social scientists brought their respective expertise to bear on these issues, much
of the underlying passion was fueled by the realization that the directions, values, and perspectives of the liberation movement were crucial to prefiguring post-apartheid citizenship. In addition, academic
assessments of capitalism's relation to apartheid had implications
for strategies of liberal reform versus Marxist theories of revolution
which, in turn, fed into the race-class controversy within the liberation movement. Whether formulated from the vantage point of Marx-
ian revolution or social democratic citizenship, the interaction of race
and class became an issue of critical significance.

In May 1977, I had an opportunity to spend four days in King
William's Town with Steve Biko, the founder and president of the
South African Student Organization (SASO), which gave rise to the
BCM, and a few of his associates, most notably Mamphela Ramphele
who now serves as the first black vice-chancellor of the University of
Cape Town. Mamphela was only able to be with us because the South
African police had spelled her name incorrectly on the banning order
that exiled her to the small, remote town of Tzaneen. Given her usual
defiant courage coupled with her lawyer's advice to ignore the banning order until the police corrected their bureaucratic error, Mamphela opted to return to King William's Town. I vividly recall that on
this occasion a recurring topic of conversation was the virtues and
limitations of Marxism for black liberation. Steve was not convinced

of the value of Marxism and generally contested its claims and positions. Despite Steve's trepidation, an increasing number of black youths shifted to the rhetoric of revolutionary Marxism largely because of their having concluded that apartheid could only be dismantled by armed resistance. By the time this discussion was taking place, the ANC in exile was becoming the primary beneficiary of the thousands of youths flowing out of the black townships to military camps in neighboring countries.

Unlike reformist, liberal multiracialism so harshly criticized by the BCM leadership, ANC-SACP Marxism represented a brand of revolutionary socialist multiracialism that was not vulnerable to the charge of accommodating apartheid. Although intellectuals associated with the Azanian People's Organization (AZAPO) also attempted to fuse revolutionary socialism with black republican thought, the ANC and its internal allies recruited by far the largest number of BCM-oriented youth; consequently, black politics swung in a nonracial direction. When so many former black nationalists turned to Marxism, race-conscious discourse was temporarily marginalized within the liberation movement—the rhetoric of class struggle became a litmus test for what constituted progressive politics. Pressured by the constant criticism that black consciousness was little more than a contrivance of "petit bourgeois" intellectuals, organizations initially associated with the BCM, such as AZAPO, distanced themselves from a public embrace of race-conscious discourse. Indeed, AZAPO outflanked the ANC and SACP on the left by adopting an extremist rhetoric of class struggle. In any case, the history of the BCM can be divided into a Biko phase devoted to public declarations of militant race consciousness and a post-Biko phase when quasi-Marxism held sway. This writer surmised that, while militant race-conscious ideology had been suppressed, similar sentiments remained strong among, what now could be termed BCM socialists. In chapter 5, I argue that, in both its Biko and post-Biko phases, the BCM grappled with political issues in ways that recast the meaning of citizenship; these issues include: inclusiveness and community; racism and social justice; and the accountability of the black elite to its working masses.

Since both disabilities were present in their everyday lives, average black South Africans continued to display a nuanced understanding of the relationship between race and class. The reciprocal nature of race and class inequality resonated in the words of a garment worker to whom I gave a ride to work one morning from Soweto to

Johannesburg, sometime in 1976. While displaying her pay stub, she eloquently described the nature of her exploitation both as a worker and as a black person: "I produce sweaters for these whites, about 250 of them a week. I have seen these same sweaters in the store; they cost thirty-two Rand each. But when they take out of my paycheck, I am left with twenty-seven Rand, less than the cost of one sweater."[15] Without being a proponent of either Black Consciousness Philosophy or Marxism, this worker spoke directly to race-class issues as they played themselves out in her daily existence.

The powerful testimony of black workers such as this one encouraged some Marxist scholars to conclude that since there appeared to be no contradiction between race and class consciousness within genuine working-class movements, black consciousness ideology had to be of petit bourgeois origin. Although doctrines of racial resistance are an unavoidable part of the study of African social classes, advocates of Marxism and Black Consciousness have traditionally been uneasy with one another's politics. All too often, it has been assumed that race consciousness is static or retrogressive. This study suggests that, to the contrary, race consciousness is dynamic, intrinsically political, and may be fused into either a progressive or conservative perspective. For example, during the latter part of the 1960s, black consciousness intellectuals extended the term "black" to include Indians and so-called Coloured South Africans. During the 1990s, identities rooted in racial oppression receded, owing primarily to the emergence of a sense of nonracial citizenship, on the one hand, and resurgent ethnicity, on the other.

With the growth of an independent black trade union movement after 1973, the old rivalry between Marxism and nationalism was rekindled in another form. A new generation of trade unionists and their intellectual allies sought to curb the influence of populist approaches to trade unionism. Most discerned, wisely, that nationalist demands tended to conflate class and race struggles to the disadvantage of workers. In other words, the specific bread-and-butter demands of black workers were usually subsumed by the broader, nationalistic demands of the urban-based African bourgeoisie. However, race consciousness was reasserted when black nationalist–oriented trade unionists successfully opposed a strict class (or workerist) interpretation of the political obligations of black workers in the anti-apartheid struggle. Similar to the reconciliation achieved by their activist counterparts, neo-Marxist and liberal scholars arrived at a common recognition of the importance of sensitivity to both race and class as interdependent variables. They were learning to live within the conceptual purgatory of race and class interpretations of liberation politics. In post-apartheid South Africa, as an essentially, if not purely, nonracial constitutional tradition takes hold, the permutations of race consciousness and nonracialism continue to stimulate innovation in black political thought.

POPULISM

In a capitalist economy that has historically excluded and disadvantaged black South Africans, democratic citizenship alone will not automatically ensure social justice. Thus, with the rise of a more multiracial bourgeoisie, populism (class, racial, and ethnic), on one side, and liberal, nonracial citizenship, on the other, are likely to become poles of debate on social policy and political thought. Skeptical of liberalism and cognizant of socialism's limited prospects, many intellectuals will resort to populism as a means to articulate the post-apartheid predicament. Race-conscious populists are more likely to concentrate on the inability of nonracial citizenship to heal the wounds inflicted by apartheid. They will remain critical of liberal democracy, point to continued white economic hegemony, and be rhetorically anti-capitalist. Socialist populists are more likely to scrutinize the involvement of the new black bourgeoisie in both government and the economy while working to build support for social democracy and a welfare state. Both breeds of populists will support many of the policies of social democracy.

Whether by the investment of worker's pension funds, demands for support of small business viewed as "people's capitalism," or numerous other policies designed to enhance black economic standing, South Africans of all political persuasions will have to fight for a socially just citizenship within the framework of a capitalist economy. What will distinguish populism (from liberalism and socialism) is its tendency to repudiate any method of analysis as well as its intrinsically anti-oligarchic posture.[16] Eager to distinguish republican from populist thought, Philip Pettit argues that "communitarian and populist approaches to politics seek to represent the people in their collective presence as masters and the state as servant, and . . . that the people ought to rely on state representatives and officials only where absolutely necessary: direct democracy, whether by assembly or plebiscite, is the systematically preferred option."[17] Pettit's point is that with respect to attitudes toward representative government, republicans are closer to liberals and socialists than to populists. However, with specific reference to South Africa, unlike the black republicans, who have tended to be more populist, multiracial unionists were specifically elitist. Advocates of the multiracial union have been—and still are—liberal or socialist. In either case, a specific class is designated as being qualified to lead or rule: socialists believe in working-class leadership and liberals in the leadership of those qualified by education, property, or both. Furthermore, when compared with the rationalism implicit in liberal and socialist thought, populism excels in its ability to synthesize seemingly contradictory ideas, intuitions, and identities into a pervasive commonsense approach to political solidarity and may surface as either right- or left-wing doctrine. Nevertheless, since as an ideological tendency it spans the multiracial–black republican divide, advocates of both positions employ populism to their own advantage.

Ironically, the struggle against apartheid provided the impetus for liberalizing black republican thought. With reference to American republican thought, Russell Hanson has observed that civil liberties understood as individual rights were not initially part of a narrow republican perspective on citizenship; rather, they were incorporated due to challenges posed by an increasingly more complex economy, society, and government. Hanson deftly refers to this process as the "liberalization of republicanism."[18] Likewise, it is important to remember that multiracial union is black republicanism liberalized under South African conditions, a process exemplified by the ideological transitions in the life of Nelson Mandela. In his autobiography, Mandela describes his personal odyssey from young ethnic royalist to college-aged black nationalist to pragmatic multiracial unionist and, finally, to world-renowned apostle of racial reconciliation and nonracial citizenship.[19] Yet in the midst of these conscious transitions, there has always been a healthy streak of populism in Mandela's thought. Mandela's championing of liberal multiracialism helped to make possible his party's stunning electoral victory of April 1994, resting as it did on the rejection of racial republicanism—black and white.

The PAC's poor showing in the first all-race elections, coupled with the refusal of groups aligned with AZAPO to participate, has relegated black republicans to the status of a relatively small fraction of the parliamentary opposition. Whatever the plight of the PAC as a parliamentary force, however, Africanism, Pan-Africanism, black consciousness, and other forms of race-conscious discourse have been far too integral to black political thought to be summarily dismissed by students of South Africa's intellectual traditions. In black South African communities, political tendencies often conform to an indigenous "two partyism," based on the cross-pressures of racial autonomy and multiracial incorporation. I have argued that these rival tendencies correspond to the distinction between black republican identity and multiracial union, a dichotomy that exists even within explicitly multiracial parties. Although traditionally black republican organizations are currently in disarray, race-conscious populism pulsates strongly within the ANC—a party that spawned not only multiracial union but also black republican identity. Historically, these alternative conceptions of community are responses to racial domination and settler colonialism and, as Nolutshungu argued above, the denial of citizenship rights on racial grounds allowed the state, as well as groups in society, to employ strategies of coercion and consent differentially within a single nation.[20]

RACIAL PROLETARIANIZATION

Linked to early forms of international capitalism, white settlement produced its own class counterpart—racial proletarianization. Settler capitalism was a social formation that sought to abate intraracial class conflict by the denial of citizenship rights to nonwhite workers, thus limiting membership in the polity to whites. The denial of citizenship rights facilitated racial proletarianization, a process that provided a social foundation for multiclass race consciousness among blacks and whites. By the beginning of the century, historian C. W. De Kiewiet could identify "a generation of natives . . . who were completely separated from the land, socially closer to the Negro populations of Chicago and St. Louis than they were to their own compatriots in the reserve."[21] Implicit in De Kiewiet's oft cited observation is the important insight that proletarianization nurtured a multiclass black consciousness which helped to remake class and racial identity.

The system of racial domination itself was grounded in white multiclass consciousness. Naturally, white settlers found more solace in racial-populist rather than working-class forms of opposition. Donald Denoon finds similar dynamics at work in settler societies as diverse as South Africa, Australia, New Zealand, Argentina, Uruguay, and Chile. In these societies, notes Denoon, European migrants, faced with free access to the land of indigenous peoples, were slow to assimilate the political implications of class struggles as these were being played out back home. Nevertheless, "if settlers were slow to assimilate the idea of class, they were quick to adopt the most up-to-date ideas about race."[22]

Unlike most predominantly rural African nations, black South Africans, over the past centuries, have been transformed into a substantially proletarianized people—wage labor was necessary for them to meet the basic requirements of subsistence. The creation of a proletariat necessitated the destruction of traditional conceptions of rights, as well as customary forms of social protection, in order to eliminate or weaken a community's control over its means of subsistence.[23] During the course of two centuries, African peoples were dislodged from their traditional means of subsistence and forced into wage labor. Several scholars contend that, in South Africa, "it was in the mining industry that racial domination became an institutionalized part of class relations and the labour process."[24] In a pioneering work on the role of intellectuals in the formation of class consciousness among mine owners, Belinda Bozzoli maintained that "the motive force of the new mode of production lay in its primary opposition . . . to black societies whose destruction would produce a proletariat."[25]

In South Africa as in the United States, the black and white working classes were divided by a race-based allocation of rights. Without recourse to basic political rights, black workers were forced to the very bottom of the industrial ladder. In 1890, the veteran communist organizer Bill Andrews reported being shocked upon his arrival on the South African gold mines where he was assigned an African worker to carry his equipment. Handing Andrews his tools, the head of the workshop said, "here's your hammer, and here's your chisel, and here's a nigger."[26]

Perhaps no South African capitalist has ever captured the connection between citizenship rights and racial proletarianization more vividly than the famous mining magnate Cecil Rhodes, who served as Premier of the Cape Province in 1894. Rhodes spoke bluntly when he asserted that "either you have to receive them on an equal footing as citizens . . . or adopt a system of despotism, such as works well in India, in our relations with the barbarians of South Africa."[27] Rhodes's objective was "to reduce the African peasantry to a labouring class and yet keep them from becoming fully assimilated and proletarianized."[28] Put in other words, Rhodes sought to racially proletarianize Africans, and he understood that the denial of citizenship was essential to the accomplishment of that task.

The form of labor exploitation envisaged by Rhodes and other white capitalists, as well as the Afrikaner farmers, could not coexist with the full extension of citizenship to black South Africans. Gradually, racial proletarianization resulted in the burial of the vaunted Cape liberal tradition that once circumscribed citizenship rights for blacks in that province. Although they could not hold office, blacks with education and property in Cape Province could vote for white representatives. Although by 1933, the black vote was merely 1.2 percent of the Union total, the Cape Colony symbolized a major alternative to white republican thought. The black vote was gradually undermined between 1929 and 1951 by the enfranchisement of white women, the removal of property and income qualifications for white males, and the removal of some 5,000 blacks from the voters' roll. The Representation of Natives Act of 1936, which removed black voters from the Cape roll, began the process of disenfranchisement completed in the early fifties, by which time Africans (1936), Indians (1946), and Coloureds (1951) had been relegated to indirect representation.

Marian Lacey provides a crisp summary of the relationship between the demise of the Cape franchise and racial proletarianization: "Cape African voters with access to political power, property and bargaining rights were a threat as they were less vulnerable to exploitation and could not be coerced in the same way as rightless workers in the northern Provinces. . . . The attack on the Cape franchise coincided with the mineral discoveries and increased demands and pressures for labor."[29]

In response to the reality of racial proletarianization, Marxist historical interpretation of South Africa has, sometimes reluctantly but properly, drawn the conclusion that, in South African society, "race and nation and constitutional rights are major determinants of political qualifications."[30] Indeed, it is fair to say that during the apartheid era, class analyses of South African history were resuscitated in harmony with the idea of racial proletarianization. Some of the best historical writings on South Africa have explored the interaction of working-class consciousness, black resistance, and capitalist development. Since it informs interpretations of modern race relations, racial proletarianization can be understood not only as a discrete historical process delineated by time and place, but also as a category of social theory and, more specifically, of black political thought. Thus, racial proletarianization can be theorized as well as periodized. However, it is important to add that the study of racial proletarianization, like that of slavery, is not the special property of black political thought but constitutes "a part of the ethical and intellectual heritage of the West as a whole."[31]

Although the concept of proletarianization does not feature as a prominent part of citizenship studies, its relevance to the subject under conditions of colonialism and segregation is entirely plausible. In African societies, liberal citizenship no less than its republican counterpart has been influenced by the origins of the state. For example, Mahmood Mamdani contends that within the confines of the bifurcated colonial state, "citizenship would be a privilege of the civilized."[32] With proletarianization in England as its background, Marshall's classic discussion can justly be read as a treatise on the extension of citizenship rights as a means to abate class conflict. While a few white South African liberals saw a similar prospect in the gradual extension of qualified citizenship to the black elite, segregation, and later apartheid, eliminated reform as an option, leaving only revolutionary action, a path that required multiclass alliances. In his spirited defense of the significance of Karl Marx's insights for American history, William Appleman Williams's explanation of the full implications of proletarianization for citizenship is directly relevant to the political history of black South Africans:

> Marx meant a good deal more by proletarianization than simply working for wages on the assembly line in an urban manufacturing plant.... He meant the loss of any participating role in the principal decisions of the capitalist marketplace due to loss of any private property, which played a part in the productive activities of the system. The overt sign of this loss of full citizenship was of course the change from entrepreneurial standing to the condition of wage labor.[33]

In the 1980s, Wilmot James lashed out at Marxists and liberals alike for their failure to explain the persistence of a racially stratified work force. Without an adequate appreciation of racism, their analyses implied that blacks were passive victims of racial oppression. James insisted that "we simply cannot account for the transformation to apartheid without incorporating black struggles into our analytical framework."[34] Times were changing and the rival ideological camps were becoming less doctrinaire. Democratic thinkers of all persuasions soon acknowledged the centrality of black politics in the transformation of apartheid. However, the populist/republican versus the liberal/populist dispute did not fade away. The former called for the leadership of the "black working class" while the latter responded with a call for "working class leadership." Fights over these two slogans reflected the rivalry between nonracial and race-conscious populism as well as the inadequacy of conventional Marxism as a template for black liberation.

2. ✿ Racial Proletarianization: Moments in the Evolution of a Concept

In South Africa, the loss of ancestral land has been transformed into a category of black political thought. The land is a metaphor for a people's deep identification with its expropriated place of origin as well as its collective memory of community life. More than mere soil, the land is the symbol of a community's cohesion and spirit.[1] The sense of land loss is a deeply significant precipitant of political anger in contemporary South Africa. A black factory worker conveys that sense of grievance: "I was not born in that township. My ancestors were born on the land, in a place where they could plough and keep cattle. . . . And I was born on the land which had always belonged to my ancestors and their chiefs. But by the time I was born, our land had been taken by white farmers."[2]

In every historical context, proletarianization has been socially traumatic; racial proletarianization doubly so. Dispossession from ancestral land on the basis of race produced a form of social alienation unlike that resulting from wars among Africans before the arrival of Europeans. The wars Africans fought throughout the nineteenth century against British and Afrikaner armies failed to prevent their being dislodged from all but the worst land in the country, making race and class but different designations for land and labor. As De Kiewiet perceptively remarks, "the land wars were also labour wars."[3]

The insistence of white settlers on exclusive occupation of any land they claimed was central to the process of racial proletarianization. Inextricably linked to white military aggressiveness and coercive labor practices, land appropriation provoked intense resistance from peoples used to communal pasturage and ownership. For such strange customs, there had been no precedent. J. B. Peires makes the point regarding Xhosa society:

> Trade in labour across the Colonial frontier eventually engendered an entirely new class of permanent labourers whose labour was directly exploited by their employers and who lost the means to

pursue any alternative existence. No such class existed in preco-
lonial Xhosa society. . . . Outsiders suffered in their transition to
membership of the community, as the Khoi and the Mfengu discovered. But even outsiders possessed their own homesteads and enjoyed equal rights to water and pasturage. . . .[4]

In South Africa, the forceful confiscation of land and exclusion of
blacks from access to citizenship ensured that proletarianization
would assume an acute racial character, thus threatening both poorer
and relatively prosperous classes of Africans. Loss of land, curtailment
of freedom, and the alteration of community life were stinging in-
sults experienced by all black people, with virtually no exceptions.
For Africanist historian Ethel Khopung, "the root of Apartheid is the
story of a dispossessed people . . . the story of land robbery."[5] Similarly, several important scholars have long maintained that the history, sociology, and anthropology of modern black South African life
should be understood, largely, as a reaction to conquest.[6]

In the arena of black political thought, conquest and proletarianization have produced powerful traditions of racial populism that are
woven into the very fabric of political discourse. Janus-like, racial
populism faces both west and east and has its negative and positive
expressions. The memory of communal life is repeatedly evoked in
denunciations of private property, capitalism, and intraracial class
conflicts while simultaneously providing the moral foundation for a
black republican identity that challenges the self-destructive tendencies fostered by racial domination.

Although there were status and class divisions, including slavery,
in traditional African societies, populists frequently reinvented a culturally and racially homogenous past as a moral measure against
which the present is judged. Embodying the aspiration for liberation,
this view of the past is deployed as if it were a mirror imbued with the
unique power to expose the perversity wrought by proletarianization.
For example, Pan Africanist Congress veteran Elias Ntloedibe sum-
mons a sublime view of the African past in order to stress the importance of black solidarity in the present: "[T]he various African tribes,
practicing the system of communalism, owned in common the land as
the chief means of production. This ruled out the emergence of a
propertied class that could dispossess and exploit its fellowmen."[7]

The impact of so disruptive a transformation of black communities alarmed one of the more astute members of the African elite.

Solomon Plaatje (1877–1932), a brilliant historian, novelist, and publicist who served as the first Secretary General of the African National Congress, was so angered by the infamous 1913 Land Act, which legally enshrined territorial segregation and the displacement of stable African communities, that he lost his generally moderate comportment. Plaatje averred, "you see your countrymen and countrywomen driven from home, their home broken up, with no hope of redress . . . you would, I think, likewise find it very difficult to maintain a level head or wield a temperate pen."[8] No less eloquent with respect to the rapidity of proletarianization, Plaatje became convinced that "the gods are cruel, and one of their cruellest acts of omission was that of giving us no hint that in very much less than a quarter of a century all those hundreds of head of cattle, and sheep and horses belonging to the family would vanish like a morning mist, and that we ourselves would live to pay 30s. per month for a daily supply of this same precious fluid, and in very limited quantities."[9]

The conquest of African land assaulted traditional notions of community and gradually provided African nationalism with a social basis that was broader than language, ethnicity, or culture.

MILLENARIAN POPULISM

Traditional African notions of community were also attacked by an enemy that was far less obviously hostile than Boer commandos or British troops. White Christian missionaries preached a gospel of "salvation" (of the savage soul), but were too often implicated in efforts to dispossess Africans from their land and separate them from their native cultures. Consider, for example, the Reverend John Philip, who was Superintendent-General of the London Missionary Society, author of *Researches in South Africa* (1828), and a powerful influence on the framers of British colonial policy. The respected liberal historian W. M. MacMillan portrays Philip as an exemplar of religious liberalism.[10] Yet, Philip's missionary humanism was replete with racial contradictions.

"Mnguni" (a pseudonym for Hosea Jaffe) of the Non-European Unity Movement seizes on such statements made by Philip as: "Wherever the Missionary places his standard among a savage tribe, their prejudices against the Colonial government give way"; or "Mission stations are . . . the cheapest and best military post that a wise government can employ to defend its frontiers against the predatory incursions of savage tribes."[11] Small wonder that many black nationalists saw evangelicals as accomplices in conquest, whose real mission was to reduce the ability of Africans to resist.

The role of religion as an instrument of imperial conquest provoked millenarian responses based on syncretic mixtures of Christian and traditional worldviews. As in the case of Khoisan[12] and Bantu (particularly Xhosa) speaking Africans, the shock of rapid land loss gave rise to a tradition of mass-based millenarian movements. Ever since, populist themes, which were explicit in many millenarian movements, have had an impact on political forms of black consciousness. Among black South Africans, some of the most colorful proponents of black nationalism have been millenarians who were quick to situate race consciousness within their programs of spiritual redemption.

Black millenarian Christianity frequently transformed white church doctrines of subordination into ideologies that stressed the redemption of lost land, culture, and community. "In Xhosa society, as in other societies," observes Les Switzer, "when military prowess failed, attempts were made to resolve crises by employing spiritual leaders whose revolutionary message generated a sense of unity and purpose that conventional political leaders could not provide."[13] Products of special circumstances, millenarian movements are the consequence of a breakdown of historical consciousness. Such movements result from severe and protracted suffering on the part of the masses of people; at the very root of millenarianism is the combined impact of poverty, low status, and a rapid descent into powerlessness.[14] With the famous Xhosa cattle killings of 1856 and 1857 uppermost in his mind, the historian Edward Roux drew an analogy between black millenarian movements in South Africa and those described by Arnold Toynbee during the decline of the Roman Empire: the masses inside the Roman Empire turned to Christianity and resorted to millenarian movements led by gentle prophets or militant leaders of war bands.[15]

While African resistance to colonial domination was punctuated by an array of millenarian movements, the Xhosa Cattle Killing Movement "remains one of the most extraordinary manifestations of its kind in sub-Saharan Africa."[16] By means of this catastrophic gesture, the Xhosa hastened their own proletarianization as thousands deprived themselves of their remaining possessions. The apocalyptic teachings of the prophet Mhlakaza, a Christianized Xhosa, prompted the vision of a young female relative, Nongqawuse. In April 1856,

Nongqawuse prophesied that, with the mass cattle slaughter and the destruction of almost everything of value, the "New People," or resurrected ancestors, would return to redeem the Xhosa nation. Mnguni offers a graphic summary of the slaughter and its aftermath:

> In 1856 and 1857 disaster overtook the Xhosa. In May, 1856, Nongquase, niece of Sareli's priest-doctor, Mhlakaza, is supposed to have begun preaching a resurrection if the Xhosa killed their cattle and destroyed their harvests. On August 15th, 1856, 40,000 cattle were killed. On the day of the full moon, February 18th, 1857, slaughter was repeated and over 50,000 died of starvation. In "Kaffraria" alone 60,000 ultimately died.[17]

The cattle killings bear directly on the subjects of race consciousness, populism, and citizenship. After some hundred years of intermittent warfare, Xhosa society was on the verge of collapse. Sir George Grey, the Governor of the Cape Province (1854–62), had sworn to destroy Xhosa political institutions, especially the authority of chiefs. Grey believed that "the Xhosa could not finally be broken until the chiefs were deprived of the material basis of their power, which lay primarily in their right to levy judicial fees and fines and receive gifts as the arbiters of Xhosa law and custom."[18] Under the tutelage of white colonial officials and in receipt of government stipends, Xhosa chiefs were transformed into "administrative chiefs," and thus co-opted into the colonial state. In this case, as elsewhere in Africa, colonialists sought to manipulate, and sometimes invent, "tribal" republicanism in order to "convert a racial into an ethnic contradiction."[19] In response, black republican thinkers sought to reinterpret ethnic citizenship in ways that would be compatible with racial liberation and territorial nationalism.

Populist dynamics were also fostered by the Cattle Killing Movement. At first, white settlers were invited to join the rituals of purification, but Xhosa believers soon decided that whites were disingenuous and, therefore, not eligible for the promised land. The more significant social antagonism, however, was between "Red" and "School Folk" cultures associated with traditional and Westernized Xhosa respectively. The School Folk consisted of those Xhosa who embraced colonial institutions, primarily market capitalism, mission schools, and the church. Switzer aptly describes the populist inclination of the movement thus: "For most believers, the cattle killing movement was their last hope to preserve the old way of life. They reasserted the traditional values of loyalty and sacrifice for the good of the community as a whole, and they condemned the unbelievers as selfish individuals who were only interested in enriching themselves."[20]

During the mid-1920s, Dr. Wellington Buthelezi reintroduced into the Transkei many of the millenarian themes that were associated with the cattle killing. This time, however, the agent of miraculous redemption was not the resurrected ancestor, but an African-American liberation army. In black South African popular culture, the image of African-Americans is frequently used to symbolize a black people who command the tools of modernity. Indeed, the rumors of an army of African-American liberators may well have started when African workers assigned to the South African military during the First World War saw, to their amazement, all-black regiments, like the "Harlem Hell Fighters," who distinguished themselves in Europe under the command of the French Army. Thus did Buthelezi, who came under the influence of Garveyism in 1925, pretend to be an African-American from Chicago. Wellington "regaled his followers with prophecies of millennium achieved through the exercise of black American power in the form of ships, troops, and bombing planes. . . . they were inspired to act by Buthelezi's warning that destruction would rain from the air, not only on Europeans, but also on Africans who did not belong to the Wellington movement."[21] Reminiscent of the Cattle Killing Movement, Wellington's followers were called upon to paint their homes black, kill their white pigs, and destroy any possessions that were white or derived from pigs. Realizing the threat his movement posed to its authority, the government banished Dr. Wellington from the Transkei. However, as Roux observed, while the Wellington movement was short-lived, "it is said that in certain districts it is still rare to see a white fowl or pig."[22]

During the 1920s, Dr. Wellington's millenarianism was paralleled by others in South Africa. In 1921, at Bulhoek commonage near Queenstown, the South African government killed 171 members of a religious sect known as the Israelites. In 1909, the group's founder, John Msikinya, had returned from America declaring himself a Bishop of the Church of God and Saints of Christ. Enoch Mgijima who lived in the Bulhoek location soon joined Msikinya. When Msikinya died, in 1918, the movement split into Mgijima's Israelites and one other faction. The Israelites believed that the reappearance of Halley's comet (1910) had revealed that the New Testament was an invention of the white man and that they must return to a form of religious practice modeled on that of the Patriarchs of ancient Israel. Nevertheless, when the Israelites built a settlement on the Bulhoek commonage, as they said Jehovah had instructed them to do, they came into conflict with the white authorities. After repeated warnings to return to their villages, a large contingent of police was dispatched to remove them from Bulhoek. When the Israelites resisted with crude weapons, the police opened fire with rifles and machine guns.[23]

In his *History of Pan-African Revolt*, C. L. R. James uses the example of a Khoisan millenarian movement to mark the transition from the phase of black peasant to that of proletarian struggle. James notes that "the post war period has given us at least two clearly-marked types of Negro revolutionary activity, the Bondelzwarts [*sic*] revolt and the Industrial and Commercial Worker's Union (ICU)."[24] The former, says James, was an anachronism when it occurred in 1922. The Bondelswart, a Khoisan people of German-controlled South-West Africa (now Namibia), did not follow either priest or prophet, but constantly resisted German efforts to conscript their labor. When under the 1919 League of Nations Mandate, South Africa assumed authority in the territory, the new power, like the Germans before them, dealt harshly with the Bondelswart. Finally in 1922, the Bondelswart revolted against the imposition of a tax on their hunting dogs by the government of General Jan Smuts. In response, the South Africans dispatched 400 soldiers, armed with machine guns and supported by two bombers, who mercilessly put down the revolt.

The flowering of Ethiopian and Zionist churches during the late nineteenth and early twentieth centuries is best understood against the background of a long tradition of millenarian populism among black South Africans. With special reference to the Christian Catholic Apostolic Church in Zion (C.C.A.C.Z.), which was founded in Chicago in 1896 and introduced into Johannesburg and Natal by 1904, Jean Camaroff concludes that Zionism offered black workers a belief system adapted to the problems of living between the impoverished worlds of rural subsistence and wage labor. Forming a bond between the two largest existing black proletariats (in the United States and South Africa), the Zionism of the C.C.A.C.Z. "involved the expression of class conflict, not explicitly voiced or nicely articulated as class consciousness, per se, but couched in the flexible symbols of Christian dissent."[25] As an extension of their efforts to adapt Christianity to their needs, church people throughout South Africa creatively pooled their resources to purchase land lost through conquest.

Shula Marks has identified millenarian tendencies among both Africans who lost their land and Afrikaners who anointed their usurpation of African land with spiritual significance.[26] The growth of capitalist agriculture was a fulfillment of "prophecy" for a small class of Afrikaner landowners. However, the majority of Afrikaners were as landless as the Africans whom their ancestors had fought so hard to dislodge, and the simultaneous proletarianization of Africans and Afrikaners predisposed the latter to embrace a virulent brand of both racial and ethnic politics, targeting blacks and English-speaking whites respectively.

Yet, to the dismay of liberal African nationalists like Plaatje, South African–style liberalism was reconciled to racial proletarianization. As Stanley Trapido points out, the major component of liberal ideology—the belief in private land ownership as a civilizing agency—was reserved for whites, whereas for Africans liberalism was associated with the dignity of wage labor.[27] Thus, Africans, Afrikaners, and British confronted one another not only with diametrically opposed political claims, but also with contradictory subjective understandings of land, law, property, and community. Europeans employed racist myths to cement class solidarity in pursuit of white supremacy, while non-Europeans invented the myth of racial solidarity to contain class divisions and mobilize blacks to fight for social justice. Moreover, both black and white nationalist movements had to cope with the grievances of a large landless class.

OMENS OF DOOM

Khoisan voices resound with the same racial indignation and sense of loss that characterize other black groups. Furthermore, individual Khoisan personalities symbolized the range of sentiments that inspired later stages of African nationalism.[28] In a real sense, the Khoisan experience can be considered an omen of impending doom—the warning that Plaatje claimed the gods had not given. For the collapse of Khoisan society, due largely to conquest and settler-carried diseases, prefigured patterns of future oppression of all Africans that were destined to endure.[29] The Khoisan of the western Cape are the oldest people of South Africa; they were also transformed into the country's first indigenous proletariat. Often compared to Native Americans, the Khoisan resisted European settlement of the interior for close to three decades, costing them near annihilation.

Although the transoceanic slave trade was abolished in 1807, it was not until 1834 that the British Governor of South Africa, Sir Benjamin D'Urban, finalized arrangements to emancipate slaves in the Cape Colony. By then, large numbers of proletarianized Khoisan had drawn progressively closer to slaves in culture, status, and economic function; together with slaves, they formed the basis of South Africa's Cape Coloured population.[30] Slaves belonged to both the Dutch East India Company (VOC), which established the colony at the Cape of Good Hope in 1652, and Freeburghers, VOC employees released from contracts to become independent farmers. While manumission by the Company was more frequent than by individual slave owners, slavery under company terms was actually far harsher.[31] When it came to the appropriation of African land or the recruitment of black labor, Freeburghers—of whom modern-day Afrikaners are the progeny—deeply resented any interference by company, government, or church. Indeed, the right to exploit the human and natural resources of the country on the basis of race was a core demand of Freeburgher republicanism. For example, in 1788, Freeburghers formed a Patriot Movement in order to confront corrupt officials of the VOC. The Patriots asserted their right to "change the form of government by violence if necessary, should the authorities no longer perform their natural task of 'standing for the people, and defending their lives, property and liberty.'"[32] One of the concessions the Patriot Movement gained from the VOC was the right to engage in the slave trade on the East African coast and at Madagascar.[33]

Marking the end of control by the VOC, the Dutch Batavian Republic ruled the Cape Colony for the brief period from 1803 to 1806. The United Provinces of the Netherlands, renamed the Batavian Republic (1795–1813), was a French protectorate and its leadership supported the ideals of the French Revolution. In the Cape, some Batavian officials were alienated from the Dutch-descended Freeburghers whose frontier lifestyle, they felt, debased the thought, speech, and customs of the Netherlands. Jacob De Mist, a well-known Batavian administrator, was reputedly one of the more enlightened officials, especially with respect to the treatment of the Khoisan. De Mist, at times, saw the Khoisan as a peasantry similar to that of his native Holland.[34] Although he understated the importance of their resistance, in 1805 he depicted the proletarianization of the Khoisan with compassion and honesty:

> On what grounds did these poor creatures deserve the persecution and ill treatment meted out to them by the company's servants from the very founding of the colony? From the caves of their fathers they watched a foreign nation take possession of their coast, offering not the slightest opposition; they gradually relented before the advance of the strangers and provided them with cattle, sheep and goats; but all this could not sate the white man's greed. . . . the colonists hounded down these timid wretches, destroyed their Kraals and villages, stole their cattle, seized the men and boys and reduced them to a state of subjection and slavery, drove others in fear of their lives, to seek shelter in the depths of wild caves and forests and callously allowed them to sink into a state of utter barbarism.[35]

The Khoisan, therefore, bore the brunt of the first efforts by white settlers to implement the logic of a herrenvolk state in which "people of color, however numerous or acculturated they may be, are treated as permanent aliens or outsiders."[36] As would be the case in the future, segregation impinged on class relations, and vice versa: chiefs loyal to the Dutch were designated "Company Chiefs," many of whom had no claim to traditional status;[37] Dutch colonial officials experimented with a pass system to control the movement of slaves and the Khoisan; and colonists proposed a reserve system to help harness Khoisan labor.[38] Similar measures would become prominent features of full-blown segregation and apartheid. By 1809, the Caledon Code had become law. This was the first piece of legislation based on the premise of a master-servant relationship between Europeans and Khoisan.

Shortly before the Batavians took charge at the Cape, the Khoisan mounted a major rebellion against the Colony that lasted from 1799 to 1802. This uprising had the spirit of a general strike. For Khoisan workers on white farms, desertion was tantamount to strike action, but it was undertaken with the hope of abandoning the labor system forever. Klaas Stuurman, primary leader of the rebellion, was apparently familiar with the conditions of Khoisan throughout the country. Stuurman was in contact with Khoisan workers on white farms, independent Khoisan bands, and empathetic Xhosa chiefs. The rebellion revealed two distinct types of coalitions: on the one hand, the Khoisan and the Xhosa formed an alliance against white settlers; on the other, Khoisan workers on farms and independent Khoi bands coalesced against the Dutch. Khoisan servants often escaped from white farms to join independent Khoisan bands that developed as an alternative form of social organization in the face of forced dislocation.

In the interior, these "primitive rebels" organized themselves under strong and able leaders such as Hans Trompetter, Boezak, and the colorful Stuurman Brothers.[39] Klaas Stuurman was described by Freund as the "Robin Hood of the Khoikhoi."[40] Stuurman, while concerned with better working conditions, exhibited a strong nationalist consciousness, clearly manifested in his stated desire to repossess ancestral land.[41] Susan Newton-King reproduces a fascinating dialogue between the English explorer Sir John Barrow and Stuurman. Barrow endeavored to convince Stuurman how little advantage the Khoisan were likely to derive from possession of a country, without any other property, or the means of producing subsistence from it. Nevertheless, Stuurman had the better of the argument. He exclaimed:

> Restore the country which our fathers were despoiled by the Dutch and we have nothing more to ask. We have lived very contentedly before these Dutch plunderers molested us, and why should we not do so again if left to ourselves? Has not Groot Baas given plenty grass roots, and berries and grasshoppers for our use; and, till the Dutch destroyed them, abundance of wild animals to hunt? And will they not return and multiply when these destroyers are gone?[42]

Autshumato (Harry), who later became an interpreter, was the first Khoisan leader the Dutch encountered. When Commander Jan Van Riebeeck (1652–1662) requested that the Khoisan under him relocate because their proximity to the colony annoyed the white settlers, Autshumato reportedly "intimated that this was our land, not yours, that we will place our huts wherever we choose and if you are not disposed to permit us to do so we will attack and kill you with the aid of many people from the interior."[43] Autshumato's threats proved idle. By 1798, population figures for Cape districts "reflect not only the decimation of the Khoi near the capital from a variety of causes but also the migration of many to the furthest reaches of the settlement in response to the colonising process."[44]

In the early years of the nineteenth century, Khoisan forced to join the so-called Hottentot Corps often did so with the hopes that their homesteads would be restored as a result of military service. In 1805, a group of Khoi captains (a term used to refer to leaders of Khoikhoi bands) petitioned their white Batavian officer to help them restore their land. The officer wrote the government as follows on behalf of the Khoisan:

> The undersigned Hottentot captains have applied to me with the request that I address you in their name in order to ask that the confiscated plaatsen listed below which have been occupied continuously by Hottentot Kraals in the time of their ancestors, be placed once again on such a footing so that old and decrepit Hottentots could maintain themselves and their families in order to prevent that when a Hottentot through old age is unable to earn anything he is placed in the unfortunate situation of dying of starvation.[45]

The range of Khoisan reactions to racial domination can be illustrated by brief reference to the lives of three early Khoisan interpreters; their respective responses to colonization suggest social-psychological implications. Autshumato, Krotoa (whose Christian name was Eva), and Doman responded to the Dutch in three unique ways. The first manipulated the Dutch for his own enrichment; the second won their affection through loyal service and intermarriage; the third resisted their colonial expansion.[46] As adaptations to racial oppression, the techniques of manipulation, cultural conversion, and overt resistance share a common ground. Within the parameters of the evolving colonial system, proletarianized Khoisan could gain goods from Europeans primarily in three ways: by trade, by raids, or by labor. However, it is also clear that the end of colonial domination was a goal cherished by Khoisan leaders like Doman.

Perhaps the most colorful of the interpreters, Autshumato was, in 1658, sent to Robben Island for his intrigues against the Dutch. The leader of a group called the Strandlopers (Beachcombers), Autshumato reputedly recruited his followers from the poor of the peninsular Khoikhoi—refugees, outcasts, orphans, and other persons without family. The Khoisan clan heads, who regarded the disaffected Strandlopers with contempt, accused Autshumato of gathering followers from the San cattle robbers, from those who were not his own people, and from those without parents or husbands. A well-informed European commander bitingly characterized the Strandlopers as the "rabble of the interior."[47] Elphick says of Autshumato, "his relations with the Dutch were so changeable that it would be wrong to call him a collaborator or a resistance leader."[48] Autshumato operated on the peripheries of black and white societies, but with total allegiance to neither. His socially marginal status allowed him to become the first intermediary in the African-European cattle trade and, for a short time, to amass considerable wealth and influence.

RACIAL PROLETARIANIZATION

Eva, a Khoisan woman, and Anna, a Benghali slave girl, are names that recur in accounts of early South African history primarily because they married prominent Cape whites. Some historians see in these personal alliances the potential for a multiracial evolution at the Cape Colony. In this vein, Fatima Meer, once associated with the Black Renaissance Convention, contends that Krotoa (Eva) of the Goringhaikona was of historical significance. Meer eloquently portrays Krotoa as one of the first in a long line of black leaders to pursue the goal of multiracial union—peaceful coexistence between black and white societies. She reflects on the meaning of Krotoa's life thus:

> Hers was a unique position in seventeenth century Cape, for she was the only person who understood the two cultures that were close to clashing on that southern shore. Product of both, she loved and respected the two equally, and in her innocent, child-like, but inspired way, she attempted to bring them together in peace and harmony. Her own marriage to the Dutchman, Pieter van Meerhoff, symbolized this attempt.[49]

Meer situates Krotoa's life within the framework of a discourse on South African race relations, but it is wise to remember that much of the conduct of whites at the Cape was no less influenced by the earlier Dutch colonial experience in the East Indies. Ann Laura Stoler emphasizes the extent to which the VOC customarily deployed sexual alliances as a means to link the potentialities of colonial settlement to the production of populations loyal to the colonial state. Stoler remarks that, since they condoned certain kinds of liaisons and not others, the rulers of the Dutch East India Company "debated long and hard over the best means to cultivate a Dutch settler population on Java, and issues of sexual management were high on the agenda."[50] What did Krotoa's life symbolize—multiracial union or the colonial deployment of sexual alliance?

At the age of thirteen, Krotoa replaced Doman and another male relative as chief interpreter at the Cape Colony; both men had, by then, become anti-Dutch guerrillas. Autshumato was also her relative. Krotoa's kinship network proved crucial to the Dutch victory during the First Khoisan-Dutch War (1659–1660). She employed her influence with her brother-in-law Oedasoa, second in command of the Cochoqua, to prevent Doman from enlisting the support of this strategic group.[51] Krotoa, through her kinship ties, not only helped to defeat Khoisan resistance, but also used her influence to undermine

Autshumato's monopoly of the cattle trade.[52] Doman, for one, considered her a quisling. He would harangue Krotoa whenever she was in sight: "she speaks on the side of the Dutch rather than of the Hottentots, and calling out when she comes. . . . 'See! There comes the Hollanders' advocate again, she is coming to deceive her own countrymen with a parcel of lies, and to betray them to the last' and other expressions tending to make her odious."[53]

The Dutch sent Doman, who has been described as a man of common origin but uncommon skill, to Java to learn their language; he returned from abroad to play a prominent role in the first of three Khoisan wars against the white settlers. By the time of the first major confrontation with the colonizers, Doman had learned the strengths and limitations of Dutch firearms, and his overall resistance to European encroachment led Van Riebeeck to consider him "three times worse and more mischievous to the Company than Harry ever was."[54]

In due time, racial proletarianization produced what Leslie Duly has referred to as South Africa's first Color Question which Ordinances 49 and 50 of 1828 were designed to resolve. The former ordinance made it legal to enlist laborers from beyond the Frontier on short-term contracts and to issue them passes, while the latter ordinance, simply stated, granted citizenship to all free persons of color living in the Cape Colony, including the Khoi. The subsequent failure of these measures highlights the long-standing difficulties faced by early colonial reformers such as Andries Stockenström Jr. Like his father before him, Stockenström was an influential government official who sought to limit some of the abuses the frontiersmen heaped upon the Khoisan. Stockenström, says Duly, had a far broader understanding of the Khoisan problem than many of his contemporaries:

> [He] saw, as few others did, that the Caledon Code of 1809 had begun a process of Europeanization of the Khoikhoi that could not be reversed. . . . [T]hese people were being made a part of the Colony's economic and social structure. . . . A more vigorous role on the part of the government was required to help the Khoikhoi complete the process of Europeanization and find a productive and equitable place in Cape society.[55]

For Newton-King, Stockenström was only set apart by his "clear and coldly cynical understanding of the process of proletarianization taking place on the eastern frontier."[56] She believes that the abolition of the slave trade in 1807 and the promulgation of Ordinances 49 and

50 are points on an historical continuum—landmarks in the early history of labor at the Cape. With respect to the recruitment of Khoisan and Xhosa into the Cape labor market, Stockenström was undeniably an advocate of clearly established Khoisan rights and, more importantly, of free labor, but his "advocacy of free labor was not unqualified."[57] Nor were the Khoisan allowed to complete the process of "Europeanization" as Stockenström advocated.

Europeanized or not, mixed-race communities were forced to function as a social stratum wedged in between black and white societies, and, as a result, Coloured identity could seem to depend on the maintenance of a racial-class position distinct from that of other Africans. H. J. and R. E. Simons go as far as to say that among mixed-race groups "colour consciousness tended to smother class and national consciousness."[58] Thus, the existence of an intraracial color line complicated the relations and attitudes of Coloureds and Africans toward one another, even as they united to fight for black liberation and full citizenship.

On the other hand, Coloureds shared language and culture with Afrikaners who were always ambivalent about where their brown brethren fit in a segregated society. Given that they were central to the development of a unique Afrikaans language and culture, Coloureds could feel the pangs of racism in ways that were both subtler and more acute than those experienced by the often more socially distant African majority. Many Coloured individuals and groups responded to white racism by affirming their non-European identity. For example, by the 1800s, miscegenation had produced mixed-race communities that were self-identified as "Bastaards." Yet, as the privileges bestowed on the basis of mixed-race ancestry were whittled away, "Bastaards" suddenly renamed themselves "Griqua." The change of name corresponded to a change of consciousness, thus the replacement of a colonial reference-point with an indigenous Khoisan clan name.[59]

Although their political outlook might display features that distinguished them from the African majority, proletarianization fostered a definite racial consciousness among the Coloured middle class while Coloured workers have always been an integral part of the non-European proletariat. In brief, there has been no time when Coloured activism was not a factor in black politics. One of the earliest black political organizations in the country was the Coloured-dominated African People's Organization (APO) founded in 1902 and soon led by the brilliant Dr. Abdul Abdurahman. The grandson of freed slaves, Abdurahman considered himself and his constituents to be true "sons of the soil." By 1909, the APO had taken up the struggle for non-European enfranchisement in the upcoming union. On numerous occasions, Abdurahman and his APO joined with Africans in the ICU and the ANC to protest the extension of segregation laws that made citizenship increasingly a preserve of whites.

Many Coloured activists, some of whom were Trotskyists like C. L. R. James himself, shared the latter's judgment that the ICU represented a movement away from peasant to worker protest. A good example is James La Guma, a man of French-Malagasy descent, who was, for a time, one of ICU founder Clements Kadalie's staunchest lieutenants. La Guma helped to establish the ICU, first in the Namibian diamond mines and, later, in Port Elizabeth. Also a member of the Communist Party, La Guma was expelled in 1925, along with all other black communists, when Kadalie passed a resolution disallowing joint membership in the ICU and Communist Party.[60] Perhaps no movement in the history of South Africa has ever gone further than the ICU in openly combining a radical race consciousness and militant working-class politics.[61] In a manner that was playful yet serious, the black workers interpreted the acronym "ICU" as "I see you white man." Sensing in the ICU a transition similar to that referred to by James, George Padmore observed that, at the height of his popularity, Clements Kadalie was as much feared by whites of his day as the Zulu warrior Dingane, at an earlier period.[62]

PARTIAL PROLETARIANIZATION: "HOMELANDS"

Ironically, the discovery of the world's largest gold deposits in the Transvaal (1886) and, before that, diamonds at Kimberley (1868) would eventually spell ruin not only for powerful African states like those of the Pedi of the northern Transvaal and the Zulu of Natal, but also for the independent Afrikaner republics. The Transvaal Republic gained its independence in 1852 followed by the Orange Free State in 1854. However, with the mineral discoveries, a cabal of arch-imperialists, led by mining magnate Cecil Rhodes, Lord Alfred Milner, British High Commissioner in Southern Africa, and Joseph Chamberlain, Britain's Colonial Secretary, devoted itself to bringing about a federal state that would be consistent with the needs of British capitalism. Given these aspirations, both Afrikaner independence and African autonomy presented considerable obstacles.[63] In 1871, Britain annexed Kimberley to its Cape colony, six years later the independent Transvaal Republic was made a British colony, and Zululand was attached to the crown colony of Natal in 1887.

During this period, British policy evolved twin objectives—the defeat of powerful African states and the imposition of union on the Afrikaner (Boer) Republics. The 1876 defeat of President Thomas Burgers's Transvaal Afrikaners by the Pedi under Sekhukhune provided the British the rationale for annexation of the gold-rich republic that next year, ostensibly for reasons of security.[64] Both Afrikaner and English aligned themselves with various African chieftaincies, even as they crushed others. Significantly, the Pedi and Zulu states were, in 1879, bludgeoned into submission by British-led armies.[65]

While Afrikaners needed support from the British army against African peoples, they nonetheless wanted to avoid British suzerainty over their republics. Placing the needs of the gold industry above all else, Britain demanded greater access to the Transvaal government in order to create coherent regional labor markets to service the mines. Afrikaner resentment and resistance festered as Britain tried to assume effective control of the bankrupt republic through the imposition of unpopular taxes and limits on a promise of internal self-rule. In 1880, the man who would come to be viewed as the father of the Afrikaner nation, Paul Kruger, fomented a yearlong rebellion against British rule, at the end of which he became the President of a new self-governing Transvaal Republic. However, President Kruger's efforts to maintain Afrikaner autonomy prompted Milner and his political allies to choose the path of war. The immediate issue was citizenship for the so-called *uitlanders* (outsiders)—mainly Englishmen who were drawn to the Transvaal by the lure of gold— who had become a majority in the Afrikaner republic. At first, Kruger's government required *uitlanders* to wait fourteen years before they could become citizens. Eventually, he offered a compromise of seven years for naturalization, but to no avail because Milner and Rhodes had set their sights on a war that would allow them to reincorporate the Afrikaner republics into a white-dominated South African union within the British Empire.

The renowned theorist and opponent of imperialism, J. A. Hobson, was deeply alarmed by the brutality of the Anglo-Boer War of 1899–1902, where 20,000 Afrikaner women and children died in detention camps while Boer commandos were methodically suppressed.[66] However, Hobson did not dwell on the plight of Africans;

during this era, the "race problem" meant the English-Afrikaner conflict. While Afrikaners enjoyed the support of groups as diverse as Europe's anti-imperialist left and the German Crown, only a few humanitarians in England protested, as morally indefensible acts, Britain's African wars or the handing over of Africans to Afrikaner rule after the South African War.[67] Clause VIII of the 1902 Peace Treaty of Vereeniging left the question of black enfranchisement to be settled after Afrikaners had been granted self-government. Black disenfranchisement followed the 1910 Act of Union and three years later the passage of the Land Act sent shock waves through the African community. Thus, it soon was evident that, similar to the Confederacy after the American Civil War, Afrikaners had lost the war, but won the peace.

Throughout the nineteenth century, African kingdoms faced a combined assault from British and Afrikaner armies, missionaries, and Africans allied with the colonialists. Sometimes withstanding this array of opponents, several African states remained intact until the last decades of the nineteenth century. However, by seizing the land everywhere, white settlers had all but destroyed the two bases of African traditional authority—common land and the chiefs as trustees of that land.[68] In 1906, amidst the rapid transformation of the Natal agricultural economy, Bambatha, a minor Zulu Chief, led a rebellion against a poll tax designed solely to encourage proletarianization. The British summarily beheaded Bambatha, and his rebellion proved to be the last one mounted by a South African chief against white authority.

By the time of Bambatha's uprising, a new race consciousness was already on the horizon; there were widespread rumors that other African groups were planning to transform this localized act of defiance by a Zulu chief into a mass black uprising.[69] Regardless of the realism of these rumors, Bambatha's rebellion marked a watershed. As the South African state was consolidated within its present borders, the primary focus of black resistance became segregation, rooted as it was in partial proletarianization.

Given that blacks were, by far, a national majority, racial policy was faced with a contradiction that segregation sought to address. Capitalist economic processes tended to blur or even eradicate customary racial divisions within the country, and partial proletarianization, it was hoped, would provide a means to reinforce those divisions so strongly that they would obstruct economic pressures for political change.[70] The myth of South Africa as a nation containing many separate nations was the core rationale for segregation and apartheid. The Land Act and its 1936 emendation legalized the creation of reserves for Africans and ultimately restricted their ownership of land and property to approximately 13 percent of the country. The Native Administration Act of 1927 supposedly restored the chiefs to their former power in the reserves; however, the South African State President was designated as the "Chief of Chiefs."[71] In the official mind of state racism, balkanization of the country, like the pervasiveness of migrant labor, was, at different points in time, thinly disguised by reference to African "reserves," "bantustans," or "homelands."

The economic theory of "bantustans," similar to its political theory, was based on myth. By the 1920s, agriculture in these areas was incapable of sustaining their black populations.[72] This fact undermined the myth perpetuated by both government and business that migrant laborers were paid survival wages because wives and family living in the homelands augmented their incomes with agricultural production. In the "homelands," which scarcely encompassed the totality of land traditionally inhabited by the various African peoples, chiefs functioned as labor recruiters and, thus, in a perverse way, regained a small measure of leverage, since men needed their permission to work. In turn, the architects of apartheid decreed that Africans should become citizens of their ethnic "homelands" rather than the South African nation.

That precept underlay the Bantu Authorities Act of 1951 which stated: "the Bantu people of the Union of South Africa do not constitute a homogeneous people, but form separate national units on the basis of language and culture."[73] It was the essential foundation of partial proletarianization as the master strategy of white rule.

CLASS, COLOR, AND CHIEFTAINCY

Immediately after Union, two prominent Afrikaner generals, Jan Christian Smuts and Louis Botha, dominated politics. Although the two Boer generals first joined forces to prevent Lord Milner from imposing a narrow and punitive peace treaty, both favored the unification of South Africa through reconciliation of the English and Afrikaner peoples. In 1911, Smuts and Botha formed the South African Party that devoted itself to the attainment of these ends. Ultimately, however, liberal Afrikaners were unable to stem the tide of Afrikaner nationalism. Expelled from Botha's 1910 Cabinet for his nationalist views, J. B. M. Hertzog founded the National Party in 1914. Ten years later, he became Prime Minister as the direct result of a labor dispute. The Rand Rebellion of 1922, with its infamous slogan "Workers of the World Unite and Fight for a White South Africa," was the bloodiest confrontation ever witnessed between workers, white or black, and the South African state; it left some 687 military personnel, workers, and innocent civilians dead or wounded.[74] The rebellion was ignited when white miners overreacted to the Chamber of Mines' intention to renegotiate the so-called Status Quo Agreement that would have retrenched some two thousand workers, replacing them with low-paid African labor. In an act that surely contributed to his lack of popularity among Afrikaners, Smuts employed the use of artillery and aircraft against the white worker protest, which he considered the work of syndicalists and white republican hard-liners. The Rand Rebellion led to Smuts's electoral defeat at the hands of a coalition formed by the Afrikaner National Party and the Labour Party.

While both parties were committed to racial segregation, Afrikaner nationalists shrewdly utilized this coalition with the Labour Party to organize Afrikaner workers into ethnic, rather than white, trade unions. Simply stated, racist socialists provided Afrikaner nationalists a means to mobilize an ethnically exclusive worker-base that might not have otherwise been so solidly constructed. Although a relatively short-lived view, after the drama of 1922, prominent white members of the newly formed Communist Party believed the largely Afrikaner proletariat to be a truly revolutionary force that with maturation and tutelage would shed its racist proclivities. In both Pact (1924–1933) and Fusion (1933–1939) governments, the implementation of segregation was central to Hertzog's overall policy agenda. By 1936, the four pieces of segregationist legislation that he put forward at the start of his tenure as Prime Minister had been distilled into the Representation of Natives Act and the Native Land and Trust Act. The first act was chiefly concerned with the replacement of the Cape African franchise, a feature of South African political life since 1853, with a complex system of indirect representation.[75] The Native Representative Councils (NRCs), provided for by the second act, would eventually cause division within African nationalist circles; some nationalists favored total boycott while others proposed using NRCs as platforms to attack segregation.

Hertzog's goal of unadulterated segregation was given an added boost when, in 1931, the British Parliament passed the Statute of Westminster, terminating any further legal authority in South Africa by the former colonial government. However, his management of the economy, in particular his inability to preserve the gold standard, forced him into a second coalition government with the South African Party. Like déjà vu, Daniel F. Malan, then his Minister of the Interior, split from Hertzog and formed the ultra-nationalist Purified National Party, the direct predecessor of the National Party that would rule between 1948 and 1994.

After the Anglo-Boer War, there was accelerated growth of urban markets in agricultural produce accompanied by the spread of railways. The expansion of agricultural capitalism would have a major impact on the structure of segregation and, therefore, labor relations, but it also generated a kind of "dual proletarianization," as large landowners swallowed up small, primarily Afrikaner, farmers. In this economic environment, white farmers and entrepreneurs were alarmed when, in 1916, the Beaumont Commission reported that African syndicates had been organized, often by churches, to purchase land on the open market. United by a common need for African labor, white farmers and other capitalists saw the advantage of forcing the African peasantry into labor tenancy.[76] While supporting segregation in principle, the Commission report fueled further controversy by asserting that it was "too late in the day to define large compact native areas or to draw bold lines of demarcation."[77]

A small, but efficient, African peasantry, that utilized family rather than forced labor, had managed to proliferate on mission stations (land owned by missionaries), especially in the Transkei and Ciskei, and on any other land available to Africans.[78] Thus, a major imperative of racial proletarianization was the creation of mechanisms to curtail the rise of an African peasantry, even on unequal terms. The largely depleted African reserves were to be the only land on which an African farming class would be allowed. Under Hertzog, existing laws implemented to limit African access to land and fair employment were augmented by a new generation of legislation aimed at restricting access to the urban areas, the prevention of black labor mobility, and the curtailment of individual civil liberties.

The class of uprooted rural Afrikaners, who were most vulnerable to the threat of an African peasantry, also faced African competition in the mining and manufacturing sectors of the economy. In the cities, the Afrikaner was confronted with his age-old African rival, now proletarianized. In the rural areas, blacks had preempted the role of agricultural labor, and in the towns, the Afrikaners had to face nonwhite competition to gain a foothold in the labor market. Craft unions, dominated by English-speaking workers, were the first to erect barriers against black workers. Initially, neither Africans nor Afrikaners possessed much in the way of union-organizing skills.[79] By contrast, union-minded European workers arrived in South Africa from societies where capitalism and trade unionism were far more advanced. Furthermore, white labor organizers were quick to augment their knowledge of trade unionism with the advantages of racism.

In the workforce, the primary means of protecting white labor from black competition was the Mines and Works Act of 1911 and the Amendment Act of 1926 (generally known as the job color bar). Ostensibly, the political rationale for the job color bar, and its predecessor, the civilized labor policy, was the protection of white workers from black competition. As we have seen, the Rand Rebellion started with charges that skilled jobs reserved for whites were going to be reclassified and made available to far cheaper nonwhite workers.[80] In this atmosphere, white nationalists could easily make the case that black working-class competition posed a major threat to white workers, especially Afrikaners. However, Martin Legassick convincingly argues that the imposition of a system of forced labor on blacks reduced their freedom and bargaining power to a point where they were never directly in competition with white workers. Furthermore, given the legacy of forced labor and statutory racism, white workers were able to steadily gain access to state power.[81]

Both racially exclusive socialism and white nationalism created favorable prospects for white workers. However, it is important to recognize the extent to which the political ramparts of race-class relations provided white workers with a rationale for demanding an extension of social rights for themselves; this had become a growing cause for workers in England and other advanced capitalist countries. T. H. Marshall observes that while class-abatement was the aim of social rights, class integration, resulting from sentiments like patriotism, gradually inspired the view that a civilized and cultured life should belong to all citizens, rather than a wealthy few. For when social rights were incorporated into citizenship, the outcome was the creation of "a universal right to real income which is not proportionate to the market value of the claimant."[82] In far less academic language, this was precisely the argument to which white workers resorted after the Rand Rebellion. The rationale for white welfare capitalism was simple: white men should not have to live at the level of Africans.

Moreover, in light of events like the Anglo-Boer War and the Rand Rebellion, white capitalists wanted to open up avenues of reconciliation between English and Afrikaner and even to find ways to involve Afrikaners in the upper echelons of the capitalist economy. De Kiewiet has synthesized the imperative toward a white welfare state thus: "South African society was being transformed. A society which was passing from a simple rural order to a complex commercial and industrial organization, and which, furthermore, was undergoing changes in the midst of an inferior subject people, could not permit a group of its own people to be lost to itself."[83]

Colonial states throughout Africa may have adapted aspects of traditional authority and culture for the purposes of racial domination, but none, outside South Africa, were forced by political and economic circumstances to fashion a large-scale system of territorial segregation, designed to simultaneously facilitate and serve as a bulwark against proletarianization. The challenge was clear: how to successfully contain revolutionary social transformation associated with capitalism by the manipulation of the very African institutions that were being undermined. Irrespective of the political features they might share, the scale of capitalist production, and therefore, of proletarianization, distinguished South Africa from other colonial systems in Africa.

Earlier, British officials, notably Sir Theophilus Shepstone, had devised policies that wed African cultural systems to wage labor regimes. Educated in South Africa at his father's mission school and fluent in several African languages, Shepstone served as Secretary of Native Affairs from 1856 to 1877. Shepstone was considered the guru of native affairs in his day, and his views, especially his belief in the need for a coherent policy on African labor and administration, greatly influenced Lord Carnarvon, Colonial Secretary in Benjamin Disraeli's 1874 Tory Government. Much of Shepstone's thinking was based on his considerable experience in Natal where he became a forceful advocate of preserving what remained of communal land tenure. After the obliteration of African communal lands, whites willing to take a preservationist stance were considered liberal. As liberals soon discovered, many race-conscious Africans considered their belated calls for land preservation to be little more than support for segregation.

With the defeat of the Zulu dynasty, Shepstone helped the British to adapt Zulu traditional authority to colonial purposes. For example, chiefs were forced to prove their loyalty by collecting taxes and providing workers for the mines. The famous Zulu warrior-king Shaka (1816–1828) had instituted a strict age-group regiment system—young men were forced to serve in the military before being allowed to marry or receive land. Shaka's custom of organizing young men by age cohorts for war was transformed into a method of labor recruitment into the gold mines. Now rather than military service, Zulu men were expected to do a stint in the mines.

In the face of the blatant misuse of traditional authority by whites, African nationalists soon recognized that a fusion of traditional and modern political institutions might more legitimately suit their purposes. During the 1920s, John Dube, the first President of the ANC, sought to enlist Zulu royal family support for the emerging nationalist movement. Similar to mother Britain herself, the royal family would serve as a national symbol of authentic African tradition, thus producing a successful synthesis of tradition and modernity. In effect, Dube proposed an alliance capable of limiting the growing influence, particularly in rural areas, of the radical worker ideology espoused by the Industrial and Commercial Workers Union, of which he disapproved.[84]

Although it was very unsuccessful in the 1920s, Dube's strategy of royalist nationalism was destined to be resurrected by Chief Mangosuthu Gatsha Buthelezi fifty years later. Like Dube, Buthelezi distrusted the radical elements of the African nationalist movement. In 1976, he founded the Zulu cultural movement, *Inkatha yeSizwe* (later *Inkatha yeNkululeko yeSizwe*, the Inkatha Freedom Party). When during the mid-1980s bitter political violence erupted, at first in Natal and later in the Transvaal, between supporters of Inkatha and the ANC, the farsightedness of Dube's vision of a united nationalist tradition became a painful hindsight.

The labor compounds (hostels) that house migrant laborers in the black townships, which provided Inkatha with its urban base of support, have long been used to handicap labor organizers, but "homeland" representatives were always granted full access to them. Over time, a close relationship between "homeland" chiefs and the administrators of migrant labor evolved. In his autobiography, Nelson Mandela gives a personal account of the cooperation that existed between authorities at Crown Mines and the ruling Regent in his native Transkei. Mandela narrates his escape and that of his friend (a young Xhosa Chief-designate) from the rural Transkei to Johannesburg. In *eGoli* (the city of gold), they hoped to avoid the positions of traditional authority for which they were being groomed in their "homeland." The *Induna* (or headman at the mines) at Crown Mines quickly discovered who these two young work-seekers were and learned that they were in Johannesburg against the Regent's wishes.[85]

Eventually, bantustans became ever more central to the apartheid regime's counter-revolutionary strategy. Instead of merely restoring the old in a new guise, the goal of counterrevolution, says Alfred Meusel, is to create "a new order in which the *ancient regime* and revolution are negated and transcended in a dialectical synthesis."[86] Although the political functions of "homelands" evolved for several decades, the legal and political fiction at the core of their very existence remained the primary justification for the entire apartheid system. Hermann Giliomee has shown that in addition to serving as the base for migrant labor, the "homelands" were used to justify the exclusion of Africans from land holding in white areas. Moreover, in order to underpin racially exclusive rule, the "homelands" were supposed to provide blacks with their own political outlet, one that had no real impact on whites, but that could still be used to deflect international pressure for black citizenship.[87]

In Morris Szeftel's view, the "homeland" policy was an exercise in conflict externalization—the state sought to displace conflict from its traditional pattern of interracial confrontation to one of intraracial competition. The larger political objective of the policy was to introduce an element of unrealistic conflict so that Africans struggled against each other for the political goods of the "homelands," rather than for those of the whole country. Through geographical relocation of social conflict, the "homelands" would narrow the scope of multiracial and multiethnic society while expanding racially and ethnically exclusive arenas. Perhaps nostalgically, the regime believed that such policies could, ultimately, return African leadership to the chiefs, with their rural and ethnically fragmented perceptions.[88] In fact, "homelands" evolved into a system of patronage for chiefs, and other black elites, who were willing to support the apartheid regime.

However, as an alternative to the liberation movement, "homelands" proved to be a very bad investment in the long term.

For as long as they existed, "homelands" remained ensconced in Shepstonian assumptions. In 1951, the all-white parliament passed the Bantu Authorities Act, which designated specific territories for Africans on an ethnic basis; this act was followed by the Bantu Self-Government Act of 1959 that granted these areas "self-government." With the largest portion of their budget coming from Pretoria, the bantustans were neither economically viable nor politically independent. Nevertheless, in 1976, the Transkei became the first of four homelands to be granted "independence"; it did not, however, receive diplomatic recognition from any country other than South Africa. Following the Transkeian example, Bophuthatswana (1977), Venda (1979), and the Ciskei (1981) opted for Pretoria-style independence. Almost comically, soldiers of their minuscule, South African–created military establishments overthrew chief-led governments in both Transkei and Ciskei. After the 1994 elections, the Government of National Unity (GNU) administratively reincorporated all of the "homelands" into a united republic.

By the time of abolition, the economic functions of the "homelands" were more pernicious than their political ones. The "homeland" myth was key to the way industrial rights came to be defined by race. Under the terms of the 1924 Industrial Conciliation Act, as well as the 1956 legislation that replaced the older regulations, blacks were excluded from the category "employee" and designated "native workers." Since the category "employee" did not apply to Africans, they were excluded from the collective bargaining system. In 1979, the Wiehahn Commission Report called for the recognition of black trade unions and the abolition of racial categorization in industrial relations policy. Nevertheless, the government, while willing to allow black urban workers legal recognition, sought to deny collective bargaining rights to migrant workers. Black trade unions, whose support the government sought to elicit, refused to even consider participation in the proposed reforms on these divisive grounds. Due to these and other differences, the white government did not remove all references to race from labor legislation until 1981.

The government's strategy hinged on the calculation that migrant workers from the "homelands," and poor neighboring countries of southern Africa, could be pitted against urbanized workers, with "section-ten" permits allowing them the right to reside in the urban areas.[89] The migrant labor system, tied as it was to the "home-lands," facilitated the state's effort to socially engineer differences in the degree of militancy between the two groups of black workers. In the "homelands" themselves, especially the Ciskei, trade unions were viciously attacked. In addition, as trade unions forced nationwide changes in industrial relations, leaders in the supposedly indepen-dent "homelands" clung to older statutes that were far more repres-sive. In the end, both black and white taxpayers subsidized a "home-land" elite that presided over extremely high levels of rural poverty. Perhaps the ugliest of all "homeland" functions was that of dumping ground for unemployed workers forcibly removed from the urban areas. Primarily through forced removals, by the 1980s "homelands," consisting of only 13 percent of the land, housed 54 percent of the African population, a 14 percent increase over the 1960 figures. During this period, more than 750,000 Africans were ejected from the urban areas and 1,250,000 were relocated from white-owned farms.

As Bill Freund noted, forced removals were a calculated part of the cheap labor system. Government officials were well aware that most unemployed black workers forcibly removed to the reserves would return to the urban areas. However, those who managed to do so came illegally or as migrants. In either case, they were far more likely to accept low wages.[90] The strange logic of forced removals guided Wilmot James to the conclusion that the "homelands" had absolutely nothing to do with ethnic partition, or the solution to the national question. These areas, in fact, had become a short-term camouflage of the unemployment crisis, which began with the eco-nomic downturn of the 1970s.[91]

BLACK CONSCIOUSNESS IN AFRICAN NATIONALISM

The origins of modern African nationalism are contemporaneous with those of Afrikaner nationalism. The first African political organi-zation, *Imbumba Yama Afrika* (Union of the Africans), was formed at the same time as the Afrikaner Bond in the early 1880s. Moreover, Afri-cans launched the South African Native National Congress (SANNC), which later became the ANC, two years before Afrikaners initiated the National Party under Hertzog in 1914.[92] As social movements, there are some striking parallels and contrasts between African and Afri-kaner nationalism. The movements were similar in that neither black nor white consciousness was exclusive to a particular social class, nor were their respective nationalist movements propelled by the masses.

One astute observer concluded that the early Afrikaner nationalist leadership was largely drawn from the ranks of "big farmers and little lawyers." Rife with racial populism and vehemently anti-liberal, the leading members of the Afrikaner nationalist elite proved to be "the poorest guides to the landless class of people who, full of irreverent national ideals," cherished "the fond delusion that they themselves are still 'the farmer.'"[93] In brief, Afrikaner populism was rooted in rejection of the reality of proletarianization. Whereas African populism often took the form of left-wing thought, Afrikaners moved in the opposite direction. Two core tenets of the National Party's doctrine of Christian-Nationalism was the glorification of God, nation, family, blood, and the cult of force together with the rejection of liberalism, Marxism, humanism, and especially the equality of humankind regardless of race.[94]

Meanwhile, black nationalism was nurtured by a growing sense of common racial identity, a shared historical experience of subordination, and the denial of citizenship.[95] Since black nationalism and trade unionism developed almost simultaneously, the relationship between black workers and nationalist movements has never been one of deference and dominance. Similar to issues confronted by Afrikaner nationalists with respect to white workers, African nationalists had to appeal to the interests of black workers, who often produced leaders from within the ordinary people. Protests by African workers often rejuvenated the nationalist movement, as in 1918, when the Johannesburg sanitary workers struck for higher wages.[96] When a wave of African strikes hit Bloemfontein in 1919, Selby Msimang, a strongly labor-oriented leader of the ANC, told white officials that African strikes had not been brought into the minds of the people by outside influences. They were "a movement that is spontaneous among the people."[97] Indeed, by the 1920s, the need to organize black workers had begun to lay the groundwork for the fraternal relationship that would develop subsequently between the SACP and the ANC.

Neither African nationalists nor communists shared the Afrikaner antipathy for all things British or liberal. Indeed, African nationalists were, for long, under the spell of English liberalism. Having served the English as laborers during the Anglo-Boer war, many Africans thought of Britain as an ally and hoped the world's most powerful nation would intervene on the side of racial equality. Unlike Afrikaners who abandoned centrists like Smuts and Botha, the liberal wing of the movement remained dominant in African public affairs, even though a race-conscious form of nationalism, which some scholars trace to the last great Zulu King Cetshwayo, did persist. (Cetshwayo, who had every reason to distrust whites, was installed as king in 1872, at a coronation presided over by Shepstone. Seven years later, he was defeated and forced into exile by Britain, at which time the Zulu dynasty was dismantled, and Zululand placed under the rule of thirteen smaller chiefs.) The original leaders of the SANNC were drawn from the largely Christian African professional class of clerks, interpreters, teachers, ministers, lawyers, and a few medical doctors. A special chamber, modeled on the House of Lords, was reserved for the chieftaincy, because it was then too influential to be overlooked. As was the case with Cetshwayo, the race-conscious militancy of the chiefs often surpassed that of Christian-educated Africans who had adopted Western notions of civilization and progress. In the main, the emerging African elite was a product of colonial assimilation. Comparing South Africa to other parts of the continent, Bangani Ngcobo observes that "the educated elite is the product of the same process of culture contact that have produced the *assimilado* in the Portuguese African possessions and the *notables evolués* or *citoyens Français* in the French African territories."[98] As in Francophone and Portuguese Africa, as well as in the Belgian Congo, colonial systems that rewarded the cultural assimilation of elites, even while they continued to discriminate against the assimilated few, stimulated a form of black consciousness that never succumbed to the influence of multiracial liberalism.

Yet, Christianized African communities often harbored deep-seated hostility toward ancestral traditions. The famous African liberal John Tengo Jabavu was Mfengu—a community of refugee groups that fled from the Zulu war machine in Natal to the Cape Colony in 1820s. The Mfengu fought with whites against the Xhosa in the Seventh Frontier War (War of the Axe) of 1846. Likewise, in 1879, Natal's African Christians fought with the British against the Zulu.[99] In the pages of their newspaper, *Isigidimi Sama Xhosa,* Elijah Makiwane and Jabavu referred to the British as "our troops, the troops of Victoria Child of the Beautiful" and to Africans as heathens who were guilty of "hostility to the Word."[100] As editor of *Isigidimi* in 1876, Makiwane warned the younger generation of Africans not to compare themselves with the people who had produced Shakespeare, Milton, and Bacon.[101]

An important segment of the black elite, including even persons with impeccable nationalist credentials, were doctrinaire cultural assimilationists. Thus, many nationalists saw African tradition as a hindrance. As late as 1959, Reverend Zaccheus Mahabane, twice President of the ANC (1924–1927 and 1937–1940), expressed his own disdain, as an educated Christian, for the traditional African way of life. Insisting that African Christians had much to overcome, he advised his parishioners that Africa had emerged from "ignorance, superstition, vice, degradation, barbarism, savagism, psychic unconsciousness, intellectual insensibility, and mental unawareness. . . ."[102] As Ngcobo suggests, Mahabane's attitudes are consistent with those of Christianized and Europeanized Africans in other parts of Africa, especially West Africa.

However, there is an important contradiction to be noted in Mahabane's position, one that reveals an unmistakable strand of black consciousness thought. Despite his firm rejection of African culture, Mahabane, like many other black Christians, believed that they, nonetheless, had a special racial responsibility to convert and uplift "raw" Africans. It was commonplace to find black evangelicals demanding that they (and not white missionaries) be anointed the sole envoys of Western, Christian civilization in Africa. Given the contradictions that race consciousness tended to produce, it was only a matter of time before a significant number of black Christians would become Africanists. For example, the Presbyterian Minister and Pan-Africanist thinker whose home was Liberia, Edward Wilmot Blyden, had, by the 1860s, begun to fashion a black cultural nationalism that would "resolve the conflict between African and European standards by accepting from Europe what appeared beneficial to Africa while preserving the best of the traditional African way of life."[103] In South Africa, black Christians were forced to swallow the racial arrogance of white settlers, most of whom considered themselves devout believers, but whose hypocrisy fueled African resistance to Christianity. Thus, elitist African nationalism, not unlike the separatist churches, had to become back-to-the-people movements in order to survive; that is, they needed to find ways to combine Western ideas, both religious and political, with the symbols of African tradition.

Yet, cultural nationalists, like Jordan Kush Ngubane, were skeptical of efforts to reconcile Christianity and African tradition within the context of liberationist thought. For Ngubane—the iconoclastic black South African journalist and Pan-Africanist thinker who helped to found the ANC Youth League, and was, at one time, the highest-ranking member of the Liberal Party—Congress's real weakness was the close association of its leaders with the church. When a new leadership emerged to challenge the conciliatory political policies pursued by the old ANC, it overreacted by turning against the Christian churches as agents of the race oppressor.[104] However, hostility toward black Christians never became a dominant sentiment in the ANC.

The need to confront the sense of hybridity produced by the pressures of African tradition and Christian conversion is manifest in R. V. Selope Thema's description of Pixley Ka Isaka Seme, founder of the ANC:

> The founder was born in Natal of a Christian family. But like an African boy of the nineteenth century he grew up in an environment which was neither African nor European: at home he was under the influence of Christian parents and the guidance of American missionaries, but outside on the hills, in the valleys and the banks of the river of his beautiful country, he came into contact with the ancient life of his people and learnt about the deeds of his warrior kings.[105]

Given the disruptive nature of racial proletarianization in South Africa, the emerging nationalist leaders were constantly compelled to rethink the meaning of African tradition. Tradition could be approached in a variety of ways: as a means to confer legitimacy upon nationalist leaders; as an important ideological resource for the mobilization of peasant and working classes; or, as an example of what hinders black advancement and, therefore, to be disregarded or condemned to extinction. In the history of black South African political thought, traditionalists—in the sense that they stressed the importance of African authenticity—have not necessarily been political conservatives, but were found in both multiracial and black republican camps. Thoughtfully blending traditionalism, Africanism, and multiracialism, Ngubane's rural populist interpretation of South African history simply dismisses proletarianization as an aberration. In his estimation, urban blacks had been deprived of their African tradition and, therefore, their true identity. A genuine African revolution was redemptive, and must originate in the countryside. Ngubane writes:

> The masses of the city are lost souls. Men who have broken with the land and thus with nature. The true African and the authentic African revolution will come from those simple men who have not lost contact with the soil or the African way . . . the seizure of African land had a graver significance for him (the African in the rural area) than the mere conquest of territory; it was a desecration of that from which he derived his being. For him, the race quarrel was defined, less in terms of colour and more in terms of ideology; there was a direct relationship between race, humiliation, the desecration of the graves of his ancestors and the land as a determinant of being.[106]

The ideological divisions of African nationalism had become evident during the decade before the founding of Congress in 1912. Within the mainstream, however, all nationalist leaders believed in what Ngubane calls Cetshwayo's doctrine of racial solidarity, but interpreted it in a variety of ways. Pixley Seme, the ANC's founder, saw racial solidarity as a means to extend the legal rights of Africans within a multiracial union. Its first President, John Dube, on the other hand, leaned toward a relatively conservative version of black republicanism, captured in his famous aphorism "where there was once a pool, water will collect again." Much influenced by Booker T. Washington, he saw solidarity as a means to accomplish African redemption and racial uplift.[107] As Kuper points out, for a long period, Jabavu's nonracialism and Bambatha's armed resistance fell outside the ambit of practical—seemingly realistic—African nationalist thought. A stronger advocate of nonracialism than Seme, Jabavu espoused South African territorial nationalism rather than black African nationalism; at the other end of the spectrum, Bambatha symbolized the spirit of armed resistance to reclaim African land. A nonracial, united South Africa seemed hopelessly remote and, until the African liberation movement embraced armed struggle in the 1960s, the symbolism of Bambatha's rebellion lacked practical appeal. However, once peaceful protest was violently repressed and the major movements were outlawed by the government, *Umkhonto we Sizwe* (Spear of the Nation), the liberation army jointly formed, in 1961, by the ANC and the SACP, vowed to install Jabavu's nonracial democracy by expanding and modernizing Bambatha's notion of armed resistance.

Ngubane's insight that the race conflict was more about ideology than color speaks directly to his understanding of the terms on which multiracial alliances were possible. In *An African Explains Apartheid,* he asserts that "Africans have generally felt that the white person who upheld the ideals for which the Africans fought was a friend, one of them. The African who supported racial segregation was an enemy."[108] Even Africanists, so often accused of black racism, did not renounce multiracial thought in its entirety. This liberal strand in Africanism serves to emphasize just how deeply the dialectic of nonracialism–race-consciousness is ingrained in black South African thought. Although preferences for black republicanism or multiracialism were often determined by political-strategic considerations, it is also thought that specific traditional cultures had their own predilections in race relations. Just as Kuper traced black exclusivism to Cetshwayo, Marks finds the origins of nonracialism in the traditional Xhosa propensity for inclusiveness.[109]

For many Africans, black republicanism was considered the most effective way to counter white republicanism. However, here and there, a rare white surmised the practical value of black republican thought. Kuper recounts the 1896 proposal of Joseph Booth, an English missionary in Natal, urging the establishment of an African Christian Union. The proposed organization would "combine religious faith, economic self-help, demands for equality with Europeans by Christian and lawful methods, and an unswerving policy of Africa for the Africans."[110] Booth's proposal was a precursor to Garvey's Universal Negro Improvement Association, but it foundered on African distrust of whites. From a black republican perspective, multiracialism represented the insertion of a radicalized version of Jabavu's early Cape politics into mainstream black nationalism; only through the influence of revolutionary multiracialists in both the ANC and the Communist Party was such an enterprise made legitimate in the eyes of many blacks. For black republicans, the worst aspect of revolutionary multiracialism was that—by aggravating the interpretive and tactical differences symbolized by Seme's Christian liberalism and Dube's traditionalism—it polarized proponents of racial solidarity.

The advocacy of militant multiracialism, more than socialism, made the South African Communist Party, formed in 1921, the major competitor of a complacent white liberal establishment, stigmatized by a long history of compromise on issues of nonracial citizenship. The ostensibly more liberal United Party was formed in 1934, an alliance between two long-time rivals, Hertzog and Smuts. Hertzog had been forced to the center of Afrikaner nationalist politics by the growing influence of ethnic exclusivists under Malan. The United Party was never prepared to support universal franchise, and seemed to offer the same old white nationalism distinguished only by its willingness to house English and Afrikaner under the same roof. In 1953, the Liberal Party, the only party other than the communists to support a nonracial constitution, was formed by a small group of white and black leaders. The Liberal Party recruited an equal number of its approximately two thousand members from white and African communities and had Coloured and Indian members as well. The party's leadership anticipated—and imagined that it would benefit from—an impending split in the United Party, whose liberal-wing had come to favor universal franchise. In 1959, the anticipated split occurred, but a new Progressive Party was formed. With the support of big English business, a well-financed Progressive Party actually undermined the parliamentary prospects of the Liberal Party; it never elected a single parliamentarian.

Now, the Liberal Party found itself politically stranded between the extra-parliamentary communists and the totally white parliamentary Progressives. In this situation, Patrick Duncan saw an opportunity for the Liberal Party to establish its militant multiracialist *bona fides* and, in the process, to contest the communists' reputation as the only whites prepared to act on behalf of racial equality. Duncan, editor of the liberal publication *Contact* and one of the most dynamic members of the Liberal Party, urged his colleagues not to give the arena of direct action over to the communist-inspired Congress of Democrats, also formed in 1953. The son of a one-time governor-general of the Union of South Africa, Duncan joined with Mahatma Gandhi's son, Manilal, and others, to make a showing in the 1952 Defiance Campaign.

In 1963, Duncan resigned from the Liberal Party, left South Africa, and in exile, joined the PAC, in effect becoming the first "white" black republican. Duncan and the leaders of the PAC shared a deep distrust, if not hatred, of the Communist Party, the ANC's chief ally. Duncan, the token PAC member, allowed the Africanists to distinguish their position on nonracialism from that of the ANC. The PAC, so it was argued, was not averse to the participation of a genuine white patriot who placed his African identity above all else and, by so doing, demonstrated that skin-color privilege could be transcended in struggle. To their way of thinking, PAC "nonracialism" was superior to the "multiracialism" of the ANC's Congress Alliance, which legitimated semi-autonomous racial and ethnic blocs inside the black liberation movement. With the ANC and PAC forced into exile, the government was unconcerned with the differences between multiracial unity and black solidarity; each was viewed as a threat, and advocates of both positions were subject to attack. However, the issue was not dead; the debate over multiracial alliances versus black solidarity would be revisited by the BCM, when it revitalized black internal opposition in the 1960s.

The transformation of the SACP, from advocacy of white workerism in the 1920s to revolutionary multiracialism in the 1950s, as well as Duncan's failed efforts to move the Liberal Party toward militant multiracialism, underscore only the practical pains taken to make socialism and liberalism indigenous ideologies—responsive to black political experience. Black political thinkers, who were usually activists too, have reconstructed liberalism and Marxism to make them better able to accommodate race relations. Despite their substantive differences, both liberalism and Marxism appeal to human values higher than race, nation, or culture, but they generate very different understandings of race relations. Compare, for example, Plaatje's *Native Life in South Africa* (1916) and B. M. Kies's *Contribution of Non-European Peoples to World Civilization* (1953). Bennie Kies (1917–1979) was an outstanding Marxist thinker who was a member of the Anti-Coloured Affairs Department group, the New Era Fellowship, the Non-European Unity Movement, and, in his later years, was an accomplished human rights lawyer.

Both Plaatje and Kies make their respective appeals to universal and humanistic values and both draw inspiration from the writings of W. E. B. DuBois.[111] John Tengo Jabavu emerges in Plaatje's *Native Life* in the same way as does Booker T. Washington in DuBois's *The Souls of Black Folk*. Washington and Jabavu began as sincere black leaders of an older generation who, compromised by white patronage, became apologists for segregation. More influenced by DuBois's efforts to grapple with race and socialism, Kies appropriated the language of historical materialism to attack white racial arrogance. As he saw it, Western civilization was not solely European; rather, it was a human achievement—the result of contributions from many cultures. Kies employed a Marxist method to argue for a multiracial and multicultural conception of civilization.

Plaatje, on the other hand, sought to exploit the discrepancy between England's rhetoric of nonracial, liberal citizenship and the actual discriminatory practices existing within the British Empire. From Kies's Marxist perspective, this would have been a futile project since racism, imperialism, and segregation are all consequences of capitalism. Kies believed that the barbarity of South African racism was an essential part of an international herrenvolk-imperialism. In short, international capitalism was inherently anti-democratic and racist.[112] Far from being naive about the racist dimension of Britain's colonial policy, Plaatje nonetheless was unrelenting in his efforts to mobilize English public opinion against Afrikaner nationalism. He appealed directly to the Victorian sensibilities of the times by providing the public with accounts of the Land Act's moral consequences—the disruption of stable African families and communities, which was especially injurious to women. Plaatje courted the sympathies of English, Afrikaner, Coloured, and African women, as he sincerely believed that females of all races were instinctively more inclined toward social and racial justice. Not far beneath Kies's Marxist scientism lay a strong moral sensibility: capitalism was the main engine of moral and cultural degradation worldwide. A genuine internationalist, Kies was deeply suspicious of racial nationalism, whether black or white. Both Plaatje and Kies were engaged in seminal efforts to ground liberalism and Marxism, respectively, in black political thought—to make these ideologies more Afrocentric.

The very essence of Eurocentric thought is the failure or refusal to take seriously the intellectual development and extension of Western political ideas in non-Western contexts. Therefore, at times, liberalism and socialism are more usefully viewed through the optic of black political thought. As Germaine Hoston has observed with respect to Marxist thought in prewar Japan, there is more at stake than the mere injection of a nationalistic impulse into some preconceived notion of Marxism.[113] As with the role of nonracialism in black liberation, the standard claims of individual rights and class conflict central to liberalism and Marxism, respectively, have been transfigured—made subordinate to a form of political struggle grounded primarily in race-conscious or multiracial populist precepts.

3. ✿ Liberalism, Populism, and Socialism

South Africa's significance in world affairs, from the dawn of the twentieth century until its final decade, is remarkable considering the relatively modest size of its population and its role as a remote outpost of imperial power and industrial development. Gold, produced in vast quantities, and racial oppression, as the central principle of South African society, account for the attention devoted to this country by social thinkers in Europe and North America. In turn, South African thinkers, black and white, have interpreted their own situation with reference to the wider world. Almost without exception, black political thinkers have conceptualized their struggle for racial liberation as part of the international democratic movement. At the Pan-African Congress, convened in London in 1900, Dr. W. E. B. DuBois spoke these memorable words: "The problem of the twentieth century is the problem of the color line." By mid-century, black South African political thinkers, like DuBois himself, appeared to agree with this influential declaration of H. V. Hodson: "[T]here are two problems in world politics which transcend all others . . . they are the struggle between Communism and liberal democracy, and the problem of race relations."[1]

The cause of racial reconciliation in South Africa had been promoted by Reverend James Kwegyir Aggrey, a Pan-Africanist from the Gold Coast (now Ghana), who visited the country in 1921 in his capacity as a representative of the Phelps-Stokes Commission on African Education. Aggrey suggested the organization of joint African-European councils which would nurture interracial dialogue and cooperation. He was a lifelong opponent of racial separation and the exclusivist philosophy of "Africa for the Africans," which he reviled as a worm of racialism in the heart of humanity's tree, an evil that might jeopardize progress toward the realization of a common human destiny.[2] Aggrey pioneered a school of thought based on the belief that Africa would advance through its mastery of Western science and culture, and not by emotional appeals to African or racial nationalism.[3]

By contrast to Aggrey's liberalism, black Marxists believed that racial conflict was an unavoidable part of the process of decolonization. From their perspectives, white-settler colonies, like South Africa, produced the objective conditions for revolutions that were not merely national, but truly social. Eschewing separatist racial populism, Marxists worked to enlist radical black nationalism for the cause of revolutionary socialism. Ultimately, however, socialism and liberalism were destined to converge in pursuit of a common goal—racial equality.

LIBERALISM AND RACIAL POPULISM

In black South African thought, populist themes of resistance and nationalism have often interacted constructively with liberal themes of assimilation and cooperation.[4] However, the barriers to fusion of these ideas were formidable. Although many black South Africans were inclined to embrace liberalism, racial segregation made it difficult for black liberals to popularize a nonracial theory of individual liberties and citizenship rights. For decades, the political values of the African elite were far from parochial. Peter Walshe has identified these early-twentieth-century influences on African political consciousness: Christianity, the Negro struggle in America, and Victorian liberalism.[5] Before the middle years of the twentieth century, the African elite did not think of itself as a segregated ethnic interest group. Its leaders wished to expand the parameters of liberty by endowing citizens on both sides of the color-line with the same rights, and they were opposed to all forms of black nativism, or the desire to rid the country of Indians, Coloureds, and whites. The African-educated elite readily associated liberal thought with humane treatment and human rights, as well as European cultural religious values. Ngubane pithily captures the worldview of African elites who were, in the main, products of Christian mission stations as a "new politico-cultural community."[6] By and large, the early founders of the ANC were Christian democrats and, as long as it remained an option, the mainstream black leadership favored the liberal democratic path. Since land tenure, citizenship, and labor exploitation were interrelated dimensions of social class formation, the collapse of Cape liberalism in the face of segregationist pressure is crucial to an understanding of the liberal-populist nexus. In brief, the aborted development of Cape liberalism compelled educated African Christians to downplay their preference for Christian liberalism.

Among South African political thinkers, segregationists were mainly white racial populists who discouraged African support of universal political ideals, but encouraged ethnic traditionalism. The salient features of pro-segregation liberalism can be summarized thus: After World War I, several important liberal capitalists, scholars, and politicians systematically elaborated the fundamentals of segregationist thought, which rejected older laissez faire, universalistic conceptions of liberalism. White republican leaders, like Botha and Smuts, espoused a unified (English-Afrikaner) South Africa, while they promoted ethnic disunity among Africans, as did racial extremists, like Malan.

Viewed as a strategy of cultural defense, intended to contain social forces unleashed by industrialization, segregationist thought played on African land hunger by linking the extension of African land rights to the denial of citizenship rights. White segregationist thinkers argued that communal and traditional forms of government were incompatible with either communism or Western democracy; they extolled the virtues of a "Bantu ethos" for Africans rather than cultural assimilation. A good deal of segregationist policy was designed to drive a wedge between the educated elite and the rural African masses.

Black republicans responded with ideas inspired by African-American separatist and communitarian thinkers—on the one hand, the moderate thought of Booker T. Washington and the rival, more radical, conceptions of W. E. B. DuBois and Marcus Garvey, on the other.[7] Even more important, however, were indigenous applications of Western religious and political thought devised by African intellectuals to counter the ideological assumptions of segregation. For example, Africans routinely criticized individualistic foundations of liberalism while they simultaneously affirmed its egalitarian aspects. The major ideological challenge faced by liberals and socialists alike was the amorphous but pervasive influence of racial populism. Race-conscious populism provided the African elite with a viable ideological approach to the problem of class division in the black community. In the religious arena, the syncretistic dimensions of racial populism served to mitigate mass resentment against the introduction of Western religious and cultural norms. This precedent was politically important since, as Leo Kuper has observed, educated Christians and the urban proletariat were the two most significant strata for African nationalism.[8]

In opposition to white racial populism, African Christians formulated their own syncretic version of Christian philosophy, one that extolled humanist unity contrary to the theologically sanctioned racism of the Afrikaner religious establishment. For this reason, the dominant non-racial tradition, often understood as a white creation, was, nonetheless, a black preference. Black Christian theology split into two ideological camps broadly identified with the European missions and African independent churches. Ngubane shows that these positions, when translated into political ideologies, became the precursors of multiracial unionism and black republicanism.[9] White South African liberalism, construed as the political counterpart of egalitarian Christianity, was damaged by its justification of segregation and its reputation as a palliative for oppression. The complicity of early white liberals in formulating segregation policy was compounded by the powerlessness of latter-day liberals to effect any concrete reforms in the structures of racial domination. By the 1960s, most black intellectuals had accepted the rhetoric of rejection for most aspects of liberal ideology. Despite his own prominence as a member of the Liberal Party, Ngubane conceded that liberalism was associated with betrayal in the African popular mind.[10]

So far did liberalism sink in the estimation of African intellectuals that the word continues to signify unacceptable compromise in contemporary black political discourse. Although this tendency has been undermined by the advent of a democratic South Africa in our time, universally accepted liberal tenets such as the rule of law, parliamentary government, and the promotion of a market economy are often overlooked in the process of belittling liberalism.[11] Yet, despite their rejection of the liberal label, African intellectuals have never failed to incorporate liberal values into their arsenal of political ideas. Indeed, the fight against a minority police state convinced many blacks of the sanctity of the rule of law and representative government. Ambivalence toward white liberals was a factor in the poor showing of the Democratic Party (successor to the Progressive Party) in the 1994 election. As an electoral strategy, the Democratic Party stressed the human rights abuses of the government and the ANC (primarily in its military camps), portraying itself as the most consistent defender of just laws and competitive markets. In the mind of the black electorate, these liberal virtues were not enough to overcome liberalism's primary vice—a reputation for political timidity on issues of racial equality.

For many years, ANC liberalism appeared to be dormant, buried beneath the ideological baggage of its revolutionary agenda. Recently, however, the ability of liberal leaders, notably Nelson Mandela, to resuscitate the liberal values of the Congress tradition has been a source of great electoral and organizational strength. At crucial moments, the old liberal tradition has been invoked to temper the wrath of both racial and class populism. Although anti-liberal socialism has been an integral part of black liberation thought for nearly two generations, awareness of liberalism's pragmatic benefits, including the prospect of nonracial citizenship, has never ceased to exist.

RACIAL AND NON-RACIAL POPULISM

The founders of the ANC envisioned the emergence of a nation that would transcend the ethnic identities of its citizens. This goal appealed to black republicans as well as multiracial unionists. The utopian vision of black republicans centered on the ideal of African civil society that would use political power to reconcile the values of tradition, social progress, and racial uplift. Meanwhile, multiracialists favored an equally compelling utopia wherein all races would recognize their common humanity under the aegis of a color-blind government.

When I. B. Tabata, founder and theoretician of the Non-European Unity Movement, reflected on the formation of the ANC, he reached the conclusion that the organization derived both strengths and weaknesses from the successful transfer of communal authority to African nationalism.[12] In a 1948 letter to Nelson Mandela, Tabata described the ANC's genesis in 1912 as "the first creation of an African organization on an individualist basis."[13] Although Tabata was a left-wing black republican and a vocal critic of the ANC's approach to liberation politics, he nonetheless acknowledged that the ANC represented a decisive step toward the realization of an African identity based on individual rights, which was essential for the achievement of majority rule.

However, black republicans generally believed that citizenship should be rooted in African communal identities, values, and virtues. For many of them, a true Azanian must be African either by descent or commitment. To be an Azanian implied a genuine identification with the right of the African people to self-rule and the reclamation of their ancestral land. It is notable that black republicans employ the name "Azania" for a truly liberated country, while the ANC shuns that name and its Africanist symbolism.[14] This enduring dispute over the name for the nation reflects the central antinomy of black political thought: black republicanism versus multiracialism. These utopian visions preoccupied leading members of the ANC Youth League (CYL), the militant organization that produced the principal leaders of both the ANC and the PAC in the 1950s. In fact, most CYL intellectuals began their active careers as black republicans, and were only won over to a multiracial perspective as Africans were joined by militants from other races who were also engaged in confrontations with the early apartheid state.

The CYL represented a new generation of largely black nationalist intellectuals who were mainly graduates of Fort Hare College. As the primary African institution of higher learning in the country, Fort Hare attracted upwardly mobile young men and women from diverse social backgrounds. In their youth, ANC leader Nelson Mandela, Robert Sobukwe of the PAC, and Gatsha Buthelezi of the Inkatha Freedom Party all attended Fort Hare and were members of the CYL. Despite his being surrounded by such capable colleagues from Fort Hare, Anton Muziwakhe Lembede (1914–1947)—who graduated from Adams College—stands out as the Youth League's most daring populist theoretician. After Adams College, Lembede acquired correspondence degrees in Philosophy and Roman Law and a Bachelor of Laws degree from the University of South Africa.

In his capacity as a journalist for *Inkundla ya Bantu* during the 1940s, Ngubane described the young Zulu lawyer A. M. Lembede as a fanatical nationalist with a narrow conception of nationhood and an uncompromising hostility to the forces of the left.[15] Nevertheless, Ngubane and Lembede, who had attended Adams College together, coauthored the 1944 *Congress Youth League Manifesto*.[16] As an explanation of his strident black republican bent, Gail Gerhart writes that Lembede's position "reflected the perspective of the Zulu peasantry for whom the memory of white conquest was fresh and bitter."[17] An even more fruitful interpretation is offered by Robert Edgar, who observes that, in his desire to formulate a pan-ethnic perspective, Lembede discounted the usual building blocks of nationalism. Working squarely within the Blydenite tradition, which encompasses Garveyism, Lembede believed that "what bound the peoples of Africa together and made them unique was not language, color, geographical location, or national origin, but a spiritual force he called 'Africanism.'"[18]

CYL intellectuals, like most of their Third World counterparts, were cognizant that nationalism and socialism represented two inter-related forms of revolutionary democratic action. Initially, however, Lembede and other CYL theoreticians considered both liberalism and Marxist socialism to be white ideologies; hence, they opted for a version of African nationalism that would be no less philosophical but more inspirational. Still, Marxist ideas on the exploitative nature of capitalism were not considered incompatible with black nationalism and were easily incorporated into Youth League thought.

During the early days of the CYL, William Nkomo was the main proponent of Marxism. Unlike most of his black nationalist associates, Nkomo, who also helped to draft the organization's founding manifesto, was active with communist students while he was attending the University of the Witswatersrand Medical School. When he was elected President, Lembede replaced Nkomo as head of the CYL's Provisional Committee.[19] In his later years, Nkomo became a prominent liberal and, just before his death, was elected the first African President of the South African Institute of Race Relations. Nkomo was also actively involved in work leading to the founding of the Black People's Convention in 1972, shortly after his death.

Motivated by the belief that African political groups were ripe for realignment, the CYL's 1944 *Manifesto* represented a determined effort by Lembede and his CYL colleagues to rethink black national-ist theory and practice. Primarily a black republican document, the *Manifesto* advanced an African-conscious program for unity and uplift as the basis of opposition to white supremacy. Inspired by a belief in African spiritual and cultural uniqueness, Youth Leaguers were essen-tially populist thinkers who demanded that political leaders represent the will of the African people. The *Manifesto* contrasted the European tendency to glorify individual power, success, fame, and control of the universe with that of African culture, where corporate life and com-munal contentment are made the absolute measure of value. Yet, most CYL members were uncomfortable with black racial chauvinism and acknowledged that African nationalism had "two streams"; hence, the *Manifesto* specifically rejected—as ultra-revolutionary and too nativis-tic—the first stream or Garveyite formulation that South Africa should be a country for none other than black Africans. Even as it identified with the more moderate and realistic second stream of African na-tionalism and acknowledged that the different racial groups in South Africa had come to stay, the CYL vowed to extend the franchise to the black majority, thus ridding the country of an exclusively white democracy.[20]

The *Manifesto* suggests that black intellectuals had begun to wrestle with competing conceptions of the nation, the people, and, unavoidably, citizenship. Although support for various forms of racial cooperation always existed, multiracial union as an alternative interpretation of political community was emerging directly from black political experience. In his important study of black politics, Tom Lodge notes that by the 1950s the two main issues confronting the black movement were the position of the multiracial Communist Party of South Africa (CPSA; after 1953, South African Communist Party or SACP) and the question of collaboration with non-African organizations.[21]

By the end of the 1940s, the African National Congress Youth League had wrested control of the parent organization from an older and more liberal generation of leaders. Central to their success was the advocacy of nationalist populism and condemnation of liberal gradualism. As long as the young turks of the CYL functioned as radical outsiders pressuring the older Congress leaders toward militant mass activity, division within the Youth League could be managed. After 1949, the year CYLers outmaneuvered Dr. A. B. Xuma to capture the leadership of Congress, serious divisions began to surface within its own ranks. More than any other question, that of multiracial alliances challenged the black republican assumptions of the CYL. This issue eventually split black activists and intellectuals into two rival nationalist traditions— multiracial union and black republican identity.

There are two core assertions that guide black republican, or Africanist, thought. First, since European settlers divested them of their ancestral lands, the African people constitute the sole source of revolutionary legitimacy. Second, since virtually all classes of whites were allied in support of racial domination, black republicans reasoned that Africans would be well advised to form their own intraracial multiclass alliance. Given its emphasis on African initiative, and in stark contrast to the assumptions of multiracial union, the black republican position was often described as "exclusivist" or one of "going-it-alone." Later, the BCM would capture this same republican sentiment with the slogan "Black man, you're on your own."

Africanists were especially upset by the prospect of privileged whites (and to a lesser extent Coloureds and Indians) benefiting from racial domination and simultaneously being allowed to sway the direction of opposition politics under the auspices of multiracial ideology. Black republican thinkers reacted at a very visceral level to the recasting of African nationalism in conjunction with the assumptions of multiracial unity. Furthermore, black republicans discerned that multiracial citizenship would undermine their most cherished political demand—return of the land to exclusive African ownership. Whether or not the land could be reclaimed was beside the point; the mere call to retake the land served to polarize black republican and multiracial visions of liberation.

Predisposed to seeing democracy and socialism as inherent in the ways of the African folk, the black republican worldview is quintessential populism. Indeed, black republicans are apt to assert, rather than explain, the historic rights and nature of the African people. Africa and its people were virtuous, their degradation being a consequence of European intrusion and the imposition of alien cultural values. Because of that assumption, black republicans concluded that the birth of Azania, either in the form of a new African socialist republic or a black social democracy, would restore the Africans' lost sense of dignity. At bottom, the African people have been deprived of their birthright, the land that was now called South Africa but that Africanists would rename Azania.

In contrast to multiracial unionists, who advocate a territorial, and therefore multiracial, view of South African citizenship, black republicans underscore African ownership of the land—a concept that they imbue with both cultural and spiritual meaning. Whereas these distinctions should not be too rigidly drawn, Africanists have tended to focus on land expropriation, while multiracial unionists stress the denial of citizenship rights and capitalist exploitation of black labor. The respective political orientations of the two positions partially help to explain the deftness currently exhibited by multiracial unionists in the practice of parliamentary politics and coalition building; by contrast, the political programs of their black republican rivals often appear to be prefaced by the demand for a more perfect past.

The lament over the forced destruction of African tradition is pervasive, especially among the older generation of nationalists. Thus, those who assert the sanctity of African tradition need not be political conservatives, or even black republicans. Defenders of tradition are of every ideological stripe, united by a sense of moral outrage at the destruction of African communal life. More properly termed neo-traditionalists, these black nationalists may reconcile the importance of African authenticity with either black republican or multiracial viewpoints.

Ever mindful of the division that can develop between the values of urban and rural Africans, Lembede, perhaps more than any other African nationalist intellectual, sought to reconcile modern black nationalism with African tradition. He viewed land reclamation as the core demand of African nationalism, and recoiled from the idea that a class struggle of African toilers against their white exploiters should take precedence over national liberation. In 1947, Lembede spoke eloquently about the inextricable links between the struggle of black workers and that of the entire African people. With the communists in mind, he declared, "[I]t is an illusion of demented political dema-gogues to imagine that African workers as such can achieve their emancipation and reach their goal of being recognized by the govern-ment on the same footing with European trade unions while the rest of the African nation is still in chains and bondage of segregation, oppression, and colour discrimination."[22]

Lembede's insistence that the emancipation of African workers would only come about in conjunction with total African liberation has been the view of the black nationalist movement as a whole, and not that of the Africanist faction alone. More than three decades after Lembede's remarks, the growth of a powerful independent trade union movement occasioned debates between so-called "populists" and "workerists" that were reminiscent of exchanges between com-munists and nationalists during an earlier period. The workerist-populist distinction was a product of 1980s debates over the proper role of the trade union movement in anti-apartheid politics. Populists advocated a deeper trade union involvement in liberation politics than did workerists, who tended to emphasize questions of union organization and the protection of gains on the shop floor.

In contrast to black republicans, multiracial unionists extended the idea of a multiracial alliance of workers to include all races, classes, and peoples opposed to apartheid. From their perspective, the liberation struggle was construed as a united front against racial domination. So did ANC and SACP intellectuals transform an idea originally drawn from class relations into a brand of multiracial popu-lism for all classes based on a racially inclusive conception of citizenship. The South African people are all those individuals, irrespective of race or class, who are willing to work for a nonracial society; this formulation made it possible for multiracialists to lay stress on national, rather than racial, identity, and it eventually became the linchpin of the ANC's approach to citizenship, thus eclipsing its older emphasis on pan-tribal unity.

Initially, the relationship between the ANC and the SACP was purely a marriage of convenience. However, in the process of carrying out direct action campaigns, ANC leaders, such as Nelson Mandela, who originally opposed communist involvement in the movement as well as coalitions with Indians and Coloureds, decided that genuine multiracial alliances were possible. Many African nationalists resented the communists' contribution to the organization of the black working class; but given the impending confrontation with the racist state, the more pragmatic in their ranks were unprepared to ignore the benefits of a communist-nationalist alliance.

In 1955, the multiracial Congress of the People organized by the ANC and SACP issued the famous *Freedom Charter,* which most consider the black liberation movement's major multiracial manifesto. The *Charter* begins with a sentence that encapsulated ANC multiracialism while it infuriated Africanists—"South Africa belongs to all who live in it, black and white." With the distinction between "multiracialism" and "nonracialism" in mind, Archie Mafeje advises that it was not until 1961 with the founding of the African People's Democratic Union of South Africa (APDUSA), another NEUM affiliate, that "[t]he term 'African' was, for the first time, in the history of the movement, extended to include *all* progressive citizens of South Africa."[23] Nonetheless, the dominant ANC-SACP faction of the black movement produced the *Freedom Charter* and that, in itself, contributed to the growing divide between multiracialists and black republicans. Despite their own use of the nonracial-multiracial distinction to criticize ANC policies, the PAC responded to accusations that their brand of Africanism was little more than racism in reverse. Africanists began to modify their own exclusivist doctrines along the lines of those articulated in defense of Patrick Duncan's participation in the PAC. Even before the PAC was forced into exile, the theoretical acceptance of non-African supporters who were ready to renounce their separate ethnic or racial status appeared to envisage a multiracial horizon. Soon a very small number of Indians, Coloureds, and the rare white were anointed African. By 1967, the Pan Africanist Congress in exile had both Indians and Coloureds on its Executive and Duncan was its representative in Algeria.

By the end of the 1960s, the PAC was joined by a new generation of black republican intellectuals and activists from the BCM who would reach different conclusions about the nature of black identity. The old guard, however, would continue to perceive these new directions in race-conscious populism through the lens of its own disagreements over the respective merits of black republicanism and multi-racialism.

SOCIALIST POPULISM

The organization of African nationalism in South Africa, as in many other African countries, involved "the interpenetration of political and labour movements."[24] This was the basis of a radical form of political action that may be identified as socialist populism.

Here, as elsewhere in the proverbial Third World, reconstructed versions of Marxism resulted in a melding of anti-colonial, anti-capitalist, and anti-racist ideologies. Fanon was on target when he asserted that in order to accommodate such a diverse array of struggles, "Marxist analysis should always be slightly stretched."[25] From the 1920s to the present, the interaction of black nationalism and socialism has added a provocative race-class dimension to the history of black political thought in South Africa, and elsewhere in the African Diaspora. Scholars of communist movements in both South Africa and the United States have traced the populist evolution of these movements to the aftermath of World War I.

African revolutionaries employed Marxism as a guide to racial, national, ethnic, and, infrequently, class struggles; therein lay the secret of Marxism's appeal in the Third World as well as its fatal flaw. In South Africa, Marxism was adapted to any number of local, non-class issues resulting in the growth of an indigenous form of socialist populism. Thus, Walshe found that the multiracial implication of Marxism was far more controversial among blacks than any particular theory of class struggle.[26] In a similar vein, Neville Alexander argued that, in the Western Cape after the Second World War, "the Westernising aspects of Marxism automatically appealed to a youth being threatened with a retrogressive policy of tribalization."[27]

In contrast to views held by many Marxists in the West, Ernesto Laclau contends that the "historical experience of the class struggle and the ascent of the masses on a world scale has progressively broken down the system of connotative articulations in which the provincial Eurocentrism of the Second and Third Internationals had encapsulated Marxist theoretical concepts."[28] Founded two years after the Bolsheviks took power in Russia, the Third International (also known as the Comintern) decided that the power of racial nationalist appeals had to be taken seriously. Soon thereafter, black Marxists, primarily from the United States and the Caribbean, influenced the thinking of Comintern leaders. Since the Comintern functioned to exert Soviet control over the international communist movement, its dictates, at strategic moments, influenced the course of communist-nationalist relations in South Africa.

Black intellectuals in South Africa, as in other African countries, often insisted that socialism and indigenous systems of communalism shared a set of communitarian values that Western capitalism violated. Thus, left-wing populists could employ cultural nationalist and race-conscious concepts to justify socialist economic organization. For example, NEUM theoreticians called for a peasant-worker alliance in South Africa, thus allowing them to combine, with some facility, the rhetoric of both racial (read land) and class struggle.[29] The need to come to terms with these two forms of struggle would, in one way or another, be played out in every black social movement in South Africa. At meetings called in 1921 to formulate the Communist Party of South Africa's first comprehensive political program, the issue of involvement in parliamentary affairs was hotly contested; finally, it was decided that the CPSA would engage in all forms of political action, including parliamentary politics.[30] For the first time, white liberals were challenged from the left regarding race relations. Specifically referring to its more uncompromising stance on multiracialism, "the irony," observes R. W. Johnson "was that the CPSA was in many ways merely an off-shoot of South African white liberalism."[31] Johnson meant to criticize the CPSA's frequent use of parliamentary politics for ostensibly extra-parliamentary goals and its rivalry with white liberals on issues of race relations. However, much of the CPSA's behavior can be understood as an adaptation to the social character of a struggle against racial domination, which confounded all efforts to propagate doctrinaire forms of Marxism.

Within the ANC and the liberation struggle as a whole, race and class were both complementary and competitive themes in black South African political thought. Philip Bonner identifies two academic interpretations of the relationship between black workers and the ANC: one represented by the works of Peter Walshe and another by that of communist scholar-activists H. J. and R. E. Simons and, to a lesser extent, Mary Benson. Walshe contends that the African National Congress never managed to transcend the non-working-class orientation of its black middle-class leadership, although it became an increasingly broad-based nationalist movement. By contrast, the Simonses and Benson insisted that the ANC, by virtue of its effective agitation and mobilization on behalf of all Africans, especially the worker majority, became the authentic vehicle of black proletarian aspiration.[32] At issue was whether the ANC had evolved from elite to mass movement politics; if so, when had that been done, and how successful had it been?

The analyses by the Simonses and Benson are consistent with the evaluation of South Africa rendered by the Sixth World Congress of the Communist International held in 1928. Over the objections of Sydney Bunting, leader of South Africa's Communist Party delegation that favored a more orthodox theoretical interpretation, the Executive Committee of the Communist International concluded on a populist note:

> there is no Negro bourgeoisie as a class, apart from the individual Negro engaged in trading and a thin strata of Negro intellectuals. . . . Negroes constitute the majority of the working class. . . . The disproportion between the wages of white and black proletariat continues to exist as the characteristic feature of the colonial type of country. . . . The Communist Party (of South Africa) must orientate itself chiefly on the national question in colonial matters.[33]

With the exception of syndicalist movements inspired by the International Workers of the World (IWW), communists were usually prepared to work within existing black movements. Initially, socialists in South Africa, like those in the United States, argued that blacks were merely exploited workers. The "Negro Question" was an expression of the black person's economic bondage, although intensified by racism. Thus, racial oppression, it was surmised, complicated black exploitation, but did not alter its essentially proletarian character. As early as 1903, the American socialist Eugene V. Debs made the point in a way that DuBois considered pure sophistry: "there is no 'Negro Problem' apart from the general labor problem."[34] White socialists decided that the political strategy of their parties should be to conduct agitation among black workers in order to unite them with all class-conscious workers. In South Africa and America, how to address issues of racial equality was an issue that divided old-style socialist reformers and pro-Soviet communist revolutionaries. As a social policy, communist parties soon realized that, in racially divided societies, proletarian solidarity translated into support for racial integration, but this reformist impulse was invariably complicated by rivalry with militant racial nationalism. As Mark Naison and Harold Cruse show for communist parties in the United States, the usual problems associated with racial integration could not be totally avoided among the communist rank and file, an observation that is equally true of South Africa.[35]

At first, communist organizers in South Africa concentrated their efforts on white workers. They were strongly convinced—especially in the aftermath of the 1922 white mine worker uprising—that the white proletariat would assume the revolutionary leadership of all workers. In the days when "white workerism" held sway, the all-too-convenient excuse for a racially exclusive worker movement was that the black proletariat was not simply unorganized, but unorganizable; even worse, "politically backward" black workers were more responsive to black nationalism than to socialism. Of course, such assessments ignored the appeals of racial nationalism to white workers. Although many communists, like their racist socialist brethren, supported the 1924 Pact Government, a wing of the communist movement rejected the view that socialism was possible without the organization of the entire proletariat. Soon, communists became active among black workers and, by the 1940s, some members of the ANC considered the CP's participation in the organization of black workers to be an invaluable resource. Making the bonds even closer, the CP encouraged its African members to join the ANC, a practice institutionalized by the exiled ANC-SACP after 1960.

The meteoric rise of the Garvey movement between 1918 and 1928, as well as its popularity among many black workers, peasants, and intellectuals, compelled communists to acknowledge the appeal of race-conscious nationalism among black workers. The existence of discernible proletarian support for Garveyite black nationalism exposed one of South African Marxism's most serious theoretical and political contradictions—an inability to come to terms with the race consciousness of black workers. Garveyism influenced leaders of the ICU as well as the ANC. Although communists had assisted Clements

Kadalie in the organizing of the ICU, he suddenly expelled them from the union in 1926.

In his capacity as Director of Negro Work for the Red International of Labor Unions (Profintern), George Padmore was a strong adversary of both Kadalie and Garvey; his views directly reflected those of the Comintern. Padmore, like most communists, considered Garveyism a demagogic, anti-democratic tendency and a major hindrance to the emancipation of black workers.[36] Much of the conflict between the ICU and various communist leaderships took the form of a debate over communism versus racial nationalism. James Gumbs, a West Indian–born President of the ICU and a strong Garveyite, accused the SACP of being a white-dominated organization.

One influential interpretation of the ICU's demise is that it was drawn into a political vacuum created by ineffectual policies of the ANC during the 1920s.[37] From this perspective, the movement failed to find a balance between its socialist and nationalist proclivities. Many commentators have questioned Kadalie's grasp of socialism, and Padmore plainly equated his leadership style with that of the famous Pan-Africanist and first President of Ghana, Kwame Nkrumah.[38] The ICU, in contrast to the ANC's method of reasoned protest, relied upon an explosive combination of political and industrial agitation. Furthermore, as a general, rather than industrial, union, the ICU was naturally inclined toward a mass black nationalist orientation. As Lodge has noted, "Kadalie viewed social conflict in South Africa in mainly nationalist and colonial terms and did not share the communist vision of class struggle complicated only by racist 'false consciousness.'"[39] It is perhaps noteworthy that Kadalie was a native of Nyasaland, present-day Malawi, not South Africa.

For their part, black nationalists began to evaluate the competition between nationalism and socialism on the basis of each ideology's capacity to energize the kind of mass movement that they felt was needed. On the left, Garveyism and communism were in competition as proven mass-mobilizing ideologies. Finally, in the 1928 Black Republic slogan, these two ideologies appeared to converge: "The Party's slogan became an 'Independent Native Republic'; and, it was this phrase that began to circulate in tandem with Garvey's 'Africa for the Africans. . . .' For the first time it appeared to some as if Africans, in the long run, might themselves have to bear responsibility for the reform and governance of society."[40]

Like most nationalists of the period, Garvey familiarized himself with radical nationalist and socialist experiments, particularly Irish and Jewish nationalism and the 1917 revolution in Russia. Of the two forms of radical democratic activity, he identified more with radical nationalism and became a vigilant antagonist of socialism and communism.[41] Similar to his guiding inspiration, Booker T. Washington, who experienced racism at the hands of white trade unionists in the West Virginia coal mines, Garvey, who began his own career as a trade unionist in Jamaica, came to despise white trade unionists, socialists, and communists. Garvey's denunciations were emphatic: Communism is a white man's creation to solve intraracial class conflict; white socialists, communists, and trade unionists fought only for economic improvements that would come at the expense of greater exploitation of weaker peoples.[42]

Garvey and his followers admired both the charismatic style of leadership and the level of mass mobilization accomplished by ultra-nationalist powers in Germany and Japan. No friend of Garveyism, Padmore observes: "Many Garveyites compare Garvey with Hitler, to the latter's disadvantage. They say that Hitler's torrential flood of rhetoric, with its direct appeal to primitive mass emotions, is similar to Garvey's oratory, but that Hitler perverted Garvey's racial philosophy and proclaimed the superiority of the German over all other races, while Garvey tried to lift up and convince the Negro that it was basically the equal of other races."[43]

Yet, for Garvey, Japan, rather than Germany, gave a glimpse into black Africa's future. Naturally, he developed a deep admiration for the nationalistic accomplishments of Asia's major power. Garvey felt that Japan, as the first nonwhite industrial power, would ultimately champion the united demands of all "Oriental Civilizations," a designation which included Africa. By 1918, the United States' Federal Bureau of Investigation began to pay close attention to Garvey's support of Japan; FBI agents filed numerous reports on his relevant speeches and remarks.[44]

Ironically, the analysis of the black struggle in South Africa rendered by two white communists, Sydney Bunting and D. Ivon Jones, was situated in what Sheridan Johns refers to as the "possibly irrelevant context of the American Negro problem or the world Negro problem."[45] Jones, as the Party's representative to the Fourth Comintern Congress held in Moscow in 1922, argued that "In Africa . . . awareness of race might break down 'tribal sectionalism' and thereby induce Negroes to transfer their loyalties to a larger cause. More important still, because there is a 'race of labourers' race conscious-ness on the part of Negroes could constitute a significant step towards class-consciousness."[46]

Less than a decade later, the Comintern imposed the Native Republic and Black Belt States policies on parties in South Africa and the United States respectively. Padmore recalls that the Native Repub-lic slogan was the brainchild of Otto Kuusinen, founder of the Finnish Communist Party and secretary of the Comintern. Padmore consid-ered the slogan, which had Stalin's blessing, a device to capture left-wing black nationalists. Few communists in South Africa, either black or white, agreed with the extreme (populist) pronouncements of the Comintern's latest effort to meld nationalism and socialism, but they at least had to appear to be implementing the top-down policy.[47] Some black communists, like John Gomas, painfully recall the vituperation between black and white comrades that accompanied the introduc-tion of black nationalist slogans into the Party's socialist programs. Starting in the 1920s, Gomas, a radical Coloured leader, was active in the ICU, the ANC, and the Communist Party. He vividly remembered being told by white comrades that non-Europeans had too quickly forgotten that trade unionism and party organization had been given to them by Europeans. Gomas's recollection of the situation was short and simple: "they [the Comintern] destroyed our Party."[48]

During the interwar years, racial liberation became embroiled in East-West conflict. This allowed the international communist move-ment to attract a number of brilliant black intellectuals who worked earnestly to reconcile the disparate elements of the Marxist theory of racial revolution. In the interim period between the two world wars, several leading Pan-Africanists applied sophisticated understandings of Marxist thought to the analysis of racial domination. The leader-ship of the 1945 Sixth Pan-African Congress, which included Peter Abrahams, Otto Makonnen, George Padmore, C. L. R. James, Kwame Nkrumah, and Jomo Kenyatta, contained many individuals with Marx-ist training. However, all of them were destined to renounce main-stream communism. In October 1956, Negritude author Aimé Cé-saire captured the sentiments of many former black communists in his famous letter of resignation written to Maurice Thorez, Secretary-General of the French Communist Party. Césaire made it clear that he wished to see "Marxism and communism harnessed into the service of coloured peoples, and not coloured people into the service of Marx-ism and communism . . . and that the doctrine and the movement be tailored to fit men, and not men to fit the movement."[49] Thus far, I have referred to three of the most significant Afrocentric Marxist thinkers—DuBois, Padmore, and James; as we shall see, Moses Kotane was instrumental in the Africanization of South African communism.

After his expulsion from the Profintern for insisting on a racial dimension to anti-imperialism, the left-wing Pan-Africanist Padmore became an articulate and informed anti-Stalinist critic of the Comintern. Padmore founded the Africa Bureau, a Pan-African organization that influenced the first generation of African nationalists, particularly Kwame Nkrumah and Jomo Kenyatta. Padmore lived in Ghana and served the Nkrumah government in the capacity of African Affairs adviser to the Prime Minister until his death in September 1959.

DuBois began his public life by helping to initiate black rights organizations both in the United States and internationally—the Niagara and the Pan-African Congress Movements. A sophisticated socialist thinker, DuBois judged political parties in light of the consequences of their policies for black emancipation. DuBois was a member of the Socialist Party only from 1911 to 1912. He joined the American Communist Party when he renounced his American citizenship in 1961, after which he moved to Ghana, where he died August 28, the day of the famous 1963 March on Washington. DuBois's formal membership in both parties was as brief and symbolic as his commitment to socialism was genuine and long-standing.

C. L. R. James was at one time Leon Trotsky's principal adviser on the so-called "Negro Question." His study of black revolution in Haiti and Ghana, his sophisticated understanding of the black American struggle, and his rethinking of the philosophy of dialectical materialism after his estrangement from the Trotskyist movement led James to renounce vanguardist ideologies as anti-revolutionary. This breakthrough made possible a flexible interpretation of black movements and an emphasis on the self-organization of the masses that became James's hallmark.

In a scholarly exploration of nationalism and communism in South Africa, Martin Legassick disagrees with Padmore's assessment that the Native Republic idea originated with Kuusinen as well as with his contention that it was merely a means to attract left-wing black nationalists. Legassick believes that there were real creative possibilities inherent in the Comintern's formulation of national struggle. He concludes that the Marxism of the 1920s and the 1930s failed only because it did not fully grasp that national liberation was a form of social revolution. While the Party explained racial oppression in terms of national oppression with the implication that imperialism was the immediate enemy, there was some confusion over the character of a South African anti-imperialist movement. Harold Cruse once quipped that, during this period, communist parties wanted to attract nationalism without nationalists. Despite the theoretical ambiguity involved with the co-optation of black nationalism, its being made a legitimate political objective nonetheless influenced race relations within the Party. For example, three Africans were elected to the Central Committee of the CPSA for the first time in 1927. Three years later, Douglas Walton, a white communist, installed himself as head of a new Central Committee, consisting of nineteen Africans and only four whites.[50]

As the CP changed internally, its criticism of the ANC leadership's reformist inclination, particularly its tendency to vacillate between the chiefs and the masses, gave way to the belief that black nationalism and socialism could become compatible. In order to recruit members of the black South African intelligentsia, the party equated the latter's plight with that of black workers. In 1933, Albert Nzula, the first African Secretary General of CPSA, then resident in Moscow, I. I. Potekhin, the acknowledged father of African Studies in the Soviet Union, and A. Z. Zusmanovich argued that the black intelligentsia, particularly black teachers, represented a stratum of African society whose material and legal position was virtually indistinguishable from that of black workers.[51]

The indigenization or Africanization of Marxism in South Africa had another important race relations dimension. Not only did the Party have to redirect its theoretical thrust, it also had to persuade white communists to recast their Eurocentric political loyalties. Perhaps no one has better portrayed the problem of Eurocentrism in the CPSA than Moses Kotane (1905–1978), who for many years served as General Secretary of the CPSA and was elected to the ANC's National Executive Committee in 1946. Kotane was much admired in the Soviet Union and was buried in Novodevichy Cemetery in Moscow. It is useful to quote at some length Kotane's 1934 letter calling for the "Africanization" of the CP, a process he equated with bolshevization:

> [O]ur party has and is suffering owing to being too Europeanized. If one investigates the general ideology of our Party members (especially the whites) if sincere, he will not fail to see that they subordi-

nate South Africa in the interest of Europe. They are foreigners who know nothing about and who are least interested in the country in which they are living. But we are living in culturally backward Africa—Africa is economically and culturally backward. In Europe self-consciousness (class) has developed immensely whilst here national oppression, discrimination and exploitation confuses the class war and the majority of the African working population are more national conscious than class conscious. My first suggestion is that the party become more Africanised that we speak the language of the Native masses and must know their demands. That while it must not lose its international allegiance, the Party must be Bolshevised, become South African not only theoretically, but in reality and not a party of a group of Europeans who are merely interested in European affairs.[52]

Nevertheless, in 1942, Kotane found himself having to combat the very kind of Garveyite millenarian populism that he associated with "culturally backward" Africa. In his pamphlet entitled *Japan: Friend or Foe,* Kotane sought to explain to black workers that even though Japan was a non-European nation, and an enemy of the South African government during World War II, the Japanese were not friends of black workers, or black people generally. Kotane's appeal was clearly designed to tone down the populist zeal of black workers whose expectations led them to believe that Japan would use its might against the white supremacist regime.[53]

With leaders like Kotane who held positions of respect in both the ANC and the CPSA, it was only a matter of time before communist and nationalist movements would undertake various types of joint action, but this could not happen until the liberal old guard was replaced. Older ANC leaders looked to the Institute of Race Relations for its white allies. James Gumede, the president most often associated with the introduction of communist ideas into the early ANC, was also influenced by Garveyism. In an effort to reestablish strong relations with white liberals, in 1930 the ANC leadership ousted Gumede, thus rejecting both Garveyism and communism. Nevertheless, the CP was always anxious to expose the white liberal establishment's complicity in racial domination and took advantage of every opportunity to stake out a militant position on the issues of racial equality.

Central to the appeal of the communists were their sympathy with mass protest and their influence with black trade unionists. The leaders of the ANC gradually recognized that elite politics would have to be replaced by that of mass mobilization. When, in 1939, Xuma took over the ANC, many Africans thought the organization had outlived its usefulness. D. D. T. Jabavu (1885–1959), the prominent Cape educator and oldest son of John Tengo, upstaged the ANC when he called for an All-African Convention (AAC) to oppose the Hertzog attack on the Cape franchise. Together with the ANC founder, Pixley Seme, Jabavu convened the AAC at a meeting in Bloemfontein during December 1935. Recognizing the challenge posed by the mass-elite divide, Dr. Xuma proposed a reorganization of the ANC along the lines of the British Labour Party.[54] Although Xuma modernized the ANC during his decade-long (1939–1949) presidency, he never transformed the movement into a vehicle of mass action.

In fact, many of the older ANC leaders did not agree with mass action. For example, Mandela recalls that Youth Leaguers tried to convince the highly venerated scholar and educator Z. K. Matthews (1901–1968) to stand against Dr. Xuma, but he would have no part of their machinations. Matthews told Mandela that he considered the Youth Leaguers young firebrands who were full of impractical dreams of mass action, and chided them by saying that he hoped that they would mellow with age. Instead, the Youth League decided to run Dr. James S. Moroka because they felt that he would be totally pliable. Moroka, an AAC man who agreed to join the ANC and to run against Xuma, provides an excellent example of how many of the older ANC leaders felt about communists. As President-General of the ANC, Moroka was the figurehead leader of the 1952 Defiance Campaign. Nonetheless, when arrested with many other prominent protestors, Moroka, despite Mandela's effort to change his mind, hired legal counsel rather than be represented by the same attorneys as communists like Yusuf Dadoo, J. B. Marks, and Kotane.[55]

As the ANC shifted from petition to confrontation politics, younger nationalists began to find communist allies to be more reliable than liberals. After all, only in the CPSA could one find whites prepared to contemplate all forms of opposition to state repression. Once the ANC adopted the 1949 Programme of Action, designed to initiate civil disobedience on behalf of full citizenship, the desire to mobilize the masses of people made trade union and communist support all the more meaningful. In the final analysis, the momentum of direct action propelled the younger generation toward a nationalist-communist–ANC-SACP alliance.

Discerning observers of the debates within the international communist movement, black Marxists were divided over which version of international communism best captured the dynamics of race-class struggle. Since both Stalinist and Trotskyist interpretations found adherents, the conflicts of the Third International were played out on a minor scale within South Africa. For example, the Unity Movement and its allies favored the short-lived Fourth International founded in 1938 by followers of Leon Trotsky in France, after he had abandoned hope of reforming the Comintern. More relevant to the South African situation than the Trotsky-Stalin controversy were the objections raised by Western European Marxists regarding the contrived universalization of the Russian revolutionary experience. It was precisely "Soviet Marxism" and the national interests of the Soviet Union imposed by the Comintern on the international communist movement that anti-Stalinists deeply resented.

In South Africa, the major project of non-European Marxism was the indigenization of Marxist theory; here, the controversies between CP and NEUM did help to enrich the black liberation movement's understanding of different schools of socialist thought. Although the dominant movements frequently dismiss NEUM, which was launched in 1943, as little more than a group of high-flying intellectuals who never developed a respectable political base, the impact of NEUM's theorization on the overall tradition of black political thought has been significant, if not mainstream. Alex Callinicos concludes that the Unity Movement, due to its political weakness, was never able to provide an alternative to the dominant populist ideologies, but that it "remains the largest organization to the left of the CP."[56] Fredrickson has aptly described the politics of the Marxist left of the time: "By the beginning of the 1940s the black left was split into those who favored working within the system in order, ultimately, to undermine it—Communists who were also ANC supporters—and those who refused to compromise with segregation—Trotskyists and independent radicals who viewed Communists as de facto collaborators with white supremacy."[57]

Motivated by a more race-conscious (yet philosophically nonracial) Marxism, NEUM galvanized left populist opposition to both the ANC and the SACP in the All-African Convention. The works of I. B. Tabata, the Unity Movement's president, and other NEUM intellectuals, including Bennie Kies, may have represented an indigenous version of Marxism, but neither the ANC nor CP were impressed. A standard CPSA criticism of NEUM was that its rhetoric was not based on any consistent understanding of Marxism, not even Trotskyism.

Such criticisms notwithstanding, NEUM opposed the ANC on a number of very basic issues: it called for the liberation movement to be organized as a federal structure with the AAC as its "parliament"; it denounced, as unprincipled and high-handed, the way the ANC and the CP had foisted multiracialism on the black movement; it criticized the Marxist ideological stances taken by the CP on the grounds that they were inappropriate to South African realities; and it demanded that noncollaboration with government institutions be elevated, from a mere tactic, to the liberation movement's basic strategy of struggle. The doctrine of noncollaboration, associated with NEUM's opposition to ANC-CPSA participation in Native Representative Councils, was, years later, destined to become a central component of black consciousness thought.

Above all else, the Unity Movement produced an indigenous tradition of socialist intellectuals, mostly Coloured Capetonians, who worked to reconceptualize South Africa's peculiar configuration of social segregation and labor exploitation. In retrospect, it is clear that they helped to lay the intellectual foundation of socialist populism. Reflecting on his political education in the Cape in the 1950s, Bojana Vuyisile Jordan, a nephew of the well-known Unity intellectual A. C. Jordan, recalls that leaders such as I. B. Tabata, Dr. Goolam Gool, Bennie Kies, Ali Fataar, and his uncle met in Marxist study groups organized by the New Era Fellowship and the Society of Young Africa (SOYA). Most of these intellectuals were educators and former Fort Hare students. According to Jordan, Leon Trotsky was the most popular foreign theorist. Rumor has it that sometime after Trotsky fled from exile in the central Asian part of the former Soviet Union, he stopped at the Cape, where he allegedly conferred with black Marxists who supported his call for an anti-Stalinist Fourth International.[58]

Many Unity Movement intellectuals began their careers in the anti-CAD movement that also began in 1943. When the South African government created a segregated Coloured Affairs Department (CAD), its radical opponents dubbed themselves anti-CADers. Bennie Kies, the foremost political thinker among them, made the important connection between the denial of democratic citizenship and labor exploitation. For Kies, the goal of the white nationalists, made so transparent by CAD, was to "disenfranchise the Non-European[s] piecemeal, to parcel out their labor supply, and to place them under the care of separate administration departments."[59] Kies regarded South Africa as a perfect example of "herrenvolk democracy"—democratic citizenship for whites in the midst of tyrannized and rightless black working and peasant classes. Offering an early theory of populist leadership, Kies and his colleagues concluded that the required answer to herrenvolkism was the organization of a strong mass movement of non-European unity under the tutelage of a committed and self-sacrificing cadre of black intellectuals.[60]

Cognizant of the need to build cadres of committed intellectuals, who would help popularize the idea of non-European unity, NEUM rooted itself among Coloured educators. The Cape African Teachers' Association (CATA) and its sister organization, the Teacher's League of South Africa (TLSA), provided some of the very first Unity Movement members. Kies, himself a teacher until he was fired for his political views in 1956, served as editor of the *Educational Journal* of the Teacher's League of South Africa. CATA was one of the first groups to become an organizational affiliate of the AAC.[61] As the AAC became a forum solely for the Unity Movement, younger militants were inclined to conflate the racial and class struggles, which caused them to forget the organization's more liberal and less anti-capitalist origins. Too often downplayed in interpretative accounts of conferences, black uplift through business was a prevalent theme at all of the AAC gatherings.

Wycliffe Tsotsi, President of the AAC from 1948 to 1959, was largely responsible for bringing CATA into the fold. Tsotsi reminded NEUM's left wing that its guiding Ten Point Programme was designed to secure for Non-Europeans equal citizenship rights in a modern, progressive, capitalist society. Tsotsi thought "it was stupid to confuse herrenvolkism with capitalism and to deny the existence of racial groups."[62] As a liberal-minded critic of dogmatism within NEUM, Tsotsi was perhaps most astute when he declared that herrenvolkism sought to prevent the extension of a modern capitalist economy to blacks, offering instead state capitalism designed exclusively for Non-Europeans. In that regard, he saw right through the government-sponsored Bantustan Development Corporations which were primarily aimed at inducing Africans to support ethnic clientelism, economic patronage, and "homeland" leadership, rather than being given equitable access to the national economy.[63]

Thus far, NEUM, anti-CAD, and the AAC have been insufficiently analyzed in scholarly works on the black liberation struggle. In the 1970s, some interest in these movements was triggered when the BCM revived the doctrine of noncollaboration and redefined black identity in terms similar to NEUM's non-European idea. During the early 1980s, exiled members of NEUM and the BCM published a short-lived journal of left-wing black consciousness thought. Inside South Africa, an alliance between AZAPO and the Cape Action League was consummated within the National Forum Committee on the basis of their common opposition to Charterism (the multiracial doctrine of the ANC's Freedom Charter).

The impact of communism on black nationalism continues to preoccupy historians and contemporary political thinkers.[64] The crux of the matter is this: Black nationalists insist that the Communist Party successfully captured the ANC; independent socialists argue that the ANC captured the SACP. The belief that the ANC has been manipulated or controlled by the SACP is central to the PAC's and NEUM's understanding of why the liberation movement has taken a liberal, multiracial course. Conversely, the ANC and SACP have always insisted that, while the two organizations have enjoyed a long and fruitful fraternal relationship, neither movement has ever controlled the other. Yet, there are socialists who, when they reflect on the Communist Party's involvement with the ANC, lament the loss of an independent workers' movement. To their minds, the CP simply turned black workers over to the African nationalists. At the opposite end of the spectrum, black nationalists consider the SACP's influence on the ANC to be the major reason for compromises that undercut the evolution of a more purely African socialist strategy of revolution. Africanists and Unity Movement Marxists have repeatedly accused the CP of working to wreck black solidarity. Mafeje, a former member of the Unity Movement, believes that the only thing that it (the ANC) seems to have learned from the CPSA was multiracialism.[65]

In retrospect, however, it seems difficult to deny that the ANC-SACP alliance has resulted in one of Africa's most complex and interesting experiments with "Afro-Marxism."[66] At a 1975 conference in Dar es Salaam, Tanzania, the late Joe Slovo, then Secretary General of the Communist Party and the first white to be elected to the National Executive Committee of the ANC, responded to doctrinaire criticism of the ANC-SACP's revolutionary strategy. In the process, Slovo explained, in simple terms, the theoretical basis of SACP's Afro-Marxism, rooted as it is in the realities of both race and class:

South Africa is clearly a capitalist society; its socio-economic structure rests ultimately on class relations of capitalist exploitation in which its race policies are rooted. But even if we accept that in a class defined society it is the struggle between historically antagonistic classes which is the main motive force of social transformation can we posit for South Africa a classical political confrontation between the working class (black and white) in alliance with the peasantry (black and white) against the capitalist class (black and white)? To South Africa's revolutionary movement, including that part of it inspired by Marxism, such a perspective in the contemporary scene is a non-sensical one.[67]

4. ✿ A New Left Battles Apartheid

Racial segregation can obscure generational identity. Yet, by the 1960s, black and white students alike became aware that "what they want subjectively from life cannot be got without a fundamental change in all society."[1] As a perceptive observer of student politics in South Africa remarked, "the splits among white intellectuals have had parallels among blacks."[2]

According to Karl Mannheim, a generation, like a class, represents a given social location. Just as a class may exist objectively but not subjectively, so a generation may be unconscious of the political implications of its own existence. Mannheim argues that a generation reflects concrete bonds of solidarity developed as the result of exposure to social and intellectual processes of change. Discrete units or cadres of intellectuals formulate the material of their common generational experience in different ways and from different ideological standpoints.[3] Given that most university education in South Africa was segregated, black and white intellectuals rarely belonged to the same generational cadres. In addition, the political environment beyond the university reinforced racial compartmentalization. By 1960, the government had outlawed all political opposition that might have produced multiracial generational cadres and, in 1968, the Prohibition of Political Interference Bill was passed. This legislation made multiracial political organizations illegal and precluded any organization receiving funds from abroad. Nonetheless, ending a nearly decade-long hiatus, a new generation of activists and intellectuals began to revitalize internal opposition to apartheid. With the liberation movements operating in exile or clandestinely, the subsequent negotiations between the new generation and the old were complex, often not seen as such, and rarely conducted with specific reference to generational differences. Indeed, many exiled leaders were, at first, suspicious of the new, youthful opposition that developed inside the country in their absence. In one of its publications, the Pan Africanist Congress honestly confronted the generational divide:

> The National will to struggle is inevitable and unavoidable but there
> is a missing link which some people attribute to a generation gap

which is not adequately understood or appreciated. The founders of the Black Consciousness Movement clearly understood it even though external conditions have distorted and transfigured some of that understanding.[4]

Before 1960, South Africa's economy was predominantly industrial and, as in all industrial economies, required an increasingly skilled labor force. Industrial nations generally exhibit a high correlation between educated labor and economic development.[5] In South Africa, the recruitment of skilled labor was fettered by the framework of apartheid. The government's constant efforts to reconcile a repressive racial order and an industrial economy led Heribert Adam to formulate his famous proposition that the state was under constant pressure to "modernize racial domination."[6] Indeed, many scholars defined apartheid (as opposed to segregation) with reference to governmental efforts to modernize white rule under the specific conditions of industrial capitalism.

The system of publicly funded, segregated university education was part of the effort to control the growth of black skilled labor. Yet, neither the subsidization of white education nor the active recruitment of whites from overseas successfully resolved the shortage of skilled whites, with the result that blacks were steadily drawn into the market for educated labor. The need for skilled and trained blacks caused a gradual expansion of university education, which, in turn, spurred the growth of a black middle class.[7] However, the unequal racial allocation of educational resources coupled with the denial of civil rights ensured that black consciousness would shape student and middle-class politics. Moreover, constant governmental intervention into the educational process made the campus a permanent site of protest. At the university level, Bantu Education (the official name given the policy of segregated schooling) was designed to structure the market for educated labor along racial lines, to channel the emerging black middle class into segregated institutions, especially the "homelands," and to deflect potential black middle-class political power.[8] In the end, however, these policies accomplished three unintended consequences; they radicalized the black middle class, racialized the class dynamics associated with industrial society, and generated a multiracial, New Left intelligentsia.

Unable and unwilling to promote collaboration or to elaborate institutional arrangements that did not result in wide-scale protest, the government's only recourse was to use repression and violence, including forced relocations, against the indigenous organizations of the black working class, the urban middle classes, and the unemployed. For as Wilmot James observed, the single most irresistible truth contained in materialist accounts of South African history is that "almost all the racial institutions of state have to do, one way or another, with controlling black labor, both in the market and in the place of work."[9] This insight was equally true for black educated labor. With respect to the expansion of black opportunity, government faced a textbook formula for revolutionary mobilization: a rising and economically strategic black middle class whose upward mobility apartheid systematically blocked.

Nearly a decade before the end of apartheid, the South African government's half-hearted reforms had produced the optimal milieu for the development of black revolutionary intellectuals. In that context, John Brewer addressed three crucial questions regarding the radicalization of the black middle class: Why are there so many middle class groups at the forefront of black protest; why is the protest movement, as a whole, more community based than plant based; and why does protest ideology tend to deemphasize concrete material gains? Brewer astutely found that South African capitalism, like capitalism in general, was becoming dependent on educated labor, especially black educated labor. By then, the country had reached the point where whites simply could no longer run the factories, produce the goods, and manage the administration without the assistance of their black compatriots. Brewer summarized the social dynamics of reform thus:

> Through its series of reforms, the government is opening occupational mobility and economic rights to a privileged section of Blacks. This is reinforcing the demographic and economic trends that are behind the creation of educated labour. Together, they have produced a restructuring of the racial divisions of labour in South Africa. The enormous growth of Black education has been both the cause and effect of this occupational restructuring. Contained herein is the essential contradiction in the government's attempt to win Black compliance and support. For it is the higher educated strata of the black population who, as educated labor, fill the middle management, technical and professional positions and who are the object of the state's co-option measures which is leading to Black protest.[10]

Similarly, a 1981 report on education produced by the Human Sciences Research Council (HSRC) found that "the highest priority is increasing the contribution of the Non-White groups to the country's high-level manpower, since the contribution that can be made by Whites is apparently already largely utilized."[11]

Both Brewer and Craig Charney estimated that there was greater support among better-educated blacks and whites for trade unionism than among black workers. The upsurge in political unionism was the manifestation of a multiclass alliance of educated labor and black industrial workers. So popular had the middle-class trade unionists become in the 1980s that "university educated whites and blacks queue to become trade union organizers, the new campus idols."[12] With reference to the growth of black intellectual cadres in the 1970s, Nolutshungu remarked that it had become difficult to distinguish between *encadrement*—the creation of intellectual cadres with a vested interest in a particular approach to political change—and *embourgeoisement*—the creation of the conditions for the emergence of a black bourgeoisie.[13]

By mid-century, professional classes had assumed increased political significance in South Africa, as in the rest of the industrial and industrializing world, and so had New Left politics. Serious analysts of industrial society could no longer ignore the political significance of professional and managerial classes or reduce them to a troublesome segment of the petite bourgeoisie.[14] Alvin Gouldner went so far as to argue that capital derived from private wealth, which formed the basis of capitalist classes in the past, had been transcended by human or cultural capital that is derived from the advanced professional education of the intelligentsia.[15] This new emphasis on educated labor, as well as the reproduction of intellectuals, forced social theorists to confront the complex interaction of class consciousness, the radicalization of new social forces, and generational identity as factors in a broadly conceived politics of human emancipation.

Erik Olin Wright has observed that intellectuals, irrespective of their contribution to revolutionary politics, have had an ambiguous status as actors and, especially, as a category within Marxist theory. He distinguishes three interconnected meanings for the expression "intellectual": it designates a general characteristic of human activity; it refers to a specific type of labor; and, of course, intellectuals are a category of people with a specific appreciation and commitment to ideas or mental labor. Marxist and neo-Marxist theory has sought to resolve the challenge posed by intellectual participation in politics by means of four alternate reductions: All intellectuals are workers; intellectuals are organic to several different classes; intellectuals are part of the petite bourgeoisie; or, intellectuals are a part of the professional-managerial class.[16] Moreover, as Edward Shils observes, intellectuals exhibit distinct ideological characteristics—scientism, romanticism, revolutionism, and populism.[17]

Often termed the decade of protest, the 1960s witnessed student revolts that rocked the universities of most industrial nations. Whether in Berkeley or Beijing, Paris or Johannesburg, New Left student movements formulated radical ideologies and designed programs of action to confront social inequities in their respective societies. So pervasive were radical student politics during this period that Shils compared worldwide student solidarity to that of the Communist International.[18] Everywhere, New Left student movements constructed a discursive insolence designed to undermine adult-controlled systems of intellectual socialization, and thus the authority of the older generation.[19] New Left thinkers either straight-out rejected or deconstructed liberalism, social democracy, and Moscow-oriented communism.[20] New Left social theory

> rejects capitalist reform, socialist and communist social systems as well as the social theories that justify them. Social inequality, elitist authoritarian hierarchy and repressive manipulation are seen as the common coordinates of bureaucratic domination which lie behind ideological mystifications buttressing each of these systems. In place of such structures, New-Left social theory posits the possibility of an egalitarian society free of the alienation characteristic of contemporary society.[21]

Despite the necessarily muted articulation of its unique position within the liberation movement, South Africa's indigenous New Left, consisting of black and white student movements, constructed a distinctive political discourse which compensated for the lack of adult leadership. Perhaps the most important aspect of New Left politics everywhere was its autonomy from, and critical standpoint toward, organizations and ideologies associated with older generations. Inside South Africa, a degree of political autonomy and a left-wing orientation distinguished both English-speaking white and segregated black universities from the Afrikaans-medium campuses. On the Afrikaans campuses, Afrikaner nationalists fought to hold sway over a new generation of students and to shield them from those influences, international and internal, that would undermine their faith in apartheid. This was not always possible; for example, in 1966, a small group of Stellenbosch students founded a short-lived chapter of the National Union of South African Students (NUSAS),[22] the significance of which will become apparent in this account. Irrespective of the important differences between education on English-medium, Afrikaans-medium, and segregated black campuses, the social forces that fostered student unrest in other industrial nations were also present in South Africa, but constrained by a society that was tightly organized into racial castes. Legassick and John Shingler eloquently capture the emotional and political context of student life under apartheid:

> South African students live in a unique environment. Crucial to any insight into their political attitudes and actions is an understanding of the main features of this environment: deep cleavage, rapid change, and bitter conflict. Extreme economic inequality, unrelenting political persecution, color bar in every walk of life—all combine to make a festering, impacted universe that every student leader must sooner or later confront, within his society and within himself.[23]

THIRST FOR THE WORLD: SEGREGATION AND INTERNATIONALISM

Upon assuming power in 1948, Nationalist politicians firmly rejected the multiracial, liberal conventions of Western democracies as being wholly incompatible with the South African way of life. The architects of apartheid clearly understood that internationalism would probably imply support for racial equality. So they resolved to instill a belief in segregation (both racial and ethnic) as a positive value in students at all levels of the educational system. Naturally, Afrikaner nationalists considered nonracial university education (even on English-speaking campuses) to be incompatible with the practice of apartheid. Government officials perceived multiracialism in every guise as a serious threat. In their minds, multiracialism was a liberal-English conspiracy against Afrikaner folkways. By 1950, the government began to commandeer the basic institutions of African education, thus defying long-established boundaries between English and Afrikaner sociopolitical establishments. In the process, educators at English-medium universities were placed under increased pressure to conform to the Afrikaners' more conservative assumptions about race relations and citizenship.[24] Despite the racial conservatism of many English-speaking educators, the debate about educational policy left little doubt but that the two white communities held distinct conceptions of university life and citizenship. Margo Russell observed that these rival approaches arose from alternative social utopias.[25] In our parlance, they are identifiable as multiracialism and white republicanism. Some liberal educators viewed their conflict with the apartheid government over university education as but another episode in a long history of cultural clash between the English and the Afrikaner:

> Among the periods in our history when inter-white racial differences have created legislative, administrative, or political problems, can be cited the period following the settlement of the Huguenots in the Cape in 1689, the period following the annexation of the Cape in 1802, the period which led up to and followed the Great Trek of 1836, the years immediately preceding and following the Anglo-Boer War of 1899–1902, the quinquennium following the outbreak of the First World War with its local rebellion in South Africa in 1914, and the present period which dates from the outbreak of the Second World War in 1939.[26]

Indeed, the Second World War drastically deepened the divide between the Afrikaner and English communities. Although South Africa entered the war on the side of the Allies, many prominent Afrikaner nationalists were interned for pro-Nazi activities. Furthermore, pro-Nazi Afrikaner groups like the Ossewa Brandwag espoused a version of national socialism and believed that "the whole future of Afrikanerdom is dependent upon a German victory."[27] To the dismay of white nationalists, the democratic pronouncements of world leaders during the era of anti-fascist resistance heightened the hopes of non-Europeans that they too would benefit from the postwar dispensation. Like other non-Europeans, black South Africans were fervent in upholding the democratic ideals of the time.[28]

Despite the influence of pro-Nazi factions within the movement, the Afrikaner leadership resolved to create an indigenous form of white nationalist supremacy. Dr. H. F. Verwoerd, apartheid's most influential proponent, and his Afrikaner nationalist colleagues were skeptical of all forms of internationalism, a category that encompassed German-inspired national socialism. In direct opposition to the major internationalist doctrines of his day, Verwoerd advocated Christian Nationalism. He warned that "During the past century the

Afrikaner has learned to strike a defense against the intrusion of the social philosophy which is coupled with British liberalism and imperialism. He also rejected the philosophy of communism. He will now have to learn to protect himself from the infiltration of national socialism."[29]

Many of the idiosyncratic and homespun values of white nationalism were soon translated into educational philosophy and policy. Eventually, Christian National Education (pedagogical apartheid) culminated in the volatile issue of Afrikaans as a mandatory medium of instruction for black school children. Ten years after Verwoerd's death, the apartheid language policy—grounded in Afrikanerdom's attempt to impose its own parochialism on Africans—proved to be the catalyst for the watershed Soweto Rebellion of June 16, 1976, an event that set South Africa on the path of irreversible change. At issue was whether black students would be allowed to learn in English, an international language, or forced to study in Afrikaans, a parochial language that they associated with racial domination. Moreover, most African teachers were not proficient in Afrikaans. A famous 1976 slogan encapsulated black student rejection of Afrikaner parochialism: "Afrikaans is not spoken north of the Limpopo River" (which separates South Africa from Zimbabwe).

The Afrikaans language requirement prefigured linguistic isolation of African students, thus allowing the government to pursue its anti-internationalist, apartheid agenda under the guise of educational policy. As John Samuel observed, the system of black education was already hopeless—the new language policy now added humiliation.[30] In the very formulation "Christian National Education," the word "national" qualified Christian universalism and suggested to blacks that Afrikaners had been appointed to dispense God's grace. Black Christians (and all black South Africans) could best seek salvation through Afrikaner Trusteeship:

> We believe that the educational task of white South Africa with respect to the native is to Christianise him and help him on culturally, and this vocation and task finds its immediate application in the principle of trusteeship, not placing of the native on the level of the white and in segregation. For this reason, we believe that any system of teaching and education of the native must be based on the European's attitude to life and the world, more particularly that of the Boer nation as the senior European trustee of the native.[31]

In reality, Afrikaners were never as isolated as they claimed to be.

Owing to early involvement in the British and Dutch colonial empires, and its own industrial revolution, South Africa developed a relatively sophisticated tradition of segregated university education. South African educational institutions are culturally European and, consequently, they have always inculcated a measure of international awareness. In the 1920s, for example, the majority of faculty was European and many white students traveled to Europe to complete advanced degrees.[32] In comparison with English-speakers, a relatively small number of African students managed to study in England or the United States. Afrikaner students who studied overseas tended to gravitate toward the Netherlands and Germany. As continental attitudes toward race began to change after the Second World War, the Eurocentrism of the South African university made white nationalists proud, in one sense, and uncomfortable, in another.

In constant contact with Western democracies, exposure to racially liberal ideas was unavoidable. Black and white English-speaking student leaders were relatively cosmopolitan and more inclined to pursue international student relations and multiracial contacts at home. Indeed, given South Africa's increasing pariah-nation status, students were expected to espouse nonracial sentiments in international forums. The National Party's fear that liberalism gave rise to multiracial relations contributed to some of its more quixotic educational policies, as well as racist public pronouncements so typical of its officials. For example, Prime Minister D. F. Malan (1948–1954) stated his reaction to multiracial student relations without equivocation thus: "An intolerable state of affairs has arisen here in the past few years in our university institutions, a state of affairs which gives rise to friction, to an unpleasant relationship between European and non-European. . . . we do not want to withhold education from the non-European and we will take every possible step to give both the natives and coloured peoples university training as soon as we can but in their own sphere, in other words in separate institutions."[33]

English-medium universities—Cape Town, Witwatersrand, Rhodes, and Natal—were modeled on British academic institutions, drew on British faculty, and refrained from imposing direct academic segregation.[34] At these universities, the minuscule black student body was segregated in sport, accommodation, and social life, but English-medium universities were, nonetheless, predisposed toward an intellectual awareness of the world beyond South Africa. By contrast, the Afrikaans-speaking universities—Stellenbosch, Rand Afrikaans, Pofchefstroom, Pretoria, and Orange Free State—remained mired in Afrikaner nationalism, with its parochial implications for culture, language, and citizenship.

By means of the Separate University Education Bill of 1957 and its revised 1959 Extension of University Education Bill, government forced black students to attend inferior, segregated universities. Fort Hare was founded in 1916 for all Africans; however, the University College of Fort Hare Transfer Bill converted it into an institution open only to Xhosa students. In addition, the legislation provided for the construction of the University of the North or Turfloop (Sotho-Twsana), the University of Zululand or Ngoye (Zulu), the University of the Western Cape (Coloured), and the University of Durban West-ville (Indian). These segregated institutions made black students more keenly aware of the wider world, as well as the indignities that apartheid imposed on non-European cultures and their educational traditions. Forced to contend with university institutions that were not only segregated but also white-dominated, blacks searched desperately and often in vain for culturally liberated educational space. Moreover, Afrikaner pedagogical attitudes directly intensified the pace of black radicalization. When compared to mission schools, Bantu Education abandoned the paternalistic interpersonal relations that were common between black students and white liberal educators. One student characterized the black universities created by apartheid legislation as institutions with "no fatherly touch."

From the Union's inception, student politics were incipient citizenship politics. Even before direct African involvement, disputes between English and Afrikaner students centered on issues related to multiracial representation in the student community. Established in 1924 as an elected student government, the National Union of South African Students (NUSAS) functioned as a federation of Student Representative Councils (SRCs) on affiliated campuses. Initially, Afrikaner students belonged to NUSAS. However, they soon seceded from that student union on the grounds that the organization was negrophilistic, imperialistic (a reference to its alleged commitment to British hegemony), liberalistic, and guided, if not controlled, by a conspiracy of international socialist Jews.[35] In 1933, they formed the *Afrikaanse Nasionale Studentebond*, renamed the *Afrikaanse Studentebond* (ASB) immediately after the Second World War. Barely autonomous, Afrikaner student associations were under constant surveillance of both the National Party and the Broederbond. Furthermore, there was always an overlap in membership between the *Nasionale Jeugbond* (the NP youth wing) and the ASB. Since they were so close, the relations between the *Jeugbond* and the ASB were usually harmonious. On those rare occasions when the ASB deviated from the National Party line, the NP used the *Jeugbond* to reestablish the party's authority (as at Stellenbosch in 1954).[36] Moreover, conservative factions within the NP organized their own independent student front organizations to ensure the ASB's political reliability. For example, the right-wing *Afrikaner-Orde*, formed in 1966, included future NP notables. Thus, Albert Hertzog went on to found the *Herstigte Nasionale Party*, after he broke with the National Party in 1969. A. P. Treurnicht (who came to be known as "Dr. No" for his opposition to any reform of the system) would serve as chairman of the Broederbond in 1972, become a power within the Transvaal NP, and lead the break-away Conservative Party (CP) in 1985.[37]

While the brunt of apartheid educational policy impacted black students, many English-speakers were alienated by constant governmental intervention into the university system, solely for the purpose of reinforcing racial boundaries. As Ngubane pointed out, a major objective of Bantu Education "was to wean the African away from the English."[38] However, Afrikaners were prevented from accomplishing this task by their often mindless belief in the righteousness of segregation. In that regard, liberals, for all their contradictions, appeared to black students as the lesser of two evils. No white educator expressed the values of educational liberalism more eloquently than the former Principal and Vice-Chancellor of the University of Cape Town, T. B. Davie. In a 1953 speech, entitled "The Four Essential Freedoms," Davie argued that a university should be able to decide "who may teach, what may be taught, how it shall be taught, and who may be admitted to study." These four freedoms became the basis of an Open University Policy advocated by a majority of liberal university educators. Considering the more racially egalitarian tradition of the English-medium universities, Davie was angered by the fact that newly planned ethnic universities were to be totally under Afrikaner tutelage and control:

> [T]he guardian university for the Coloured university was to be Stellenbosch and not Cape Town, and for the African-Sotho university, Pretoria and not Witwatersrand—significant because while at present the Universities of the Witwatersrand and Cape Town ac-

cord full academic equality to Europeans and Non-European students, the Universities of Stellenbosch and Pretoria have not at any time knowingly admitted a single Non-European student, Coloured, Asian, or African.[39]

In 1945, the English-speaking students of NUSAS welcomed the participation of black students at Fort Hare—then the nation's only black university. The efforts of the liberal left to include Fort Hare students required a constant assault on the parameters of citizenship established under segregation and apartheid. Among students, the political left was broadly conceived to include all opponents of apartheid—liberals, socialists, and African nationalists. Indeed, communist and liberal students were competitors as advocates of multiracialism and internationalism. Over the years, only a small number of student radicals became communists, but the CPSA exerted considerable influence on English-medium campuses, especially at the University of the Witwatersrand. The late Ruth First, a world-renowned radical scholar, wife of Joe Slovo, and long-time member of the Party, provides an interesting example of a communist student activist. In the 1940s, she was involved in the Federation of Progressive Students (FOPS) at the University of the Witwatersrand. FOPS consisted of a left-liberal/communist alliance of students who were disenchanted with the conservative orientation of NUSAS policy. Such was CPSA's influence in FOPS that many liberals considered it a front organization. A primary goal of FOPS was to push NUSAS to the left, an objective that it frequently accomplished. FOPS activists were militant multiracialists and fought pitched battles with those opposed to Fort Hare's participation in NUSAS.[40] Subsequently, Ruth First, the Party's most important campus organizer, toured China and the Soviet Union in 1954 as a member of the International Union of Students and the Democratic Federation of Youth.[41]

Unlike Fort Hare of old, the power structure of the university under Bantu Education was made to replicate that of the larger society and, in the process, black student consciousness was transformed. A far more visible form of repression characterized black educational institutions under apartheid.

> The "tribal colleges" are more directly under state control. The Rector, corresponding to the Principal or Vice-Chancellor at the other universities, is appointed by the Minister of Bantu Education. Members of the Council (White) and the Advisory Council (non-

white) are appointed by the State President, who also designates the Chairmen. The Council only has such powers as the Minister may care to delegate; it is the stated intention of the Government that the Advisory Council is gradually to take over the functions of the Council. There are also a Senate and Advisory Senate, with similar relations, whose members are selected by the Minister in consultation with the Council.[42]

In his famous 1972 graduation address, Ongokopotse Ramothiki (Abraham) Tiro, President of the Student Representative Council at the University of the North (Turfloop), told the audience that white administrators, who strongly recommended apartheid as the solution to South Africa's race problem, "failed to adhere to the letter and spirit of the policy."[43] In other words, although white officials publicly advocated separate development, they used black educational institutions as an arena of primarily Afrikaner professional advancement. As late as 1979, the councils, staffs, and administrations of black universities were dominated mostly by Afrikaners. For example, 441 of the 621 lecturers at African universities were white. At the University of the Western Cape, established for Coloureds, 185 of 247 lecturers were white. At Durban-Westville, founded for Indians, there were 224 white lecturers out of 346.[44] Black participation on governing councils at segregated universities fared no better. The Western Cape had five Coloured council members and eleven whites and Durban-Westville had four Indian members compared to eleven white ones. At African universities, the black-white ratios were as follows: Turfloop had only five black council members out of thirteen; Fort Hare had four blacks as opposed to thirteen whites; and Ngoye's governing council consisted of four blacks and eleven whites.[45] Even more insulting, black and white faculty and staff facilities were segregated on black campuses. Since it equated demands for desegregation with communist agitation, the National Party was extremely hostile to the Black Academic Staff Association (BASA) which was formed at Turfloop in 1973. BASA was founded only after the white staff association refused to address black grievances.[46]

Many respectable black educators shunned involvement with segregated universities, which students dubbed "bush colleges." African nationalist and scholar Z. K. Matthews was offered the Rectorship of the new Fort Hare on the condition that he renounce the ANC. He refused. In 1961, Matthews delivered the annual T. B. Davie Memorial Lecture that he entitled "African Awakening and the Universities."

The venerable professor argued that South African universities were an integral part of the African awakening and, as such, had a special role to play in transnational African education. Furthermore, South Africa's role in the African awakening could make it pivotal in the international community of universities. Matthews commended Fort Hare for the educational service it had rendered to the High Commission Territories—the Rhodesias, Nyasaland, Tanganyika, Kenya, and Uganda.[47] A confirmed liberal Africanist, Matthews held out the future prospect of a nonracial, democratic South Africa motivated by its responsibility to Africa as a whole. For the moment, however, Afrikaner nationalism, with its hostility to Africa and the world, was ascendant.

After the Second World War, Afrikaner identity was used to legitimate not only ethnically exclusive student groups, but trade and professional unions, boy scouts, and commercial and women's organizations.[48] Isolationists themselves, Afrikaner nationalists were infuriated by NUSAS's international involvement. A *Die Transvaler* editorial of July 20, 1961, registered the extent to which Afrikaners were incensed by a NUSAS call for overseas organizations to protest South Africa's apartheid legislation. The editorial went on to demand that NUSAS's "internationalism be eradicated in favor of the South African nationalism of the ASB."[49]

The strenuous effort of dissident students to keep up with international political currents was an integral part of their struggle against apartheid. Progressive students in South Africa professed solidarity with their counterparts overseas and especially with the fight for black civil rights in the United States. At English-speaking universities, white students were involved with recognized international student bodies. International student politics provided an important outlet for progressive whites, but were not as accessible to black students. Black student leaders, nonetheless, held strong, informed opinions about international student affairs. It is evident from annual resolutions at NUSAS conferences that student leaders, black and white, kept abreast of domestic, regional, and international affairs. The NUSAS leadership participated in two important student associations formed after the war. These were the pro-communist International Union of Students (IUS) and the noncommunist International Student Conference (ISC). Historically the more important of these two youth associations, the IUS was founded in Prague in 1946 at the first World Student Congress arising out of the International Student

Council. The aim of the IUS "was to be a representative international student organization which strives for the right of all young people to enjoy primary, secondary and higher education regardless of sex, economic circumstances, social standing, political conviction, religion, colour or race; world peace, international friendship among all peoples and the employment of advances in sciences and culture for the benefit of humanity."[50] The establishment of IUS reflected the firm commitment by European students to the goals of anti-fascism and anti-colonialism.[51] After the war ideological tensions between communist and noncommunist student associations split the international student movement.

Like student organizations in most African nations, NUSAS, in 1946, affiliated with IUS. However, in 1953, NUSAS disaffiliated from IUS and eventually joined ISC. According to NUSAS leaders, the dissatisfaction with IUS stemmed from the "conduct of the IUS in furthering a particular ideology, its lack of attention to the views and wishes of those who did not accept the views of the majority, expulsion of the Yugoslav student union in furtherance of the policies of certain governments wholly irrelevant to the purposes of the IUS . . . its refusal to defend the rights of those members who did not agree with its views."[52]

Black students opposed disaffiliation from IUS, whose membership was drawn from primarily communist and colonial countries, with very few Western democracies represented. Conversely, students from Western Europe and the United States dominated the ISC. Motivated, in part, by their overall distrust of NUSAS leaders, black radicals regarded affiliation to the ISC as evidence that whites were easily intimidated, quick to compromise, and disposed toward the imperialist camp. To be sure, white students were wary of the catch-all communist label that could be pinned on dissenters under the 1950 Suppression of Communism Act. Highly suspicious of the switch from the IUS to the ISC, and generally resentful of its claim to represent blacks in the international arena, students aligned with the Unity Movement took this, and every other opportunity, to disparage NUSAS as an agency of white domination.

Criticisms of NUSAS by Unity Movement student groups and others were reinforced in the mid-1960s when it was disclosed that ISC had received Central Intelligence Agency funding since 1953.[53] NUSAS leaders reacted firmly and promptly: "NUSAS notes the allegations that the ISC has been receiving financial support from the

CIA and that although the ISC has denied that it receives such support, no independent enquiry has been set up, [NUSAS] expresses its grave concern at the possible influence of the CIA in the ISC."[54]

In the course of its international affairs, NUSAS delegates were also forced to grapple with intellectual issues such as the nature of apartheid, particularly the rivalry between race and class explanations. At the first Pan-African Student Conference, held in Kampala, Uganda in July 1958, disputes flared between those African students who supported the ISC and those who were affiliated with the IUS. Pro-IUS students distributed pamphlets reporting on a meeting held earlier in the year and announcing an IUS Congress scheduled for that September in Beijing. Of direct concern to NUSAS, IUS, and ISC, student groups held different positions on the racial composition of student delegations from white-ruled countries in southern Africa. Paradoxically, the South African delegation was multiracial while the Rhodesian delegation was all white. The lack of African representation prompted a resolution by the Tunisian students calling for the reduction of the Rhodesian delegation to observer status. After an initial tie vote on the issue, a woman member of the Ghanaian delegation and a black male delegate from Fort Hare successfully defended full membership for the Rhodesians.[55]

In addition to the specific controversy over the status of the Rhodesian delegation, the larger issue of the colonial versus the racial character of apartheid was heatedly debated: "The South African delegation fought a long struggle with the Tunisian delegate and his block over the wording of the resolution strongly criticizing South Africa. The South Africans wanted the main attack to be on the issue of racialism. The Tunisians felt colonialism was the major villain. The strong South African mixed delegation persuaded the majority to support it in condemning South Africa on racial grounds."[56]

In this international forum, NUSAS leaders argued that racism was the social disease that made apartheid possible, and that multiracialism was the proper antidote. But this argument created a lasting blind spot for NUSAS with respect to black republican identity. Ten years later, in 1968, black students (African, Indian, and Coloured) formed the South African Student Organization (SASO) which gave rise to the Black Consciousness Movement. NUSAS leaders sought to defend their multiracial stance by equating black consciousness with Afrikaner racism. Of course, the social contents of these two forms of race consciousness were completely different. At a time when Africans stood firm against fascism, many Afrikaner student leaders found solace in National Socialism's vindication of white supremacy and racist nationalism. Especially in its antipathy to liberalism, Christian Nationalism sounded like little more than a homegrown variety of fascism. Whenever Afrikaner student movements involved themselves in international student associations, they were extremely uncomfortable and their politics fit nowhere. For example, Afrikaner students were alienated from the IUS because of communism and the ISC because of liberalism and multiracialism. Nevertheless, goaded by the thought of NUSAS representing—or to their minds misrepresenting—South Africa in an important international body, Afrikaner student leaders made a vain bid for ISC recognition. However, the ASB was denied delegate status because membership in the association was based on the unacceptable principle of racial segregation.[57]

EMBATTLED AND DIVIDED

In order to intimidate potentially radical white students, the government clamped down on selected activists for their social as well as political transgressions. Passports were withdrawn, leaders banned, and radicals from other countries, such as Rhodesia, deported. In response, NUSAS activists encouraged international scrutiny of the repressive character of apartheid legislation as well as the government's repeated violations of academic freedom. Thus, in 1966, NUSAS President Ian Robertson was banned for sponsoring a South African tour for the popular American Senator Robert Kennedy. Slapped with a banning order by the government, Robertson was prevented from participating in the activities surrounding Kennedy's visit, in spite of the fact that he was principal organizer. Once in South Africa, Kennedy visited Robertson amidst great media fanfare. This was precisely the kind of publicity student leaders hoped to generate and the government worked to avoid.

Like extremist elements of the international New Left, a small number of former white student activists opted for political violence as a means to combat the government. During the 1960s, all of the major liberation movements organized sabotage operations. *Umkhonto we Sizwe* was organized by the ANC-SACP, *Poqo* by the PAC, and the smaller Yu Chi Chan Club drew its membership from NEUM. With the formation of the amateurish and short-lived African Resistance Movement (ARM), white New Leftists tried their hand at sabotage. Among the persons detained by the government for ARM activities were two former NUSAS presidents, Neville Rubin (1958–1959) and Adrian Leftwich (1960–1962). As an indication of just how sensitive the government was to student politics, NUSAS President Jonty Driver caused a storm of controversy when, at a 1964 conference in Dar es Salaam, Tanzania, he referred to NUSAS as a wing of the African liberation movement. Although it may have reflected the sentiments of some NUSAS leaders, Driver's assertion was never an official policy.

In stark contrast to NUSAS, Afrikaner nationalists managed to contain the consciousness of Afrikaner youth within the parameters of National Party ideology, and to channel their energies toward defense of the regime. Thus, Afrikaner students were mobilized to attack English-speaking students who participated in anti-apartheid protests. During 1968, students at the University of Cape Town sat in at Bremmer Hall in opposition to the government-orchestrated firing of Archie Mafeje, a black lecturer and research associate of the well-known Professor Monica Wilson. Mafeje was also a prominent member of the Unity Movement. Outraged that white University of Cape Town students would dare to make demands on the government for racial justice, approximately one thousand Afrikaner students from Stellenbosch University, joined by other Afrikaner toughs, descended on UCT. Under threats of violence, the Cape Town protesters were forced to disperse.

In the IUS, NUSAS leaders came to appreciate that anti-colonialism was as important a political posture for Afro-Asian students as anti-fascism was for their European counterparts. This understanding also had ramifications at home. The growth of African nationalism and Pan-Africanism reinforced the need for NUSAS to dramatize the prospect of multiracial citizenship in a predominantly African nation. For example, in 1962, Nobel Peace Laureate Chief Albert Luthuli, then President of the ANC, was made honorary president of NUSAS. During this same period, Thami Mhlambiso, a former president of the Student Representative Council at the University of Natal (Non-European section) became the first, and only, African elected to the NUSAS vice-presidency (1961–1962) during the apartheid era. Several years later, Mhlambiso served as ANC representative to the United Nations in New York. In reality, however, the black student left was more diverse than the ANC tradition with which NUSAS felt most comfortable.

Although the NUSAS left fought to incorporate black students at Fort Hare, the latter remained ambivalent about affiliation with

NUSAS—a perennially controversial issue on the new black campuses as well. This was particularly the case during periods when NEUM-affiliated groups such as the Society of Young Africa (SOYA) or the Progressive National Student Organization (PNSO) held sway; student leaders from these organizations regarded liberals, in general, and NUSAS, in particular, as agents of colonialism, imperialism, and white rule. Moreover, NEUM had a reputation for dogged criticism of its opponents. In the final analysis, peer ostracism and an inclination toward African nationalism tended to make black students view affiliation with NUSAS as a risky undertaking with few concrete benefits, and this judgment was widely shared among black students. Not surprisingly, Fort Hare students decided against forming an SRC, thereby rejecting participation in NUSAS throughout most of the 1950s.[58] However, the ANC Youth League began to view affiliation with NUSAS as a means to enlist white support in the fight against university apartheid and, by 1957, the Youth League had gained sufficient influence to bring Fort Hare into the NUSAS fold.[59]

This development had significant indirect consequences. NUSAS leaders were placed under increased pressure to recognize both multiracialism and Pan-Africanism as progressive aspirations. By 1969, NUSAS's Department of International Relations openly acknowledged the positive role of Pan-Africanism, but gave it a multiracial twist. NUSAS accepted that the concept of Pan-Africanism "has at its heart loyalty to the African continent, which implies political and economic control of the resources of Africa by the people of the African continent on the basis of self-determination and democracy . . . defining as an African any person who is a national of an African state."[60]

In brief, NUSAS leaders took pains to distinguish their position on Pan-Africanism from the race-conscious version propounded by the PAC. Furthermore, NUSAS condemned colonialism and neo-colonialism and professed a principled opposition to imperialism which, it argued, took "many forms and cannot be viewed solely as the culmination of a particular economic system or as the natural expression of a particular ideology."[61] Perhaps influenced by the organization's experience in the IUS and the ISC, NUSAS leaders insisted that both capitalist and socialist countries could be agents of imperialism. NUSAS leaders were also well aware that black student opinion was influenced by identification with factions of the black liberation movement that held different views on such issues.

After their banning in 1960, supporters of both the ANC and the PAC formed separate student associations, the African Student Association (ASA) and the African Student Union of South Africa (ASUSA), respectively, while NEUM-aligned students founded the Progressive National Student Organization. A 1967 Annual Assembly resolution instructed the NUSAS Executive to find out whether the ASA and the ASUSA still existed. Since student groups affiliated with the PAC and Unity Movement were opposed to multiracial student cooperation on philosophical grounds, NUSAS felt more comfortable with the ASA. However, the report acknowledged the existence of three black student organizations, assessing each one based on its attitude toward NUSAS. The following profile of black student associations was offered to the 1968 Annual Assembly:

> ASA was founded in 1960–61; was strong on the campuses of University of Natal, Non-European, Fort Hare and in Johannesburg; was uni-racial in composition, but philosophically non-racial based on the Freedom Charter; and that its membership was split on its attitude to NUSAS. The ASUSA was founded in 1960–61 (just after the ASA); was strong at Turfloop and in Johannesburg; was uni-racial in composition but non-racial Africanist in philosophy; and its membership was usually hostile to NUSAS, but understanding. The PNSO was founded in 1961–62; had a few members primarily at Fort Hare; was affiliated with NEUM, embraced Unity's Ten Point Programme, and stood for non-racialism and non-collaboration with anyone including (especially) NUSAS.[62]

In addition, the report stated that the ASUSA appeared to be defunct and the ASA had been reconstituted at a January meeting in Soweto and consisted of 200 to 300 high school students.

Black Consciousness and the New Left

As a rule, the NUSAS leadership was far to the left of the overall white student population; one of the organization's primary missions was, therefore, the radicalization of a complacent white student body derived largely from the racially and politically insular white middle class. However, relations with black student leaders posed problems that were more serious. Even black supporters of multiracialism found it hard to ignore the asymmetry of social privilege existing between whites and blacks. How then could students share a common political perspective across the racial divide? After the government smashed adult African resistance, black students were recruited clandestinely to replace African nationalist cadres in jail or exile.[63] The student organizations with which they were affiliated were not autonomous student movements; moreover, they mirrored the political divisions that characterized the nationalist movement. The pro-ANC ASA and the pro-PAC ASUSA did not survive.[64] For want of other political outlets, many African students had begun to focus their attention on NUSAS, whose leadership had become outspokenly anti-government. By 1964, however, NUSAS began to shift to the right.[65]

The political give-and-take in NUSAS between black and white students was not by any means markedly hostile; yet, tensions in race relations remained a constant in student politics. After 1960, the delicate balance which NUSAS leadership had orchestrated between white and nonwhite centers became harder to maintain. NUSAS leaders "were fully conscious that they were relying more and more on non-white centers and failing to liberalize white student attitudes as fast as that of the National Assembly which included black and white student leaders."[66] In other words, although Student Representative Councils on all-white campuses might be racially conservative, student representatives from black campuses were gaining greater influence at the annual meetings of the National Assembly. In that respect, black influence in NUSAS was not always fully revealed by their token numbers. In this way, NUSAS became one of the sources of SASO leadership. For example, Steve Biko was a former NUSAS representative.

Black student leaders were all too aware of the fact that a truly nonracial, democratic student organization would contain a black majority. Thus, NUSAS multiracialism translated into a disadvantage for black students—it tended to constrain their ability to pursue the political agenda they deemed relevant and necessary. Black student leaders saw that NUSAS provided white students with political legitimacy and an unavoidable institutional advantage derived from a university system based on racial privilege. Gradually, they could no longer reconcile the hassle of fitting into NUSAS with the limited gains derived from participation. For one thing, the degree of state repression faced by black students on campus and in the larger community tended to undermine their sense of multiracial student solidarity. Reflecting on the period, Baruch Hirson noted that white students were preoccupied with the government's whittling away of democratic rights, while black students faced concerns that are more basic. "[T]he Blacks' concern was to secure the most elementary of such rights. The white students did not often feel the need to take their political demands outside the campus: the Blacks were always conscious of the fact that they came from an oppressed majority, and could not divorce the demand for national liberation from their own student demands."[67]

Furthermore, NUSAS was perhaps not the best standard-bearer of multiracial commitment. The University Christian Movement (UCM), another multiracial organization, provided far fewer institutional impediments than NUSAS to the growth of black political and ideological influence. Biko and other black consciousness–minded student leaders realized that the UCM—founded in 1966 as a more liberal alternative to the racially divided Student Christian Association—could provide black students with greater influence than was possible in NUSAS. UCM also had a highly developed network of independent international contacts that were made available to black students.[68] By 1968, the UCM had some 20 branches and over 3,000 members.[69]

Similar to black consciousness thought, the radical Christian transcendentalism of the UCM was grounded in a praxis of redemption and, when transformed into political ideology, it was less plagued by ideological divisiveness than Marxism or by social hypocrisy than liberalism. Much to its credit, the black caucus of the UCM gave birth to Black Theology, the religious counterpart of Black Consciousness Philosophy. The UCM was very conscious of theological and political developments among African-Americans and influenced by black theologians like James H. Cone. In a letter to the wife of slain American civil rights leader Dr. Martin Luther King Jr., UCM President Basil Moore wrote "non-violence presents us with an alternative both to doing nothing in the face of injustice and responding with hatred and despair."[70] Indeed, black influence in the organization in the early 1970s was so pervasive that the BCM's annual journal *Black Review* concluded that UCM should be considered a black organization.[71] Sharing the fate of most black organizations, by 1971 the UCM leadership was forcibly suppressed; Basil Moore, Sabelo Ntwasa, and Justice Molotho were all banned.[72]

Both NUSAS and UCM contributed to the growth of black student autonomy. Within these groups, black caucuses became the nuclei of independent black student organizations. Blacks used NUSAS and UCM as forums for their views, but did not consider them to be "leading the overall struggle for both black and white students."[73] Therefore, black students always participated in NUSAS with some trepidation. Even as they defied government restrictions against participation, black student leaders regarded NUSAS as an arena of white privilege.

In 1968, students at Fort Hare organized a major sit-in protest leading to the suspension of over 350 students. University administrators used mass suspensions followed by a highly selective readmission process to weed out radical students. Outraged, NUSAS leaders wrote to overseas organizations about the treatment of Fort Hare students. In its press release, NUSAS clearly spelled out the dictatorial powers of the white Rector on the black campus:

> No student may leave the campus without permission from the Rector or his deputies; No student organization can be set up without prior approval of the Rector; No student meetings can be held on campus without the permission of the Rector; No magazine, pamphlet, or publication for which students are responsible can be circulated without permission of the Rector; No statement can be given to the press on behalf of students without the Rector's permission; and No outsider may be upon the College grounds as a visitor and no Fort Hare student may visit any other institution without the permission of the Rector and then only under certain conditions.[74]

The tyranny of white officials at the university and the long arm of repressive government beyond the campus radicalized many black students.

> For the average black student, apart from his or her private life, the most important thing in life was "the political struggle." And since politics intruded into almost every aspect of private life, for some students politics was deemed more important than private life. The political struggle embraced every aspect of life so that the distinction between university politics and national liberation politics was an artificial distinction with little or no meaning except at the tactical level. Unless this point is understood . . . students are puzzling and even incomprehensible to the outsider.[75]

A revealing study of the political socialization of black South African students studying abroad in the late 1960s found five recurring attitudinal patterns: intense politicization, oppositionalism (the rejection of all forms of authority), nationalism, socialism or populism, and incivility (the tendency to see those who disagree as enemies). The author concluded that black South African students saw multiracialism as an impediment to self-liberation; they did not reject it out of any deeply rooted anti-white sentiment.[76] Black student attitudes at home were strikingly similar.

Whether or not black students agreed with all aspects of NUSAS politics, they viewed the formation of a Student Representative Council on a black campus as an act of defiance. Ultimately, this was not enough. In 1968, Biko and his associates founded the South African Student Organization (SASO), which rapidly became the most vocal black opposition inside the country. SASO's first order of business was to clarify its break with NUSAS. Biko offered a concise and pithy summary of political problems for black students in NUSAS: The Union was ineffectual; it repeated shopworn liberal dogmas; within NUSAS itself, blacks and whites formed separate and opposing camps; and within NUSAS, black students could not do what the struggle required of them.[77]

Toppy Mtimkulu, the student representative from the University of Natal (Non-European Section), explained to the 1969 NUSAS Executive why black students on his campus chose to disaffiliate and join SASO. Mtimkulu acknowledged that the ideal university community should transcend barriers of race, color, or creed; however, he said:

> [T]he non-white student finds himself faced with problems unique to him and his kind; there was a lack of fruitful and worthwhile participation by most non-white institutions of higher learning in the student organizations of the country; most non-racial student organizations have inadvertently allowed themselves to be influenced by the social and political stratification in this country to the extent where their priorities are made to suit the more privileged and affluent groups such that the non-white students and their problems have become an appendage of these organizations; there is a need for the students from underprivileged groups to amalgamate their resources and strength into one concerted effort so as to be able to bargain from a position of strength.[78]

When they criticized NUSAS, SASO leaders discovered that student activists from the Unity Movement had already covered most of the ground. Hirson observed that in an early SASO publication, black-conscious intellectuals described the Unity Movement–aligned PNSO's attitude toward affiliation with NUSAS as "emotional." But soon thereafter, SASO denounced NUSAS in similar terms.[79]

There was, however, a significant difference between SASO's judgment of NUSAS and that of the PNSO, which flatly dismissed the multiracial Union. The views of many SASO leaders were crystallized through personal contacts with their fellow NUSAS members at Annual Assemblies and other meetings. At these gatherings, white students exhibited little concern about, or awareness of, the racial indignities—such as remote, segregated accommodations—that their black colleagues had to endure merely to be there. SASO was formed after one such NUSAS conference where black students decided that they simply had had enough of the charade of racial equality. Under apartheid, progressive whites could not reform the system and could do little more than express their personal abhorrence of racism. Yet, up-close observation of white student lifestyles often triggered black student anger. In that emotional context, NUSAS's appeal for multiracial unity antagonized black students who responded by demanding that whites renounce skin-color privilege before they could be taken seriously as radicals.

By 1973, NUSAS representatives encountered hostility from black students at a conference on the university campus in Roma, Lesotho. Geoff Budlender of NUSAS reported that the majority of students present felt that a white-dominated organization should not be allowed to participate. Budlender surmised that Lesotho student leaders were uncomfortable with the way he was treated. However, Abraham Tiro and Jeff Baqwa, two central SASO figures, insisted that white involvement would only hinder the prospect for black liberation. The SASO leaders prevailed: the Southern African Student Movement (SASM) which grew out of the Roma meeting sought to "bring together under a common banner all students of the black nations of Southern Africa."[80]

The interaction of these two organizations posed important analytical questions thus: What does the relationship between NUSAS and SASO reveal about the evolution of a transracial, generational discourse on South African citizenship; and to what extent did the black component of the New Left offer an innovative perspective on racial segregation in Africa's most advanced capitalist country? Whatever its shortcomings from a black perspective, NUSAS proved to be useful to black student leaders in some important respects. First, it offered a few of them a range of resources, contacts, and experience that might not otherwise have been available. Moreover, those SASO leaders who had participated in NUSAS learned that they did not need the Union as an intermediary to attract support and resources, domestically or internationally. Indeed, shortly before his murder by the South African police, Steve Biko had begun to serve as a fundraiser for Black Community Programs, an outreach arm of the BCM.

Second, although both NUSAS and SASO were involved in student outreach into the community, the older NUSAS tradition appears to have influenced SASO's recognition of the importance of such endeavors. Since SASO outreach programs were not fundamentally different from those of NUSAS, Hirson concluded that SASO's break with NUSAS was organizational rather than ideological.[81] Explicitly dismissing the political content of black consciousness, Hirson compares the two student groups in order to make his main point— SASO was no more than an organization of black liberals. As we shall see, this was a standard Old Left criticism of the BCM as a whole.

Third, NUSAS took an early interest in worker issues and began to establish Wage Commissions. Nolutshungu believes that this prompted SASO to also get involved with black workers.[82] Eventually, both black and white students began to include the concerns of workers at their annual conferences and to pass resolutions opposing the exploitation of black labor. Although Fozia Fisher contended that SASO showed no awareness of worker issues, in time, black consciousness–oriented unions such as the Black Allied Workers Union (BAWU), under the leadership of Drake Koka, did become involved with the organization of black workers.[83]

Last, but certainly not least, government antipathy toward NUSAS liberalism inadvertently helped to create the window of opportunity required for SASO to become established on black campuses. At a crucial juncture, government officials naively interpreted SASO's race-conscious denunciation of white liberals as evidence of the group's affinity with apartheid. For a fleeting moment, some government officials even believed that the BCM could be used to undermine the influence of the exiled liberation movement.[84] The opposite proved true as black youth left the country to join the armed struggle. However, when young recruits reached its exile bases with black republican ideas, the ANC became acutely aware of the BCM's ideological influence at home. The ANC leadership feared that "if recent exiles are allowed freely to espouse ideologies of racial or class exclusivism . . . they could open movement-wide schisms that, for now, lie buried while waiting for liberation."[85]

Perhaps the black movement that felt the pangs of generational change most acutely was Inkatha. During the year of the Soweto

Rebellion, Chief Gatsha Buthelezi's support was weakest in the Transvaal and the Cape, where student power was strongest, but it was a counterweight to student organization in his home province of Natal. There, he was able to prevent widespread student violence and even to recruit many youths into Inkatha.[86] "Homeland" leaders were considered legitimate targets of radical student anger. Chief Buthelezi readily acknowledged the generation gap between himself and student radicals. Nonetheless, he was clearly appalled by student resentment of elder (his own) authority. Responding to attacks on him by Soweto Student Representative Council President Tsietsi Mashinini in 1976, Buthelezi pondered the difference between his generation and that of Mashinini. He agreed that he and his young Fort Hare contemporaries also criticized venerable leaders such as Z. K. Matthews. However, he recollected, "although we criticized these great sons of Africa, we never despised them, as Tsietsi Mashinini and his cronies despise us."[87]

Actually, Buthelezi was not the only leader concerned about the influence of the BCM. The conference in Roma, Lesotho, mentioned above is another example; the occasion of black students from inside South Africa successfully promoting black nationalist ideas at a regionwide student gathering alarmed the white liberal left and the multiracial ANC. Black Consciousness Philosophy could be distinguished from the larger body of African nationalism by the extent of its race-conscious rhetoric; this made many members of the older generation uncomfortable. Critics of the BCM pointed to its adaptation of Negritude and Black Power and questioned the relevance of Black Consciousness Philosophy for South African conditions. Since SASO leaders had cultivated a detailed understanding of trends within the civil rights and black power movements in the United States, they were also charged with having no originality and foolishly imitating African-Americans. However, BCM leaders were aware of trends in Africa as well as in its Diaspora. With respect to the differences drawn between African socialism and Afro-Marxism, the early BCM advocated communalism as an alternative to capitalist values. The BCM also faced several concerns of a more practical nature. Not unlike the problems faced by the Old Left, the attempt to consolidate a new student movement posed two related issues: How should the student organization relate to the larger black community, and was internal opposition possible given the degree of state repression? By merely attempting to operate openly inside the country, SASO was immediately forced to explore the limits of government repression. With respect to the larger community, in July 1972 SASO launched the Black People's Convention in an effort to expand beyond the campus, help build autonomous community organizations, and bridge both the class divide and the generation gap.

5. ✿ The Black Republican Synthesis

By the mid-1970s, three distinct political forces, associated with "homeland" leaders, militant youths, and black workers, combined to revive black politics in South Africa. Although chiefs, youths, and workers had been active politically in the past, they were now on their own without effective guidance from leaders of the banned political parties, who were either in exile or in prison. In the absence of authentic national leaders for the black majority, the government backed various neo-ethnic politicians, among whom Chief Mangosuthu Gatsha Buthelezi proved to be the most viable. R. W. Johnson summarized the new configuration of internal political forces thus: "The PAC, ANC, and CPSA had all virtually ceased to exist inside South Africa. . . . These movements thus effectively abdicated from any significant role in shaping the burgeoning African movements of the 1970's. This new wave represented by the radical Bantustan leader, Chief Buthelezi, the Black Consciousness Movement, the striking black workers, the Soweto students, owe virtually nothing to the revolutionary exiles."[1]

Dramatized by the 1973 Durban Strikes and the 1976 Soweto Rebellion, youths and workers were largely responsible for the revitalization of internal protest. Through such organizations as the Black People's Convention (BPC) and the Soweto Committee of Ten, many members of the previous generation became active politically once again. Thinkers associated with the BCM undertook to both clarify and revise the meaning of black liberation.

Until then, Black Consciousness Philosophy was primarily a discourse on liberation with little or no attention given to the question of citizenship in a democratic country. When the BCM attained preeminence among internal opposition groups, its leaders addressed issues that impinged on the subject of citizenship. Their efforts to redefine the meaning of political community, in particular, revived latent tensions between liberal and republican ideals. The BCM's main contribution to republican thought on citizenship resulted from its staunch opposition to the contrived "tribal republicanism" which lay at the core of apartheid ideology.

Conceived by thinkers of apartheid as an antidote to the danger of African solidarity, ethnic self-government was central to the strategy of white supremacist rule. In this connection, it is worth repeating that apartheid policies were designed to foment both class and racial divisions. The government's utopian vision of African advancement was that of a conservative, state-aligned black bourgeoisie whose political loyalties were circumscribed by ethnicity and whose aspirations did not transcend the boundaries of homeland institutions. It was within the framework of official ideology that neo-ethnic politicians made their impact on internal politics.

Dependent on government patronage, and with hopes of wielding power in rural and urban migrant communities, Bantustan politicians sought to forge new constituencies from old ethnic loyalties. Well into this century, "chiefs still had considerable power over the daily lives of their subjects and it is this, in part, that explains the retention among migrants of the ideology of precapitalist social formations."[2] Moreover, Bantustan chiefs incarnated vestiges of an ethnic republicanism that held sway among many rural and some urban Africans.

The pathologies of racism, political corruption, and class exploitation associated with the Bantustans are well-known features of the apartheid system. Less well understood is the extent to which the Bantustan policy fostered an anachronistic form of ethnic republicanism. South African segregation denied full citizenship to black people by preventing the evolution of common political institutions—a strategy that required the manipulation of ethnic identities. The isolation of republican sentiment to discrete ethnicities within segregated races, it was wistfully thought, would thwart the demand for full and democratic citizenship grounded in an African, or South African, identity. For example, government officials were fond of saying that Africans had full citizenship, but in the Bantustans, not the republic. Indeed, the troublesome 1983 reforms, which produced a tripartite legislature, elevated the idea of "own affairs" for whites, Indians, and Coloureds to a contentious constitutional principle.

The major contradiction faced by the white government was all too obvious: since all people not of European descent were treated as black, racial oppression overrode ethnic identity. It was natural, therefore, for the oppressed races to proclaim black solidarity as the liberationist alternative to apartheid's strategy of divide and rule. Building on the older notion of non-European unity, the BCM extended the logic of racial solidarity to include Indians and Coloureds. Even among staunch African nationalists, there were always those who felt that Indians and Coloureds comprised a vital part of the black nation. By the time of his death in 1978, Robert Sobukwe of the PAC had renounced his earlier rhetoric which depicted Indians as an alien merchant class. During the last years of his life in Kimberley, many of his closest friends and strongest supporters were Indian. Historically, Afrikaners were also divided over the social status of Coloureds. A few Afrikaner leaders urged the incorporation of mixed-race communities as a means of racially integrating Afrikanerdom based on a shared language and culture. However the Afrikaner majority, including many white republicans, rejected Coloured incorporation and projected onto them, along with Indians and Africans, a racial construct grounded in their own heart-felt separatist precepts.

Thus, the alchemy of black South African nationalism lay in its ability to transcend the legacy of bifurcated citizenship by the positive use of both liberal and republican ideals as a means to combat the ideologies of white supremacy. Where segregation has persisted, the major challenge of liberal citizenship is to foster political institutions that reflect the diversity of civil society while remaining true to the principle of legal equality. Concurrently, the republican dimension of citizenship has involved the appropriation of sentiments associated with communal life in order to provide the struggle for citizenship an emotional content. In South Africa, however, apartheid made communal life and racial identity virtually inseparable.

BLACK REPUBLICAN AND LIBERAL CITIZENSHIP

Black consciousness thought is relevant to both the liberal and the republican theories of citizenship. Although apartheid over-determined racial identity, the role of tradition in the modern construction of citizenship would, in any event, have been controversial in African nationalist thought. Colonial regimes in Africa, particularly those in the British colonies, regularly manipulated ethnic republican sentiments to quell liberal demands for independence. In contrast to France's policy of universal citizenship through gradual assimilation of French culture, Britain appealed directly to ethnic republican ideals in order to bolster its policy of indirect rule. In response to Britain's support of conservative, traditional authority, African nationalists evoked radical liberal conceptions of citizenship. With special reference to Nigeria, Richard L. Sklar has described the dramatic rivalry between African nationalists and colonial officials over the rights-content of postcolonial citizenship thus:

> Against the conservative doctrine of historic rights, Nigerian nationalists invoked the principle of popular sovereignty to vindicate the radical doctrine of "natural rights." Whereas the colonial theory assumed the functional rationality of the social order, the logic of the nationalist theory postulated the rationality of the individual. Whereas the colonial theory accepted the premise that in African society men and women were functional parts of the social organism, the nationalists believed that every person was an end in him- or herself. Whereas colonial theory valued the preservation of a hierarchical order, the nationalists adopted the doctrine of progress and looked ahead with optimism to an egalitarian new order in which communal values would survive, but not at the expense of individual rights.[3]

With distinctive variations, the two major colonial powers, England and France, sought to justify their systems of rule in Africa by drawing on the ideals of republican and liberal citizenship respectively. In South Africa, the apartheid regime's Bantustan policy represented a further perversion of ethnic republican sentiment, a kind of internal indirect rule placed at the service of racial domination. White settler colonialism began at such an early stage and racial proletarianization was so pervasive that left-wing intellectuals coined the phrase "colonialism-of-a-special-type" to describe the South African case.[4]

The kind of ethnic consciousness that Bantustans were designed to propagate was generally resented and scornfully rejected by African nationalists. Yet, South African officialdom clung tenaciously to the hated designation "Bantu" (connoting "tribal" consciousness) and refused to countenance the word "African" (which signified multiethnic, national consciousness). To be sure, many of the mission-educated, older African nationalists were not as hostile to ethnic identity as were the SASO activists. With its growing number of young members, who viewed themselves as victims of oppressive retribalization, the Black Consciousness Movement evolved as a counter-ethnicity social force. The ethnic preoccupations of apartheid ideologues drove Neville Alexander, one of South Africa's most articulate theorist-activists, to the conclusion that in modern social theory "ethnicity is a substitute for the concept of 'race.'"[5] In the face of state-sponsored ethnic nationalism, the BCM was prompted to reconstruct black nationalism as a theory of citizenship based on anti-ethnic premises. Race consciousness, specifically the term "black," was understood to signify an explicit rejection of apartheid categories. For example, some of the most well-known Indian members of the BCM refused to join specifically Indian organizations on the grounds that they fostered ethnic division.

The attempt to transcend ethnicity—to construct black unity as a new culture of resistance—constituted simultaneously the most utopian and radical dimension of the Black Consciousness platform. The rejection of neo-ethnic politics led the BCM to assert Black Consciousness as the nemesis of ethnic identity. Yet, questions of how black consciousness theory should interpret ethnicity, relate to ethnic politicians, and deal with the ethnic sentiments of the black masses were recurring theoretical problems, even while the official anti-ethnicity stance of the BCM remained inviolate. Reflecting on the possible confusion between black and ethnic republican thought, Hirson insisted that Buthelezi's revival of Zulu nationalism posed theoretical and practical problems for the black consciousness concept of non-collaboration with ethnic organizations.[6] Logically, he wondered why ethnic consciousness should not be an acceptable part of black consciousness, particularly if Coloureds and Indians were included in the movement?

While the BCM's solidaristic attack on the Bantustan policy was extremely important, there were other, equally important dimensions to black consciousness thought. The Black Consciousness Movement offered a critique of capitalism that was both radical, without being explicitly Marxist, and democratic without yielding to the Eurocentric pressures of South African liberalism. The most important critical imperative of the early BCM was its refusal to allow the demand for black solidarity to be subsumed under liberal or socialist perspectives. As a matter of principle, the BCM openly demanded that themes emerging from liberalism, socialism, and African nationalism be judged from the perspective of black solidarity. Indeed, the BCM's most fundamental criticism of the Bantustans was that they constituted a crude and blatant attempt to fragment the black majority. Moving far beyond a mere celebration of racial pride, the BCM proposed a new foundation for the republican theory of citizenship: racial domination, rather than African tradition, provided the basis for a sense of peoplehood and national solidarity. Thus, black consciousness thought staked out a middle ground of citizenship identity between multiracial union and old-style black republicanism.

The BCM's racial populist theory of citizenship created a high degree of anxiety in many members of the older generation. By emphasizing the subjective dimension of black identity, this movement of black intellectuals revitalized an indigenous tradition of racial populism, one that the ANC and its Charterist allies had worked to banish from the arsenal of liberatory weapons. As a subjective understanding of politics, populism provides a set of values for everyday life that enables it to blend smoothly with liberalism as well as socialism. What Craig Calhoun sees as the real strength of English populism during the Industrial Revolution can also be said of black consciousness thought: "Populism was not so much a distinct set of political opinions as a mobilization of people who shared a common understanding of how life ought to be. Not that all people were mobilized at any one time, but the mode of understanding was wide spread."[7]

Ironically, the initial negative reaction to the BCM transcended party affiliation; much of the distrust was a combination of a generational bias and the jealousy that exiles often feel toward activists who have remained at home. Indeed, ANC nonracialism, SACP and NEUM Marxism, and even PAC Africanism had become, in James C. Scott's sense, the "public transcripts" of the generation that came of political age in the 1940s. Racial populism, while never totally eliminated, was relegated to the role of a "hidden transcript"—a discourse that takes place beyond the formal political arena.[8]

Marxist thinkers were even more strident than traditional liberals in their attacks on Black Consciousness Philosophy; particularly fervent were those with Unity Movement backgrounds. For example, No Sizwe (Neville Alexander's pseudonym) criticized the movement as a retrogressive occurrence, although he did concede that it made "important rediscoveries of deep-rooted political traditions."[9] Archie Mafeje granted that the BCM was a step forward if for no other reason than its ability to convince some Coloureds to proclaim a black identity for the first time in South African history; however, he believed that the movement was inadequate in that it did not see anti-racism in the context of class struggle and socialist transformation.[10] From a white Marxist perspective, Eddie Webster observed that the rise of Black Consciousness Philosophy in South Africa coincided with the renewal of Marxist thought in British, European, and North American universities. Marxism, he noted with candor, was the radical alternative to racial populism: "The emphasis of Black Consciousness on the need for blacks to mobilize as a group left white liberals with a deep uncertainty about their role in change in South Africa. Marxism, with its bold claims of class as the motor of history, offered a new generation of white academics an intellectually coherent political alternative to Black Consciousness."[11]

Liberal thinkers were often disposed to treat black consciousness with respect; some of them even postulated its counterpart in the form of conciliatory white consciousness. For example, this statement by Paul Pretorius, NUSAS President in 1972, exemplified liberal deference: "NUSAS would have to reject many existing White liberal policies and institutions if it were to avoid obstructing Black development as it had in the past. . . . Even our much lauded self-help programmes can best be initiated by Black community leaders and if our help is needed it will be called for."[12]

Unlike liberals, Marxist critics of the BCM were not at all inclined toward retreat. They deeply believed in the superiority of revolutionary Marxism and, as Anthony Marx has shown, gradually won many former black nationalists over to their position.[13] Assessments of the success or failure of the BCM depend, in large measure, on whether it is viewed as a student vanguard organization or a more diffuse intellectual and cultural movement. The litmus test imposed by Marxist critics measured the BCM against the organizational and ideological norms of scientific socialism. Marxists often claimed to be annoyed by the BCM's refusal to behave like a vanguard party or to provide leadership to youth and worker movements, although it is doubtful that any form of organization would have mollified ideological distaste for the BCM and its principles. Nonetheless, Steve Biko, the preeminent BCM theorist and political leader, was extremely sensitive to the fact that his generation—the SASO generation—was politically pivotal. Intellectuals of the Old Left insisted that Black Consciousness Philosophy was hopelessly mired in a retrogressive form of race-conscious liberalism. For example, Toussaint, writing in the *African Communist,* the official organ of the SACP, accused Biko, the BCM leader, of being a liberal, an idealist, and a pacifist; one who was insufficiently anti-capitalist and deficient in understanding of the mass struggle.[14] Toussaint chided the black consciousness thinkers for wasting so much time and energy on criticisms of white liberals, who were a tiny ineffective minority with minimal influence on black thought or action. Comparing the thought of the BCM with that of the ANC-SACP alliance, he concluded: "Black liberalism . . . compared with the forthright radicalism of the national liberation movement, developed in depth both in the realm of ideas and in the fields of action by the African National Congress and the Communist Party . . . is a puny and inadequate ideology indeed—even when given a radical-sounding cloak of Black Consciousness."[15] In a 1972 issue of *Azania News,* the PAC, which was philosophically closer to black consciousness than its ANC-SACP rivals, echoed the same sentiments: "We specifically want to warn against the promotion of black consciousness which seems to be gaining foot in our country today. Black consciousness is a racial reaction to White racism and white liberal paternalism. It is not a solution to either."[16]

Often criticisms of the BCM's alleged ideological limitations were disguised or confused reactions to the revival of internal opposition by groups that were not controlled by the older liberation organizations. From that standpoint, both the BCM and the independent trade unions were viewed with suspicion by the parties in exile. Even before the growth of the BCM and independent trade unions, the exiled leaders had discounted the possibility of aboveground internal opposition to the government. After the Sharpeville Massacre of 1960, the ANC and PAC concluded that armed struggle was the only possible and appropriate response to the white regime. Within the liberation movement, as Dennis Davis and Robert Fine observed, "a tendency was born which equated armed struggle with revolution and legal struggle with reformism."[17] They speculate that the anti-legalism of the ANC and the SACP may have been over-compensation for their own reliance on a legalistic strategy before they were banned. Now, however, the old guard concluded that any group "allowed" to operate inside the country was presumptively counterrevolutionary. Ultimately, governmental repression of spontaneous internal opposition quelled the suspicions of most leaders in exile. In addition, the exiled parties developed their own legal internal wings by the early 1980s. Organizations like the United Democratic Front and its offspring, the Mass Democratic Movement, were aligned with the ANC while the National Forum Committee was supported by AZAPO and other anti-Charterists; however, both groupings had former BCM members among their leaders and activists. For example, Cyril Ramaphosa, who honed his skills in the BCM, was a central figure in the launch of the National Union of Mineworkers, Africa's largest trade union.

When the BCM took shape as a broad alliance of black organizations in the early 1970s, Biko and his associates were acutely sensitive to leftist criticisms. But they were even more troubled by the specter of failure, and the possibility that their SASO generation would be spurned as "sell outs" by a younger generation of militant students. BCM leaders were also concerned by the formation of alliances between liberals, both black and white, and moderate "homeland" leaders, notably Chief Buthelezi.

In a 1972 article, Biko explained why so much of his verbal artillery was aimed at liberals. He wrote that "after a brief spell of silence during which political activity was mainly taken up by liberals, blacks started dabbling with a dangerous theory—that of working within the system."[18] The policy of noncollaboration as a response to cosmetic reforms was central to Biko's understanding of the politics of internal opposition.

Also in 1972, a new SASO President, Temba Sono, advocated the development of a working relationship with progressive homeland leaders and opposition candidates in Bantustan elections. In addition to his contention that Sono had failed to properly consult the SASO executive before announcing his controversial policy, Biko wholly rejected the new direction and successfully worked behind the scenes to have Sono deposed. The Sono affair provides an example of how BCM leaders could respond to any policy that might confuse black and ethnic republicanism in the public mind or the anti-apartheid opposition as a whole.[19] Biko's own relations with various liberals inside South Africa (e.g., Donald Woods and Aelred Stubbs) may have served to reinforce his undoubtedly liberal inclinations. It was Stubbs's impression of Biko that neither Lenin nor Trotsky would have been at home with him or the BCM.[20] This writer's own conversations with Biko in May 1977 confirm Stubbs's observation. By inclination Biko was a social democrat. He believed that a redistribution of wealth implied the adaptation of socialist policies to a capitalist market economy.[21] Donald Woods, who did much to popularize Biko as a personality and as a thinker, insisted that his contribution to black consciousness thought was sincerely derived from a combination of philosophical and tactical considerations.[22]

Possessing an uncanny awareness of the limits of identity politics, Biko understood that a realistic strategy of internal opposition required a reconsideration of the role of progressive whites who opposed apartheid and conservative blacks who were connected with it. However, the BCM did not believe that the best way to influence white liberal opposition was to condone black participation within the existing system. On the contrary, it challenged the legitimacy of collaboration with apartheid in any form. Biko and his associates formulated a race-conscious republicanism that extended African nationalism while defending it against ethnic nationalism. Whether one believed in black republican identity or multiracial union, the main criteria of black leadership must be struggle and sacrifice for the sake of liberation. Biko contended that "People like Mandela, Sobukwe, Kathrada, M. D. Naidoo and many others will always have a place of honour in our minds as the true leaders of the people. They may have been branded communists, saboteurs, or similar names—in fact they may have been convicted of similar offenses in law courts but this does not subtract from the real essence of their worth. These were people who acted with a dedication unparalleled in modern times."[23]

Biko's desire to combat the influence of white liberalism was reminiscent of the revolutionary tradition of Georges Sorel and Frantz Fanon. Sorel, the theorist of revolutionary syndicalism, believed that liberal reforms undermined class polarization; therefore, he opposed ameliorative social legislation regardless of its immediate benefit to workers. For Sorel, "the path to change is not gradual but apocalyptic, involving a confrontation of the chief rivals for power in any given age."[24] In similar fashion, Fanon, a black Martinican, applied the notion of revolutionary catharsis to colonial struggles. Biko did anticipate a necessary period of polarization between blacks and whites in South Africa. But, he did not publicly advocate interracial conflict, since that would have made it easier for the government to outlaw the BCM, which it did in 1977. As racial populists, Biko and his comrades believed that black liberalism was nourished by a lingering desire on the part of the missionary-educated elite for white acceptance. Biko's republican conceptualization stressed the Eurocentric impulse in liberalism; from this racialized view of liberal ideology, many socialists were regarded as liberals by BCM thinkers.

As a prelude to Biko's synthesis of the several distinct strands in black liberation thought, let us compare his concept of black consciousness with that of Jordan Ngubane, another important race-conscious, Africanist thinker. This comparison affords an insight into the differences between old and new approaches to black republican thought. In an exploration of the limits of Western liberalism, Ngubane attempted to reconcile republican and liberal thought by analyzing the differing conceptions of the individual held by Africans and Europeans. Reminiscent of Hegel's dialectical approach to the history of ideas, Ngubane shows how the political contradictions in one period of reaction to white domination gives rise to the next phase of African ideology. The "Sudic Personality," Ngubane's term for authentic African consciousness, like Hegel's Idea, works its way through the antithetical, Eurocentric values imposed by racial domination. Ngubane's African consciousness is timeless and ultimately incorruptible; it moves through history without being a product of history. Since the Sudic Personality cannot be reconciled with a Eurocentric worldview, their encounter causes a "conflict of minds," a process that provides the title for Ngubane's book.[25]

Biko's conception of black consciousness is far less essentialist. Black consciousness for him is the outcome of struggle and introspection. A famous passage from his essay "We Blacks" makes Biko's point:

> It becomes more necessary to see the truth as it is if you realize that the only vehicle for change are these people who have lost their personality. The first step therefore is to make the black man come to himself; to pump back life into his empty shell; to infuse him with pride and dignity, to remind him of his complicity in the crime of allowing himself to be misused and therefore letting evil reign supreme in the country of his birth. This is what we mean by an inward-looking process.[26]

Many of the important intellectual characteristics of the New Left as a whole were evident in Biko's political thought. Although he was primarily concerned with black liberation in South Africa, Biko was aware that a significant political discourse was taking place worldwide. Nyameko (Barney) Pityana, Biko's closest intellectual collaborator and an important black consciousness thinker and activist in his own right, captures the connection between Black Consciousness Philosophy and the intellectual themes of the New Left thus:

> The late 60's saw in America and Europe a great tidal wave of campus power, a rejection by young people of the decadent values of the passing generation and a challenge to authority that was unprecedented hitherto. In Sorbonne and Berkeley, California, students sought to exert their power and idealism. There was a serious examination of the norms of society and an attempt at evolving societal values, meaningful examination of the self, and a redirection of the collective perspectives of the oppressed people.[27]

During this same period, many white radicals were engaged in a similar process of rethinking the meaning of class, and the relationship of class struggle to politics in contemporary capitalism. New

Leftist innovations in revolutionary thought often violated established ideological boundaries in order to cope with the issues of human emancipation as a transnational project. In South Africa, Biko saw that elements of liberalism, Marxism, and even African nationalism were often used in defense of the status quo or to explain the meaning of liberation in ways that obscured the political and psychological dynamics of racial oppression. Having studied the works of such left revolutionary thinkers as Frantz Fanon, Aimé Césaire, Malcolm X, and Amilcar Cabral, Biko stressed the responsibility of revolutionary intellectuals for cultural and psychological as well as political emancipation. Like Fanon, he criticized Western education for its tendency to undermine the commitment of black intellectuals to their people and cultural values.[28]

In brief, Biko tried to construct a new theory of political consciousness for black South Africans. He believed that a transformation of consciousness precedes mass action. Common to many student ideologies of his era was a focus on culture, community, and the dimension of everyday life as the most important reference points for political activity. In addition, mass protests during the 1960s had persuaded many student radicals that a mass movement was the most genuine expression of mass consciousness.[29] New Left thinkers everywhere were inclined to detach the notion of an advanced political consciousness from the Leninist dogma of the vanguard party. Most Old Left revolutionaries believed that education of the masses required leadership. By contrast, Biko concluded that committed intellectuals armed with knowledge of popular culture could accomplish mass education without a party apparatus. Popular culture could be harnessed to help "breathe life back into the oppressed."

SNCC AND SASO: BLACK POWER AND CONSCIOUSNESS

SASO and the American Student Non-Violent Coordinating Committee (SNCC) shared a strikingly similar commitment to populism. Carson notes that by 1965 SNCC had become, in the eyes of supporters and critics, not simply a civil rights organization but part of the New Left—an amorphous body of young activists seeking new ideological alternatives to conventional liberalism.[30] The BCM was one of the few African organizations to unreservedly identify with blacks in the Diaspora and to assimilate international resistance against racial domination into its political outlook. In South Africa, Biko and other members of the BCM encouraged a dialogue between intellectuals in Africa and the African Diaspora. This led some of Biko's critics to charge him with being contaminated with foreign ideas and to dismiss the BCM as a parody of America's Black Power Movement.

The very phrase "black consciousness philosophy" suggests a discourse unique to the victims of white racism; it posits the existence of a transnational tradition of black political thought. By contrast, African nationalist thought is more parochial and, unlike Black Consciousness Philosophy, often rejects the idea of "black power." Black power politics does not limit itself to identification with a particular nation-state or even to Africa as a continent; people of African descent are called upon to seek empowerment wherever they find themselves and to fight racial oppression wherever it exists. Black power represents the internationalization of black nationalism and this has important theoretical implications.[31]

Their willingness to make international black power a public transcript was another significant distinction between the thought of the BCM and that of the previous generation, especially the ANC. In the United States, as E. Victor Wolfenstein observes, the identification of the Black American and African struggle culminated in Malcolm X's fervent belief in "linking the national struggle to the international one."[32] It was, therefore, inevitable that the two most historically significant student-led struggles for racial liberation would draw sustenance from one another. So it was that these two movements, with very few formal links, drew upon one another for inspiration and as evidence of the international significance of their domestic struggles. Moreover, their deep empathy revitalized a long history of synergy and concrete interaction between South African and African-American intellectuals.

In America, the black minority dominated SNCC. In South Africa, the black majority constituted a minority voice in NUSAS. Hence, SASO began with the call for black consciousness while the call for black power was made toward the end of SNCC's organizational history. Black Power and Black Consciousness were designed to initiate a new approach to struggle by distinguishing SASO and SNCC from both white student radicals and black moderates. In the final analysis, neither SASO nor SNCC were organizationally capable of supplanting the multiracialism of the older generation of elites in either the national liberation or civil rights movements. Nonetheless, the influence of their race consciousness ideas had tremendous public appeal. Both SNCC and SASO learned an important lesson from their distinct experiences with multiracial student organizations. In the words of Howard Klare, these black students came "to understand that the struggle against racism is not an afterthought of revolution but its precondition."[33]

Both in South Africa and the southern United States, students began to stress the uniqueness of black struggle and to relate African liberation, civil rights, black power, and Third World politics within the framework of New Left discourse. The focus on racial liberation was an ideological bond between the two black student struggles as well as a shared component of their generational understanding. John Lewis, Chairman of SNCC during the famous 1963 March on Washington, was forced by the more established civil rights leaders to tone down his black conscious utterances for the sake of unity. Implicit in his comments about the civil rights legislation, which grew out of the massive demonstrations of the period, is a close identification of the black American and South African struggles. Toward the end of his speech, Lewis proclaimed that "one man, one vote is the African cry and it is ours, too."[34] The flourishing interest of SNCC in African liberation movements was to be reciprocated by SASO. Gail Gerhart observed that black South Africans followed with great interest the 1954 American Supreme Court school desegregation decision and the Montgomery bus boycott of 1955. "But never had social and political ideas originating in black America been subject to as wide and searching scrutiny as the ideas emanating in the Black Power aftermath of the civil rights movements."[35]

Although several of the early leaders had been active in multiracial politics, both groups drew their following from segregated campuses. It was only a matter of time before SASO and SNCC would articulate go-it-alone positions. In an early discussion of the BCM, Heribert Adam contended that those black South African students who were involved in NUSAS suffered from an "interaction disability;" they found it difficult to function on an equal basis with whites who enjoyed superior resources and social standing.[36] This had little or nothing to do with the leadership ability of black students, many of whom went on to become important national figures.

SNCC, unlike SASO, began as a student coordinating body for the spontaneous defiance of black university students against segregated lunch counters in the South. However, SNCC's and SASO's main strengths rested with their autonomous student origins. In large part, SNCC's autonomy can be attributed to the farsightedness of Ella Baker. A veteran activist, Baker helped the youth to organize themselves and to escape control by the established civil rights leadership, dominated as it was by the male clergy of whom she had grown wary. Baker, along with SNCC's first Chairman, Bob Moses, worked vigilantly to protect the political autonomy of the fledgling youth movement. In his award-winning history of SNCC, Claybourne Carson emphasizes the fact that black activists were always in control of field operation and, therefore, white recruits from northern colleges were, usually for the first time, under the supervision of black leaders.[37]

Just as SASO produced many of the new leaders of the internal opposition, SNCC was a training ground for a large number of the New Left activists who gravitated toward anti-war, feminist, and revolutionary nationalist causes. Only SNCC, of all the civil rights groups, refused to include a loyalty statement in its foundational documents or to bar communists or ex-communists from membership. For SNCC, the only test of loyalty was a willingness to confront the racist southern authorities. Similarly, Biko and the BCM refused to renounce black leaders because they were, or had been, communists.[38]

As SNCC attempted to extend its operations beyond the South and into the major urban centers of the North and West, the organization declined as a political force. Ironically, the conditions which prevailed in American cities made "black power" an ever more popular slogan. In South Africa, as we have seen, the ANC and its allies were able to contain the influence of black consciousness ideas at home and in its military camps, but, as the Truth and Reconciliation Commission Report revealed, this was not accomplished without incident.

As relatively open student organizations, SASO and SNCC were unable to adapt to the escalation of political violence in South Africa and the United States respectively. The more violent periods in the two countries were initiated by the 1965 Watts rebellion in America and the 1976 Soweto uprising in South Africa. Some of SNCC's most prominent members joined the paramilitaristic Black Panther Party for Self-Defense, while thousands of youths formerly associated with BCM left the country to join the military wings of the ANC and, to a lesser degree, the PAC. This turn toward armed struggle by a new generation exposed the gulf between subjective and objective dimensions of liberation. Despite its ardent commitment to revolutionary action, the BCM could not launch and sustain its own armed struggle, even though it made a concerted effort. Thus, reality imposed limits on the Sorelian/Fanonian conception of revolutionary struggle with its emphasis on the subjective dimension of violence. No thinker has understood the implications of armed struggle for the BCM and the entire Soweto generation better than the late Sam Nolutshungu: "It is the subjective apprehension of the armed struggle in its relation to the psychological process of liberation that Fanon grappled with . . . and which, in the end, evaded even his own powerful vision and translucent prose. It is an elusive thing, perhaps impossible to describe with precision. By defining state power as white power they subordinated its reality to ideology, making it, too, subjective, and subjectively everything seemed possible."[39] While the conditions for black revolution never actually existed in the United States, it is, nonetheless, noteworthy that virtually all of the organizations founded after the mid-1960s adhered to some form of black republican thought and espoused either armed self-defense or more aggressive revolutionary measures.

The revolutionary conditions which existed in South Africa, the leadership vacuum left by the destruction of the older nationalist organizations, and the sheer weight of the African majority placed SASO in a position completely different from that of SNCC. In South Africa, black control of the state was a real, if seemingly remote, possibility. The SASO leadership was well aware of the potentially powerful position of the black majority when compared with the African-American minority. At a 1970 training seminar, a member of the SASO Executive spoke to this difference: "Afro-Americans accept that they will never be in a position to change the system in America, and adopt the approach that if you can't beat them, join from a position of strength. . . . Purely from a consideration of who we are, we realize that it is we who must be allowing others to participate in our system. We must not be the ones to be invited to participate in somebody else's system in our own private yard."[40]

SASO and SNCC also shared a strikingly similar commitment to populism. Indeed, the main means employed by SASO and SNCC to move beyond liberalism was to infuse black conscious radicalism with new forms of populism. Michael Rogin notes that New Left thought constituted a significant extension of the radical, pre-Marxian liberal tradition and that young radicals raised many of the questions posed by earlier radical democrats such as Rousseau and Mill.[41] The political thought of SNCC and SASO, like most New Left student movements, tended to be populist rather than Marxist, emphasizing communitarian rather than class theory. New Left movements did not view the working class as the sole agency of revolutionary change; they instead sought to build movements encompassing alienated students, middle-class professionals, and the poor as well as workers.[42]

The populist impulse of SNCC and SASO can be seen in the thought of their two founding presidents, Robert Moses and Steve Biko. Moses was noted for his skeptical approach toward ideology and organization, including SNCC's own. As intellectuals seeking to relate to less-educated blacks, Biko and Moses played down education and were concerned with the danger of intellectual isolation from the masses. Moses, a Harvard philosophy student, was deeply influenced by the works of Albert Camus, particularly *The Rebel.* He was moved by Camus's existentialist assessment that anarchism was essentially more radical than Leninism.[43] Camus understood Leninism to justify revolution by remote control; the vanguard party represented the ultimate form of alienation and emotional detachment from the very process that was supposed to bring about personal and social transformation. Moses, like Biko, opted for populism rather than vanguardism.

The populist goal of Black Consciousness thinkers was to articulate popular sentiments which serve to unify intellectuals and the masses. Tiro, in his famous 1972 speech, asserted that "the magic story of human history gives irrefutable proof that as soon as nationalism is awakened among the intelligentsia it becomes the vanguard of the struggle against alien rule."[44] It is in this light that Biko's famous comments about education should be understood:

> The attitude of some rural African folk who are against education is often misunderstood, not least by the African intellectual. Yet the reasons put forward by these people carry with them the realization of their inherent dignity and worth. They see education as the quickest way of destroying the substance of the African culture. They complain bitterly of the disruption in the life pattern, non-observation of customs, and constant derision from the non-conformists whenever any of them go through school. Lack of respect for the elders is, in the African tradition, an unforgivable and cardinal sin. Yet how can one prevent the loss of respect of child for father when the child is actively taught by his know-all white tutors to disregard his family teachings? How can an African avoid losing respect for his tradition when in school his whole cultural background is summed up in one word: Barbarism?[45]

Biko's comments on education were intended to be non-elitist and, concerning intellectuals, introspective. They confirm, rather than disguise, BCM's relationship to the average black South African. Spokespersons for the BCM understood that black solidarity required every effort to transcend intraracial class differences. In 1974, Mafika Pascal Gwala insisted that if the BCM were to succeed, it would have to become a "Back-to-the-People-Movement":[46]

> [W]e cannot talk of Black Solidarity outside of class identity. Be-
> cause as our Black brother has put it, it is only the elite that are
> plagued by the problem of identity. Not the mass of the Black
> people. The common Black people have had no reason to worry
> about their blackness. They never in the first place found them-
> selves outside or above their context of being black. But the student,
> the intellectual, the theologian, are the ones who have to go through
> foreign education and assimilate foreign ethical values.[47]

By the incorporation of a populist conception of class, the young members of the BCM began to consider professional advancement within a system structured by racial segregation as a degrading com-promise. In the words of another important African revolutionary, Amilcar Cabral, the BCM began to advance a theory of class suicide. So powerful was this view that many black South African intellectuals when discussing the subject of intraracial class relations would con-tend that there was no such thing as a black bourgeoisie (or middle class) under apartheid. From the writings of Rousseau to the debates between Russian populists and Lenin, the contention that capitalist values, and for that matter class stratification, could simply be resisted by the force of social solidarity has been a central feature of populist thought.[48] The BCM renounced capitalism in populist rather than Marxist terms. Capitalism's primary sin was that it infringed upon the expression of black people's cultural and political will. Given this intellectual trajectory it was not difficult for AZAPO, during a later period, to develop the idea of racial capitalism, a conception central to Black Conscious socialism.

TRADITION AND INNOVATION: BIKO'S SYNTHESIS

After Biko's tragic death in detention in 1977, his writings rapid-ly gained international renown. In addition to his collected essays, Biko's published testimony at the trial of South African Student Or-ganization and Black People's Convention leaders enabled people throughout the world public to read the thoughts of this important black intellectual.[49] In his speeches and writings, it is apparent that Biko assiduously avoided the temptation of trying to convert black consciousness into a form of racial fundamentalism. In other words, without compromising racial liberation as a core political value, he did not reduce all political conflict to racial factors. For this reason, most commentators rightly assert that there is no evidence of reverse racism in Biko's thought.

Biko was an avowed humanist. His best-known essay, entitled "Black Consciousness in Quest of a True Humanity," relates the black experience to processes of change which have shaped the modern world. His starting point was the black nationalist tradition reformulated from the perspective of a sorely oppressed but politically awakened generation. His method was predicated on the idea that political tradition is the raw material for intellectual reconstruction. As Russell Hanson observed with reference to the United States, discursive activity rather than retrieval of timeless ideas reproduces intellectual traditions. "It is common action that binds generations to one another and identifies them as different moments in the same political tradition. The specific arguments that are the product of this activity may or may not show signs of continuity. They are incidental to the activity itself, and it is the activity that constitutes a tradition."[50]

Biko's thought was ordered by the concept of dialogue between his insurgent generation and the grand tradition of African resistance to alien rule. He conceived of Black Consciousness Philosophy as a synthesis of the fundamental political principles of the three most prominent black liberation organizations, namely the African National Congress, the Pan Africanist Congress, and the Non-European Unity Movement. From the elements of these distinct parts of the nationalist tradition, Biko proposed to reconstruct its successor. As Anthony Giddens has explained, theoretical reconstruction "signifies taking a theory apart and putting it back together again in a new form in order to attain more fully the goal it has set itself."[51]

A crucial issue for Biko's reconstruction of theory was the so-called land question: Should the land belong to all, including European settlers, or be returned to the dispossessed African majority? On this issue, Biko's view was forthrightly republican rather than multiracial unionist. He upheld the principle of racial nationalism by endorsing the view associated with the PAC that the land belonged to the African people. However, he departed from the camp of African exclusivism by including Africans, Coloureds, and Indians in the category of "black." Although the BCM objected to separate ethnicity-based organizations, it was influenced by the idea of programmatic unity among existing black organizations; different versions of this position were associated both with the ANC (Charterism) and the Unity Movement (federalism). By eliminating the direct involvement of whites and making Indians and Coloureds "black," at least in theory, Biko resolved the PAC's objection that ANC Charterism facilitated minority control of the liberation movement. The BCM made *black* nationalism superior to ethnic—African, Indian, or Coloured—nationalisms. Thus, it strengthened the call for non-European unity that had long been championed by NEUM; Coloured and Indian communities were invited to unite with the African majority.

In this way, the BCM challenged the white government's power to decide the most basic question of citizenship, "who are the people." Just as Biko modified the Africanist definition of "black people" to incorporate all "non-Europeans," he altered the notion of multi-racialism to exclude formal alliances with whites. The decision to avoid alliances with whites was based on the assumption that their participation would undermine the prospects for black solidarity. Formally, the ANC endorsed alliances with progressive whites over the PAC's ceaseless objections, but, in reality, the issue remained difficult to resolve in both camps. As we have seen in the case of Patrick Duncan, the PAC eventually defined "African" as a behavioral rather than a racial category, so that progressive whites might be members of the nation. Similarly, the BCM contended that white South Africans who opposed apartheid should educate their racist brethren, should not attempt to control black organizations, and should learn to accept terms of interaction established by the black majority. This amounted to a call for a white consciousness movement that ran parallel to the activities of the BCM, and for a short time, a small number of white students at the University of the Witwatersrand did organize such a movement. In actuality, Biko did not see "race" purely as a biological category; like ideology, it too was a social construction. He and his associates maintained that black people, despite class and ethnic divisions, shared a common experience of oppression, which whites could not fully realize.

Biko's synthesis redressed the balance between civil society and the state by reviving NEUM's principle of noncollaboration with government-sponsored institutions as a new theory of community-based protest. Biko argued that black South Africans could choose *not* to participate in "the system." Noncollaboration, as a positive act of re-fusal to participate, constituted a negative theory of political partici-pation. Put another way, the refusal to participate in racist institutions empowered majority communities and required a reformulation of legitimate standards of civic participation. Again, Biko's understand-ing of legitimate politics was derived from his critical synthesis of the liberation tradition. He put it this way: "I completely discourage the movement of people from the left to join the institutions of apartheid. What seems to me to be logical at this stage is for the left to continually pressurise the various apartheid institutions to move in the direction of testing the limits of possibility within the system to prove the whole game a sham and to break off from the system."[52] By the 1980s, the black liberation movement as a whole had adopted Biko's position on the possibilities of internal protest.

Theoretically, nonracialism and racial nationalism offer alterna-tive prescriptions for political action, although in practice they have produced similar outcomes. Within the framework of black political discourse, cooperation with nonblacks usually reinforces liberal con-ceptions of citizenship and can be read alternatively as "negotiation" or "co-optation." As political actors, black leaders seeking to trans-form the racist character of the dominant institutions from within the system can be subjected to the charge by separatists that they perpetu-ate those very institutions simply by cooperating with them. On the other hand, black republicans who have claimed to operate indepen-dently of dominant institutions rarely ignore legitimate opportunities to work with nonblacks in order to "pressurize" the system as Biko advised.

Consistent with his contention that politics had an undeniable psychological dimension, Biko evolved what can be referred to as a prefigurative approach to politics: for emancipatory politics to achieve a social transformation, new values and practices would have to be *prefigured* in the opposition movement. "Conscientisation" of the masses remained integral to the process of liberation and constituted a way to understand the need for permanent revolution, not in the Trotskyist sense, but as a recurring subjective rejuvenation of black political awareness.[53]

Biko's synthesis was a means to confront the real divisions in the black liberation movement and, by so doing, come to terms with the primary antinomy in black political thought—nonracialism and ra-cial nationalism. Both as analytical categories and as race-relations strategies, the permutations that result from interactions of these two poles of possibility are central to periods of revitalization in black political thought. Given the situation of racial domination, these two approaches reflect an unavoidable dimension of black life that confound liberal and Marxist ideological distinctions. In his early study of race relations on the American left, Harold Cruse contended that, with respect to black political thought, it was necessary to separate "Negroes proper from Marxist politics and examine their politics purely within the context of nationalist vs. integrationist trends."[54] Although the legacy of Biko's thought can rightly be appropriated for many purposes, the originality of his contribution to black political discourse is undeniable.

The transition to black consciousness socialism during the years of 1977 to 1979, so ably treated by Anthony Marx, is usually interpreted as a rupture between the race-conscious and class-conscious phases of BCM development.[55] Due to his premature death, Biko's thought belongs to the earlier phase only; his intellectual influence was most manifest in discussions of the meaning of black consciousness, racial liberation, and internal opposition. Although some legitimate heirs of Biko's legacy decided to forswear racial populism, the tendency to organize the history of the BCM into neat, mutually exclusive black nationalist and socialist phases may only serve to mask the ongoing tension between nonracial and race-conscious conceptions of liberation. In addition, such interpretations may stem more from a multiracialist bias than an honest interpretation of the murky realities on the ground.

In the new South Africa, race-conscious political assumptions remain controversial among intellectuals. Nonracial political parties have not been able to suppress the racial questions addressed by Biko and his generation. Even within an ANC government firmly devoted to building a nonracial democracy, multiracialists accuse high-ranking ANC officials—notably Mandela's heir apparent and the new President of South Africa Thabo Mbeki—of harboring Africanist sentiments. Biko and his associates played a vital role in reshaping South African society by pursuing strategies of struggle based on republican traditions of African resistance. In this respect, the legacy of Biko and black consciousness thought will continue to influence the evolution of post-apartheid South Africa.

6. ❀ An Enduring Duality

In democratic thought, citizenship is a moral conception as well as a legal category. This dual connotation is particularly pertinent to the evolution of democracy in South Africa. Since the demise of apartheid in that country, liberationist thought, which provided the main basis of political morality for black South Africans, has encountered a powerful challenge in the form of nonracial, constitutional democracy. Despite the ascendancy of liberal constitutionalism, populist beliefs—associated with class as well as racial identities—persist strongly in the arenas of both mass and legislative politics.

In racially stratified societies, democratic development is affected profoundly by traditional polarities of thought that were enumerated in the first chapter (separation vs. integration, racial consciousness vs. nonracialism, and black power vs. civil rights). The issues reflected by such polarities are relevant to the distinction between moral and legal conceptions of citizenship in a society such as South Africa, which was divided forcibly and for centuries along lines of race and class as well as rights and justice. Following his first visit to South Africa in 1991, Francis Fukuyama concluded that black South Africans would have to work hard to construct a civil society comparable to that of whites.[1] In response to Fukuyama's observation, are we not justified to pose this query: Would so protracted a struggle for liberation—with its considerable social sacrifice—have been possible without the support of a highly developed black civil society? The idea of duality in the meaning of citizenship—republican and liberal—is an extension of the core argument of this work: Non-racial and race-conscious populist discourse bisects every other ideological confrontation in black South African political experience.

As Yoav Peled has observed with respect to Arab citizenship in the Jewish state of Israel, "Unlike the liberal citizen, who is a passive bearer of status (a mere bundle of rights), the republican citizen experiences citizenship as practice (active participation in the determination, protection, and promotion of the common good)."[2] From this insightful perspective, participation in a black community organization, a National Party caucus, or a Zulu cultural organization would be citizenship in practice. Yet, with respect to the historic bifurcation of black political thought, a serious question remains: Can the liberal-republican dichotomy be bridged, or will it continue to be a turbulent dividing line in the post-apartheid South Africa?

CITIZENSHIP AND POPULISM

Populist thought thrives in the interstices between conceptions of popular and democratic government. Popular sovereignty—the right of ordinary people to self-rule—is a fundamental principle of government for democrats and populists alike. Historically, however, populism has been the universal mode of expression for unique national, cultural, class, ethnic, or racial identities of "the people," derived from interpretations of national experience.[3] In multiracial societies, including South Africa, the challenge is often to make nonracial citizenship a popular identity. Yet, an inclusive national identity for the black majority will necessarily derive a substantial measure of its emotional force and indigenous character from the legacies of racial domination.

Rival populisms, nourished by competing visions of liberation, are bound to have an impact on the evolution of South African citizenship. In addition, popular democratic traditions, of which populism is one manifestation, are among the most durable sources of inspiration for democratic thinkers.[4] After centuries of racial domination, it would be unrealistic to expect an ethos of nonracial citizenship to prevail unchallenged by older political perceptions. Eventually, the black liberation struggle may come to be viewed by all South Africans as a national achievement and, therefore, a cornerstone of nonracial citizenship identity. For the immediate future, however, successive governments will have to cope with the implications of both nonracial and race-conscious political sensibilities.

The South African government confronts an awesomely complex challenge: it must implement radical education reform, solve the housing crisis, combat crime, establish police accountability, alleviate poverty, reduce black unemployment, and promote economic democracy. Every proposed reform has implications for race-class relations. Each one requires a stressful accommodation of affirmative action values with those of racial reconciliation. The viability of ANC party rule, as well as the durability of constitutional democracy in South Africa, will depend on the ability of national leaders to channel the energies of social movements—both old and new, and black and white—toward mutually satisfying goals. Nonracialism is now, and will surely continue to be, the government's official stance. However, a government popularly elected by the black majority must also avoid the temptation to transform racial reconciliation into a public orthodoxy that discourages constructive race-conscious dialogue and the inclusion of indigenous forms of black republican citizenship participation. New forms of populism are bound to give voice to those inescapable fears and frustrations that accompany rapid political and social change.

Alan Scott has correctly observed that populist segments of a formerly disenfranchised people are often apt to regard the fight for citizenship rights, and by extension racial reconciliation, as co-optation, designed to blunt the radical edge of social movement politics.[5] Ambivalence regarding the value of nonracial citizenship has plagued the black nationalist wing of the American civil rights movement, particularly as its influence has spread in an atmosphere of renewed racial tension precipitated by controversies over the proper relationship between equal protection of the law and social mobility (issues such as affirmative action, civil rights, and social welfare). So, too, in South Africa, racial and class-conscious conceptions of citizenship strongly persist with regard to similar public concerns, including affirmative action, black empowerment, economic equity, and land redistribution. Given the legacy of racial proletarianization, and despite an exponential growth of the black bourgeoisie, Africans are still the principal victims of inequitable past public policies. Although democratic elections now provide the black majority with a powerful means of influencing government policy, the impact of reform on the daily lives of most South Africans will be incremental for years to come. As is widely acknowledged, the post-apartheid government faces a difficult challenge: to transform incremental changes in social policy into massive progress before the onset of pervasive disillusionment.

Whether or not they develop new avenues of expression, populists therefore will remain critical of aspects of liberal democracy and capitalism. Hence, racial, ethnic, and class populism, on one hand, and (liberal) nonracial citizenship, on the other, are likely to remain polarized in policy debates. Distrustful of liberalism (more than capitalism alone) and aware that they must now fight for a social welfare state within a capitalist economy, many intellectuals use the rhetoric of populism to articulate the needs of the common people in post-apartheid society. Race-conscious populists are even more likely to concentrate on the inability of nonracial citizenship to heal the specific wounds inflicted on blacks by apartheid. Populist movements like the Azanian People's Organization and the Pan Africanist Congress will remain critical of liberal democracy, highlight continued white economic hegemony, and revile capitalist society.

Since apartheid was antithetical to the development of an acceptable national identity, black liberation thinkers sought alternative conceptions of citizenship in socialism, populism, and liberalism; furthermore, they often fused elements of these distinct systems of political belief. More often than not, black South African intellectuals reacted to white nationalism with their own populist strategies of racial liberation, many of them designed to address the race-class divide.[6] Understandably, South Africa boasts a rich populist tradition. As racially divided working and bourgeois classes developed, two forms of populist ideology became evident: a nationalist populism, which reduced class differences to assertions of national, racial, multiracial, or even ethnic solidarity; and a socialist populism, which asserted that the termination of capitalism would, automatically or in successive stages, resolve the dilemmas of racial and ethnic conflict.

Both race-conscious (nationalist) and nonracial (socialist) populism harbor nascent conceptions of citizenship. Thus, there are a variety of populist rhetorical devices. For example, black intellectuals champion the unified spirit of the African people while seeking to transcend ethnic determinations and, at the same time, uphold the dignity of African tradition. Some conceptualize the African masses (and sometimes the African elite) as an exploited working class; many stress black solidarity and thus contain intraracial class and ethnic divisions; others define the people of the nation (or segments of it) in terms of multiracial or multiethnic opposition to apartheid. All such conceptions have implications for populism and citizenship.

Reflecting the interplay of class, nation, race, and ethnicity, populist political movements often promote and rely upon multiclass alliances. Where persons deemed to be outsiders or enemies dominate local markets, populist thought tends more often toward vaguely anticapitalist, rather than specifically socialist, conclusions. The South African populist idea of "racial capitalism," developed by black consciousness–oriented socialists during the 1980s, provides an example of that transition. Grounded in both working-class and black nationalist assumptions, the doctrine of racial capitalism teaches that racism

135

and capitalism in South Africa have been far too interconnected for nonracial democracy to be attained under capitalist conditions.[7] The 1994 election demonstrated a lack of public support for this position; since then much of the zeal for socialist populism has surfaced as opposition to neo-liberal elements of the ANC's economic policy.[8]

While black-conscious populists do not necessarily embrace socialism, many do demand an accessible people's capitalism. Socialist populists, including those in the South African Communist Party, are more likely to scrutinize the involvement of the new black bourgeoisie in both government and the economy while, at the same time, they work to construct social democracy and a welfare state. The prevalence of black faces in the bourgeoisie will, to their way of thinking, finally confirm the nonracial character of class struggle. Nevertheless, socialist populists will also be tested by new approaches that challenge old conceptions of the capitalist-socialist divide such as the advocacy of "corporate unionism" by former trade unionist and ANC leader Cyril Ramaphosa. Indeed, the powerful Congress of South African Trade Unions (Cosatu) has established its own business arm known as Kopano ke Matla Investment Company. Tumelo Motsisi, the head of the company, sees no contradiction whatsoever between Cosatu's commitment to socialism and the federation's business arm. As he puts it, "[t]he driving objective within Cosatu is the ultimate seizure of economic power from a few powerhouses to the majority."[9]

During the 1980s, a distinction between populists and workerists gained prominence among socialist intellectuals as debates raged over the role of black trade unions in the larger anti-apartheid struggle.[10] In this context, populism connoted worker or trade union involvement in political movements with broader social bases of support. Workerists were concerned that trade union gains would be compromised by protests that could accomplish only dubious outcomes. Although the label "populist" was used derisively by workerists, populist movements—alliances of workers, intellectuals, youths, and community activists—did reflect the interplay of class consciousness and racial militancy. In post-apartheid South Africa, both populists and workerists joined the government and portions of each group disagree with some of its economic policies.

In the past, faced with the reality of white supremacy, socialists and communists have not been able to avoid issues that are emphasized in the liberal and populist traditions, including citizenship, equal rights, the rule of law, popular sovereignty, the nature of political representation, and the content of popular culture. South African communists, for example, have often co-opted liberal and populist issues for their own purposes. Some of these instances have been discussed in previous chapters: the formation by communists in 1929 of the League of African Rights, whose liberal orientation troubled more orthodox members of the SACP; the call for a Native Republic in 1928 as a stage of worker and peasant government; and the controversial participation of the ANC and the Communist Party in government-sponsored Native Representative Councils of the 1940s. These and other cases illustrate the degree to which conjunctures of race and class stimulate populist approaches to thought and action. The apparent convergence of racism and capitalism also contributes to the left-populist view that black liberation and capitalism are necessarily incompatible. In the 1980s, a popular slogan called for "the leadership of the working class." Since white workers functioned primarily to police black labor, left-wing black republicans concluded that what this slogan really meant was "leadership of [i.e., by] black workers."[11]

According to Ernesto Laclau, progressive populist movements have flourished when and where working classes themselves incorporate context-specific, popular-democratic themes and defend egalitarian values rather than national, ethnic, or racial chauvinism.[12] By that standard, strictly applied, no populist movement would be deemed progressive. Populist movements never fail to draw on the energies of intellectuals and political elites or to promote solidarities based on divisions other than class. Produced by the interaction of autochthonous social thought and more formal ideologies, populist ideas readily penetrate other traditions of thought. For example, in the rhetoric of contemporary liberal democracy, core conceptions of equality, justice, and individual liberty easily coexist with constant references to the "people." In his exploration of the fundamental characteristics of fascism, Umberto Eco has described the syncretic quality of populism as well: "Syncretism is not only, as the dictionary says, 'the combination of different forms of belief or practice'; such a combination must tolerate contradictions. Each of the original messages contains a sliver of wisdom and whenever they seem to say different or incompatible things it is only because all are alluding, allegorically, to the same primeval truth."[13]

Cultures, nations, peoples, and, for that matter, constitutions are founded on complex social identities, themselves combinations of myth and reality. As with all others, South Africa's political culture consists of a medley of old and new values and identities placed at the service of present-day political needs and desires. Many Afrikaners, for example, now stress their African identity and distance themselves from the old designation of Africa's "white tribe." And indeed, the Inkatha Freedom Party has recruited a noticeable number of so-called "White Zulus." Conversely, black populist thinkers have injected their own lived-experience into European-derived systems of political thought, as exemplified by the concepts of racial capitalism, Afro-Marxism, and nonracial liberalism, among others. From the perspective of indigenous African populism, the vice of Eurocentrism can be defined as a failure or refusal to take seriously the intellectual expansion of Western political ideas into non-Western environments.

While this discussion has focused on race-class populism, others have specified ethnic identity as a salient factor in post-apartheid South African politics.[14] There are indeed ethnic populists, most notably Zulu and Afrikaner, who have demanded ethnic nations within the country. While Zulu republicanism constitutes a powerful political sentiment, its discourse falls outside the mainstream of black liberation thought. Based on a deep-seated historic grievance against white conquest and the suppression of its monarchy, Zulu nationalism and individuals of Zulu ancestry have greatly contributed to liberation politics. However, ethnic populism of the IFP (whose members are mostly Zulu) extols earlier Zulu participation in the ANC and the larger liberation movement solely for the purpose of appropriating black struggle on behalf of ethnic mobilization.[15] Recently Kenneth Anderson has defined populism as "a sensibility inculcated into a class over a long period of time by a form of production."[16] Ethnicity, to be sure, has been crucial to the organization and control of production throughout Africa. Here we need only reflect on the extent to which chiefs have acted both as political authorities and labor recruiters. Due to its deep involvement with both the apartheid state and capitalism, many South African progressives believe that the institution of the chieftaincy is virtually indistinguishable from state-engineered ethnicity. However, the complicated politics of Chief Mangosuthu Gatsha Buthelezi's leadership of Inkatha—an ethnicity-based populist movement—and the broader ANC-led liberation movement, as well as the former apartheid state (especially its police and military establishment) accentuate both the appeal and ambiguity of African ethnic mobilization.

No mere chimera, the resurgence of Zulu nationalism, which culminated in the IFP's insistence on greater autonomy for KwaZulu/ Natal and constitutional recognition of the Zulu King, dramatizes the strength of ethnic populism. The IFP has made KwaZulu/Natal regionalism, the call for a federal state, and containment of ANC authority its primary objectives. Yet, seen through the prism of citizenship rather than ethnic identity, Buthelezi's ability to forge an indigenous multiracial alliance of conservatives—the Freedom Alliance—may prove more significant than the resuscitation of Zulu nationalism.

Indeed, careful consideration of Buthelezi's ethnic nationalism reveals a tension between liberal and republican conceptions of citizenship. During the height of calls for economic sanctions by the black liberation movement, Buthelezi was an outspoken proponent of market-based strategies to transform apartheid. He was, therefore, a vocal opponent of employing sanctions as a means to force the NP government to negotiate a new democratic dispensation. Buthelezi defended his opposition to restrictions on loans and new investment by insisting that black workers would be disproportionately affected by international sanctions. During this same period, Buthelezi urged white governmental and business leaders to experiment with federalism as a means to generate political reform. With respect to both market-based strategies of transformation and reform through federalism, Inkatha would have been the primary beneficiary in KwaZulu/ Natal.

Despite his advocacy of capitalism and federalism as alternatives to strategies pursued by the mainstream of the liberation movement, Buthelezi was well aware of the political implications of an independent black business (and professional) class in KwaZulu. Therefore, while advocating liberal citizenship for the country as a whole, he leaned toward a populist-republican form of citizenship for his own KwaZulu homeland.[17] Inkatha's use of Zulu nationalism to thwart and co-opt independent labor organizations is well known. Less understood is Buthelezi's deployment of ethnic populism in an effort to control or contain the political influence and independence of the KwaZulu business community. In his desire to shape the interests of KwaZulu labor and capital, Buthelezi readily resorted to the rhetoric of Zulu populism. Moreover, his actions suggest that he clearly comprehended capitalism, like labor, as a social movement, and one that could challenge or bolster Inkatha's hegemony in the province.[18]

During negotiations to end apartheid, white conservatives recognized that interracial alliances were unavoidable; in the IFP, they discovered a black movement with accommodative political assumptions, based on ethnic populism. More troubling for Buthelezi's reputation as an independent black conservative was the IFP's complicity with violent anti-ANC operations sponsored by elements within the South African police and defense forces. Still, Buthelezi, Minister for Home Affairs in the first post-apartheid government, appeals directly to an indigenous strand of conservatism that reflects many of the social values of an older generation of Africans. In the face of numerous developments that many South Africans associate with moral decay, especially the crime epidemic, social conservatism with a populist mooring finds adherents across the ideological spectrum. While it provides him with a loyal Zulu constituency, Buthelezi's image as a narrow ethnic nationalist tends to limit his political prospects, constrain the formation of broader alliances, and undercut his desire to galvanize a conservative opposition to the ANC.

As in many other African countries, South African ethnic traditions of authority need not be interpreted solely from the vantage point of the centrifugal forces of ethnic populism. Richard L. Sklar observes that African political identity often involves the recognition of dual authority. In addition to the domain of state sovereignty, there is an older "second dimension of political space behind the sovereign states."[19] With this insightful formulation, Sklar captures the complex interface between traditional and modern forms of social control. Rarely do traditional elites seek to dominate central governments of multiethnic African states, yet they can, and do, play constructive roles in the variegated process of citizenship identity formation, especially at the level of local government. It is important to note that Sklar does not identify dual authority with ethnicity, but with a second dimension of government—ethnic identity need not imply traditional authority.

The recent founding of an organization for traditional rulers, the Congress of Traditional Leaders of South Africa (CONTRALESA), suggests that these ethnic elites are prepared to work with the new government in an effort to reconcile modern and traditional conceptions of political community. Concerning the specific question of what role traditional leaders should play in a modern democracy, one constitutional analyst notes that there is little distance between the positions of the IFP and the ANC.[20] However, civic activists, such as those affiliated with the South African National Civics Organization (SANCO), are not sanguine about the perpetuation of chieftaincies.

Many leaders of civic organizations spurn the entire chieftaincy structure in rural areas and believe that, in principle, hereditary and democratic leadership are irreconcilable concepts.[21] Ironically, CONTRALESA and SANCO are both allies of the ANC. Clearly, all traditionalists are not conservatives, and prominent ANC populists, most notably Winnie Mandela-Madikizela, have taken up CONTRALESA's cause with apparent conviction.

In South Africa, as elsewhere on the African continent, traditional elites do not usually represent a rarified "tribal" consciousness. Many have long been simultaneously traditionalists and modernizers. On this point, there may be no better South African example than Nelson Mandela. What makes Mandela at once a unique individual and symbol of his party and people is the way these forms of consciousness cohere in his principled thought.[22] Although Mandela's life story has come to epitomize the moral high ground of nonracialism, a difficult question remains to be answered: Will South Africans continue to share his abiding sense of nonracial citizenship? It is widely recognized that these are precisely the kinds of questions a post-Mandela administration under the leadership of Thabo Mbeki will have to address.

The process of democratization will certainly test South Africa's commitment to nonracial citizenship. In the democratic elections of 1994 and subsequent local elections, the ANC translated its status as the senior liberation movement into that of a dominant political party. If South Africa continues to evolve as a democratic country, its political leadership will increasingly reflect the characteristics of local constituencies rather than the corporate culture of party stalwarts. However, such a transition may be hampered by the constitutional provision that requires an elected official to vacate the seat should that person "cease to be a member of the party which nominated him or her as a member of the National Assembly."[23] For, in black communities, political tendencies often conform to their own indigenous "two partyism" based on the cross-pressures of racial autonomy and multiracial assimilation.

These rival tendencies correspond to the distinction between black republican identity and multiracial union, a dichotomy that exists even within explicitly multiracial parties. Although specifically black republican organizations are currently in disarray, race-conscious populism pulsates strongly within the ANC. Even before the new South Africa celebrated its first birthday, astute observers noted the growing intensity of interactions between nonracial and race-conscious political attitudes. Contrasting the tolerant nonracialism of Nelson Mandela with the restless racial populism of his former wife, Winnie, *New York Times* correspondent Bill Keller captured this tension with a provocative question: "His South Africa or Hers?"[24]

SYNCRETIC CITIZENSHIP

In every community, moral standards are derived from interpretations and misinterpretations (the use and abuse) of common experience; moral claims drawn from presumptive authenticity regularly prove to be more important than historical accuracy. In fact, populism can be thought of as a social movement that appeals to some conception of cultural or national authenticity. Ideological by their very nature, claims of authenticity are not as easily dispensed with as some postmodern interpretations of political culture would lead us to believe.[25] Nationalism and many other deep political attachments would be impossible without claims of authenticity. As Max Weber once observed, nationalism is one of the few modern inventions that can give meaning to death.[26] Citizenship, on the other hand, is one of the primary means of socializing the burdens and benefits of national life. Nonetheless, powerless or threatened communities are far more likely to resort to some form of hyper-authenticity, whether in the form of hyper-nationalism, hyper-ethnicity, or, for that matter, hyper-masculinity.[27]

It is precisely the explosion of communal identities worldwide that currently presents liberal citizenship theory with its most significant challenge. That provocation will also face the new South Africa. Will Kymlicka argues that there is a need to learn to use what he terms "societal cultures" as a foundation for a multicultural theory and practice of citizenship.[28] In a recent article devoted to America's search for an expanded philosophy of citizenship, Michael Sandel asserts that "a growing aspiration for public expression of communal identities reflects a yearning for political arrangements that can situate people in a world increasingly governed by vast and distant forces."[29]

Despite their failures and successes, African democracies have had to experiment with various forms of dual authority and citizenship as well as mixed government. Sklar argues that regrettably the theoretical importance of mixed government has been largely overlooked:

Political scientists have neglected to articulate the reality of this circumstance, although its manifestation in contemporary Africa is pervasive. As in previous (both ancient and modern) epochs of mixed government, African polities today are governed by unified sovereign authorities. However, there are also two separate dimensions of government authority, as there were in medieval Europe. These back-to-back domains of authority are readily identifiable as the realm of state sovereignty and the realm of traditional government; both systems effectively govern the same communities of citizen-subjects.[30]

In this work, I have used the liberal-republican dichotomy to capture the "duality" of the citizenship experience in a racially stratified society. In an important essay on divided citizenship loyalties in Africa, Peter Ekeh examines the way attachment to a primordial ethnic community within the modern African state bifurcates public life. Ekeh's notion of "dual publics" in Africa is based on his contention that colonialism tended to encourage Africans to place stress on rights rather than duties. In this case, dual publics are a manifestation of dual citizenship consciousness, which fosters the belief that the state can be raided with impunity; whereas traditional office holders are often less corrupt and more accountable.[31] Moreover, Ekeh contends that a mix of rights and duties, which are largely determined by culture and national experience, structure the content of citizenship.[32] In this respect, Ekeh's view coincides with T. H. Marshall's famous assessment that in every society citizenship is a developing institution and that there is no universal combination of civil, political, and social rights for all nations. Although Ekeh explores what he terms "African bourgeois ideologies of legitimation," his primary concern is with ethnicity; as a result, he tends to pay less attention to the class analytic themes in Marshall's work. While the evolution of citizenship and capitalism coincide, the two systems rest respectively on the assumptions of equality and inequality. In contradistinction to most Marxist interpretations of bourgeois legality, for Marshall, citizenship is a strategy of class abatement in that workers and capitalists benefit (if not equally) from a regime of rights.[33]

The South African experience with law and citizenship has been shaped by segregation. In his analysis of South Africa's 1927 Native Administration Act, Martin Chanock highlights the impact of segregation on law and, therefore, on citizenship. He observes: "Black liberation movements have given little attention to the questions of cultural differentiation and institutional separatism which concern minorities in plural societies elsewhere. . . . Yet, in thinking about the shape of a future legal system in black-ruled South Africa in light of the experience of inherited legal pluralism based on racial and cultural differentiation in the rest of Africa, the place and content of black law needs to be considered."[34]

Thus, it is useful to think of dual citizenship as political pluralism that may, or may not, develop a coherent system of legal norms. Legal pluralism can be construed as a reaction to segregation, colonialism, settler colonialism, or institutional racism. Common in Africa, legal pluralism is primarily a compromise between indigenous African and European colonial legal systems, where the balance of power may or may not be contested. On occasion, and particularly during periods of social unrest, the pressure for an alternative legality may become evident. During the height of the 1980s black resistance, People's Courts evolved a theory and practice of popular justice (on many occasions not fair and on others pure vigilantism). In what may prove to be an impetus to populist reaction, black South Africans are discovering that citizenship rights are attached to duties that obligate them to political and economic arrangements that sometimes appear unfair in light of the apartheid past—for example, payment for township housing after years of rent boycott.

All too often, racial segregation and colonial intrusion have bifurcated liberal and republican dimensions of citizenship in the black experience. Consequently, liberal citizenship assumed the form of a struggle for equal rights while republican citizenship sought to build institutional and communal autonomy; both are components of a holistic citizenship consciousness. For black South Africans, as for African-Americans, segregation nourished a civic republicanism rooted in racial identity as well as in a host of black community institutions. Although republican sentiments are evident to varying degrees in all such institutions, nonracialists and black nationalists coexist. Indeed, the overwhelming rejection of the PAC by black voters may have had more to do with that party's failure to produce a realistic black republican agenda rather than with a more general rejection of racial populism.

Thus, black republicanism is a complex set of ideas and sentiments that embrace and extol the communal virtues of the African people. Many of the practical and ideological compromises that liberationists have made over the course of the struggle may only serve to disguise a deeper core of black republican belief. The dichotomy between multiracial union (nonracialism) and black republicanism, therefore, cannot be too rigidly drawn, for as sociologist Leo Kuper once noted, "these positions tend to shade off into one another."[35] In South Africa, they are virtually inseparable and clearly complementary. Failure to comprehend the dual nature of citizenship has encouraged the abandonment of black civic republicanism to those populistic leaders who are least likely to value it as a constructive political resource.

Entrenched norms of civic accountability reassert themselves in novel ways and at unanticipated times. Under pressure to give real substance to the designation "new," South Africans have produced a constitution that reflects many of the time-honored values of Western citizenship, especially those associated with rights, equality, and justice. But, as Africa's first industrial power and last bastion of overt white supremacy, South Africa may also encourage democrats in all parts of the world to consider the imprint of indigenous thought and experience on democracy and citizenship.

Notes

1. NATIONALITY AND RACE

1. J. G. A. Pocock is one of the first and, perhaps, the most well-known exponent of the liberal-republican dichotomy in the study of citizenship. Although present in some of his earlier writings, Pocock makes a clear statement on this issue in his classic, *The Machiavellian Moment* (Princeton, N.J.: Princeton University Press, 1975), pp. 460–461. Since the publication of this work, several scholars have questioned treating liberalism and republicanism as if they were mutually exclusive. See, for example, Russell Hanson, *The Democratic Imagination in America: Conversations with Our Past* (Princeton, N.J.: Princeton University Press, 1985); Jeffrey C. Isaac, "Republicanism vs. Liberalism? A Reconsideration," *History of Political Thought* 9, 2 (Summer 1988), pp. 349–377; Philip Pettit, *Republicanism: A Theory of Freedom and Government* (Oxford: Clarendon Press, 1997); Richard Dagger, *Civic Virtues: Rights, Citizenship and Republican Liberalism* (New York and Oxford: Oxford University Press, 1997).

2. Peter Riesenberg, *Citizenship in the Western Tradition* (Chapel Hill: University of North Carolina Press, 1992), p. 25.

3. Thomas Janoski, *Citizenship and Civil Society* (Cambridge: Cambridge University Press, 1998), p. 11.

4. Ibid., p. 6.

5. Peter Ekeh, "Colonialism and the Development of Citizenship in Africa: A Study in Ideologies of Legitimation," in Onigu Otite, ed., *Themes in African Social and Political Thought* (Enugu, Nigeria: Fourth Dimension Publishers, 1978), pp. 302–334; see also Ekeh, "Colonialism and the Two Publics in Africa: A Theoretical Statement," *Comparative Studies in Society and History* 17, 1 (January 1975), pp. 91–112.

6. Ekeh, "Colonialism and the Two Publics in Africa"; C. S. Whitaker, *The Politics of Tradition: Continuity and Change in Northern Nigeria, 1946–1966* (Princeton, N.J.: Princeton University Press, 1970); Richard L. Sklar, "The African Frontier for Political Science," in Robert Bates, V. Y. Mudimbe, and Jean O' Barr, eds., *Africa and the Disciplines* (Chicago and London: University

of Chicago Press, 1993), pp. 83–110; C. R. D. Halisi, "From Liberation to Citizenship: Identity and Innovation in Black South African Political Thought," *Comparative Studies in Society and History* 39, 1 (January 1997): 61–85; Stephen N. Ndegwa, "Citizenship and Ethnicity: An Examination of Two Transition Movements in Kenyan Politics," *American Political Science Review* 91, 3 (September 1997), pp. 599–616; Mahmood Mamdani, *Citizen and Subject: Contemporary Africa and the Legacy of Late Colonialism* (Princeton, N.J.: Princeton University Press, 1996).

7. Although Oliver C. Cox does not use the term "racial proletarianization," I am indebted to his work for this conceptualization of black South Africa's social evolution, especially this observation:

> While race relations and the struggle of the white proletariat with the bourgeoisie are parts of a single phenomenon, race relations involve a significant variation. In the case of race relations, the tendency of the bourgeoisie is to proletarianize a whole people—that is to say, the whole people is looked upon as a class—whereas white proletarianization involves only a section of the white people. The concept of bourgeoisie and white people sometimes seems to mean the same thing for, with respect to the coloured people of the world, it is almost always through a white bourgeoisie that capitalism has been introduced.

See Cox, *Caste, Class and Race* (1948; New York: Modern Reader Paperbacks, 1970), p. 344.

8. Sam C. Nolutshungu, *Changing South Africa: Political Considerations* (New York: Africana Publishing, 1982), pp. 60–61.

9. The term "Coloured" refers to people of mixed-racial descent. Although the designation precedes the apartheid era, it was central to official racial classification during apartheid, and as a result, its use may be controversial. For example, the Black Consciousness Movement rejected the term. Nevertheless, "Coloured" is still, and always has been, widely used in South Africa.

10. See for example, Joy James's chapter on "Disappearing Race Women and Civil Rights Radicals," in her *Transcending the Talented Tenth: Black Leaders and American Intellectuals* (New York: Routledge, 1997), pp. 83–97.

11. George M. Fredrickson, *Black Liberation: Comparative History of Black Ideologies in the United States and South Africa* (New York and Oxford: Oxford University Press, 1995), p. 23.

12. W. E. B. DuBois, *The Souls of Black Folk* (1903; New York: Bantam, 1989).

13. James H. Cone, *Martin and Malcolm and America: A Dream or a Nightmare* (Maryknoll, N.Y.: Orbis, 1992).

14. Anthony W. Marx, *The Lessons of Struggle: South African Internal Opposition, 1960–1990* (New York and Oxford: Oxford University Press, 1992).

15. This was related to me by an African woman to whom I gave a ride from Soweto to her place of employment in Johannesburg sometime during December 1976.

16. Ghita Ionescu and Ernest Gellner, eds., *Populism: Its Meaning and National Characteristics* (London: Macmillan, 1969), which remains the most comprehensive collection of scholarly essays on populist thought. In addition to theoretical exploration of the term "populism," actual movements in North America, Latin America, Russia, Eastern Europe, and Africa are examined in separate chapters.

17. Pettit, *Republicanism*, p. 8.

18. Hanson, *The Democratic Imagination*, p. 63.

19. Nelson Mandela, *Long Walk to Freedom* (Boston: Little, Brown and Co., 1994).

20. Nolutshungu, *Changing South Africa*, pp. 60–61.

21. C. W. De Kiewiet, *A History of South Africa: Social and Economic* (London: Oxford University Press, 1957), p. 219.

22. Donald Denoon, *Settler Capitalism: The Dynamics of Dependent Development in the Southern Hemisphere* (Oxford: Oxford University Press, 1983), p. 210.

23. Enzo Mingione, *Fragmented Societies: A Sociology of Economic Life beyond the Market Paradigm* (Cambridge, Mass.: Basil Blackwell, 1991), p. 100.

24. Wilmot Godfrey James, "From Segregation to Apartheid: Miners and Peasants in the Making of a Racial Order, South Africa, 1930–1952" (Ph.D. dissertation, University of Wisconsin, Madison, 1982), p. 33; see also Fredrick Johnstone, *Race, Class, and Gold: A Study of Class Relations and Racial Discrimination in South Africa* (London: Routledge and Kegan Paul, 1976).

25. Belinda Bozzoli, *The Political Nature of a Ruling Class: Capital and Ideology in South Africa, 1890–1933* (London: Routledge and Kegan Paul, 1981), p. 51.

26. R. K. Cope, *Comrade Bill: The Life and Times of W. H. Andrews, Worker's Leader* (Cape Town: Stewart Printing Co., 1944?), p. 27.

27. Quoted in Alex Hepple, *South Africa: A Political and Economic History* (London: Pall Mall Press, 1966), p. 198.

28. Marian Lacey, *Working for Boroko: The Origins of a Coercive Labour System in South Africa* (Johannesburg: Ravan Press, 1981), p. 16.

29. Ibid., p. 53.

30. Leo Kuper, "Review of *Class and Colour in South Africa, 1850–1950*," republished in his *Race, Class, and Power: Ideology and Revolutionary Change in Plural Societies* (Chicago: Aldine Publishing Co., 1975), Appendix I, p. 283.

31. Paul Gilroy, *The Black Atlantic: Modernity and Double Consciousness* (Cambridge, Mass.: Harvard University Press, 1993), p. 49.

32. Mamdani, *Citizen and Subject*, p. 17.

33. William Appleman Williams, *The Great Evasion* (New York: New Viewpoints, 1974), p. 114.

34. James, "From Segregation," pp. 5–6; see also Wilmot James, "The Life Trajectories of a Working Class: South Africa 1969–1981" (paper presented to the Africa Seminar, Centre for African Studies, University of Cape Town, Cape Town, May 9, 1984), p. 4.

2. Racial Proletarianization

1. See Ferdinand Tonnies, *Community and Society* (East Lansing: Michigan State University Press, 1957).

2. Ari Sitas and Debbie Bonnin, "Lessons from the Sarmcol Strike," in William Cobbett and Robin Cohen, eds., *Popular Struggles in South Africa* (Trenton, N.J.: Africa World Press, 1988), p. 43.

3. C. W. De Kiewiet, *A History of South Africa: Social and Economic* (London: Oxford University Press, 1957), p. 180.

4. J. B. Peires, *The House of Phalo: A History of the Xhosa People in the Days of Their Independence* (Berkeley and Los Angeles: University of California Press, 1982), p. 106.

5. Ethel Khopung, *Apartheid—A Story of a Dispossessed People* (Dar es Salaam: Sharpeville Day Association Mbizana, 1972), p. 1; for a similar discussion with the same title and within the same tradition of thought, see Motsoko Pheko, *Apartheid: The Story of a Dispossessed People* (London: Marram Books, 1984), and for a more polemical account see David Dube, *The Rise of Azania, the Fall of South Africa* (Lusaka: Daystar Publications, 1983).

6. For example, see Monica Hunter Wilson, *Reaction to Conquest: Effects of Contact with Europeans on the Pondo of South Africa*, 2nd ed. (London and New York: Oxford University Press, 1961), and for a recent testament to the continued importance of the reaction to conquest approach see Jean Camaroff, *Body of Power, Spirit of Resistance: The Culture and History of a South African People* (Chicago and London: University of Chicago Press, 1985), p. xii.

7. Elias L. Ntloedibe, *Here Is a Tree: A Political Biography of Robert Mangaliso Sobukwe* (Gaborone, Botswana: Century-Turn Press, 1995), p. 1.

8. Solomon Plaatje, *Native Life in South Africa* (London: P. S. King and Son Ltd., 1916), p. 14. This work was reissued by Ohio University Press in 1991.

9. Solomon Plaatje, "A Retrospect," chapter 1 of his *Native Life in South Africa,* reproduced in Brian Willan, ed., *Sol Plaatje: Selected Writings* (Johannesburg: Witwatersrand University Press, 1996), p. 196.

10. See W. M. MacMillan, *The Cape Coloured Question: A Historical Survey* (London: Faber and Gwyer, 1927).

11. "Mnguni" (Hosea Jaffee), *Three Hundred Years: A History of South Africa* (Cape Town: New Era Fellowship, 1952), pp. 69–70.

12. Khoikhoi herders and San hunter-gatherers are referred to jointly as the Khoisan. According to geographer James L. Newman, *The Peopling of*

Africa: A Geographic Interpretation (New Haven: Yale University Press, 1995), p. 185, the Khoisan remain an intriguing ethnographic puzzle with some scholars portraying them as immigrants from as far away as Egypt. However, based on linguistic studies, Newman believes that the Middle Zambezi Valley is where the Khoikhoi originated over 2,000 years ago, with the acquisition of livestock playing a key role in their development. After migrating into the Kalahari and the swamplands of the Okavango Delta, the Khoikhoi followed watered routes to find suitable habitats along the Orange and Vaal rivers and near the Cape of Good Hope. Richard Elphick, *Kraal and Castle: Khoikhoi and the Founding of White South Africa* (New Haven and London: Yale University Press, 1977), p. 72, speculates that cattle must have been introduced in the Cape about a century before 1488, when the Portuguese explorer Bartolomew Dias observed Khoikhoi with large herds as far south as Mossel Bay in the western Cape. The introduction of cattle into the area caused what Elphick calls the "Pastoral Revolution." Khoikhoi herders most likely developed from San hunter-gatherers, but never totally abandoned the latter's skills. Elphick believes that herding gradually became the dominant mode of economic development, but coexisted with older modes of economic activity. The region came to be characterized by well-established political and social relations between those owning cattle and those without.

13. Les Switzer, *Power and Resistance in an African Society: The Ciskei Xhosa and the Making of South Africa* (Madison: University of Wisconsin Press, 1993), p. 67.

14. Yonina Talmon, "Millenarian Movements," *Archives Europeans de Sociologie* 7, 2 (1966), p. 173.

15. Edward Roux, *Time Longer Than Rope: A History of the Black Man's Struggle for Liberation in South Africa* (1948; Madison: University of Wisconsin Press, 1964), pp. 10–15.

16. Switzer, *Power and Resistance*, p. 66.

17. "Mnguni," *Three Hundred Years*, p. 85.

18. Switzer, *Power and Resistance*, p. 66.

19. Mahmood Mamdani, *Citizen and Subject: Contemporary Africa and the Legacy of Late Colonialism* (Princeton, N.J.: Princeton University Press, 1996), p. 29.

20. Switzer, *Power and Resistance*, pp. 70–71.

21. George M. Fredrickson, *Black Liberation: Comparative History of Black Ideologies in the United States and South Africa* (New York and Oxford: Oxford University Press, 1995), p. 167; Fredrickson's account of the Wellington Movement is based on Robert Edgar's seminal essay "Garveyism in Africa: Dr. Wellington and the American Movement in the Transkei," *Ufahamu* 6, 1 (1976), pp. 31–57.

22. Roux, *Time Longer Than Rope*, p. 141.

23. On the Israelites see ibid., pp. 135–142, and Peter Walshe, *The Rise of*

African Nationalism in South Africa: The African National Congress, 1912–1952 (Berkeley and Los Angeles: University of California Press, 1971), p. 73.

24. C. L. R. James, *A History of Pan-African Revolt* (Washington, D.C.: Drum and Spear Press, 1969), p. 63.

25. Camaroff, *Body of Power*, p. 177.

26. Shula Marks, "African and Afrikaner," *Journal of African History* 11, 3 (1970), p. 442.

27. Stanley Trapido, "'The Friends of the Natives': Merchants, Peasants, and the Political Ideological Structure of Liberalism in the Cape, 1854–1910," in Shula Marks and Anthony Atmore, eds., *Economy and Society in Pre-Industrial South Africa* (London: Longman Group, 1980), p. 258.

28. Shula Marks, "Khoisan Resistance to the Dutch in the Seventeenth and Eighteenth Centuries," *Journal of African History* 13, 1 (1972), pp. 55–80. Marks has shown the extent to which Khoisan groups in the seventeenth and eighteenth centuries exhibited patterns of resistance and collaboration associated with colonized peoples of later periods.

29. For a nationalist account that incorporates the experience of the Khoisan, see W. M. Tsotsi, *From Chattel to Wage Slavery: A New Approach to South African History* (Maseru: Print and Publishing Co., 1981); Tsotsi was, for many years, the Vice-President of the Non-European Unity Movement.

30. Richard Elphick, "The Khoisan to c. 1770," in Richard Elphick and Hermann Giliomee, eds., *The Shaping of Southern African Society, 1652–1820,* 1st ed. (Cape Town: Longman Press, 1979), p. 30; see also Martin Legassick, "Gold, Agriculture and Secondary Industry in South Africa, 1885–1970: From Periphery to Sub-Metropole as a Forced Labour System," in Robin Palmer and Neil Parsons, eds., *The Roots of Rural Poverty in Central and Southern Africa* (Berkeley: University of California Press, 1977), p. 176.

31. Orlando Patterson, *Slavery as Social Death: A Comparative Study* (Cambridge, Mass.: Harvard University Press, 1982), p. 245.

32. Gerrit Schutte, "Company and Colonists at the Cape, 1652–1795," in Richard Elphick and Hermann Giliomee, eds., *The Shaping of South African Society, 1652–1840,* 2nd ed. (Middletown, Conn.: Wesleyan University Press, 1988), p. 309.

33. Ibid., p. 314.

34. J. S. Marais, *Maynier and the First Boer Republic* (Cape Town: Maskew Miller, 1944), p. 75n.

35. Quoted in William Mark Freund, "Society and Government in Dutch South Africa: The Cape and the Batavians, 1803–1806" (Ph.D. dissertation, Yale University, 1971); a major part of this dissertation was published as "The Cape under the Transitional Governments, 1795–1814," in Elphick and Giliomee, eds., *The Shaping of South African Society, 1652–1840,* 2nd ed., p. 253. De Mist's humanism was compromised later in his career.

36. George M. Fredrickson, *White Supremacy: A Comparative Study in*

American and South African History (New York: Oxford University Press, 1981), p. xii. Among nationalist intellectuals, the idea of the South African herrenvolk was popularized by the Unity Movement; see Bill Nasson, "The Unity Movement Tradition: Its Legacy in Historical Consciousness," in Joshua Brown et al., eds., *History from South Africa: Alternative Visions and Promises* (Philadelphia: Temple University Press, 1991), pp. 144–164; see also Allison Drew, ed., *South Africa's Radical Tradition: A Documentary History* (Cape Town: Mayibuye Books, University of Cape Town Press, 1996–1997), 2 vols.

37. V. C. Malherbe, "The Khoi Captains in the Third Frontier War," in Susan Newton-King and V. C. Malherbe, eds., *The Khoikhoi Rebellion in the Eastern Cape, 1799–1803* (Cape Town: Centre for African Studies, University of Cape Town, 1981), pp. 67–68.

38. Freund, "Batavians," p. 247.

39. Marais, *Maynier,* p. 105.

40. Freund, "Batavians," p. 60.

41. Ibid., p. 109.

42. Susan Newton-King, "The Rebellion of the Khoi in Graaff-Reinet, 1799–1803," in Newton-King and Malherbe, eds., *The Khoikhoi Rebellion,* p. 17.

43. I. D. MacCrone, *Race Attitudes in South Africa* (Oxford: Oxford University Press, 1937), p. 25.

44. Malherbe, "The Khoi Captains," p. 68.

45. Freund, "Batavians," p. 305.

46. Elphick, *Kraal,* p. 103.

47. Ibid., pp. 94–96.

48. Ibid., p. 146.

49. Fatima Meer, "The Black Woman in South Africa," in Thoahlane Thoahlane, ed., *Black Renaissance, Papers from the Black Renaissance Convention, December 1974* (Johannesburg: Ravan Press, 1975), p. 35.

50. Ann Laura Stoler, *Race and the Education of Desire: Foucault's History of Sexuality and the Colonial Order of Things* (Durham and London: Duke University Press, 1995), p. 40.

51. Elphick, *Kraal,* pp. 34–35.

52. Ibid., p. 108.

53. Marks, "Khoisan Resistance," p. 62.

54. Elphick, "The Khoisan to c. 1770," in Elphick and Giliomee, eds., *The Shaping of South African Society,* 1st ed., p. 12.

55. Leslie Clement Duly, "A Revisit with the Cape's Hottentot Ordinance of 1828," in Marcelle Kooy, ed., *Studies in Economics and Economic History, Essays in Honour of Professor H. M. Robertson* (Durham: Duke University Press, 1972), p. 32.

56. Susan Newton-King, "The Labour Market of the Cape Colony, 1807–28," in Marks and Atmore, eds., *Economy and Society,* p. 172.

57. Ibid., p. 195.

58. H. J. and R. E. Simons, *Class and Colour in South Africa, 1850–1950* (New York: Penguin, 1968), p. 120.

59. Martin Legassick, "The Northern Frontier to 1820," in Elphick and Giliomee, eds., *The Shaping of Southern African Society*, 1st ed., p. 268.

60. Fredrickson, *Black Liberation*, p. 195; Roux, *Time Longer Than Rope*, pp. 164–165.

61. Robert H. Hill and Gregory A. Pirio, "'Africa for the Africans': The Garvey Movement in South Africa, 1920–1940," in Shula Marks and Stanley Trapido, eds., *The Politics of Race, Class, and Nationalism in Twentieth Century South Africa* (New York: Longman, 1987), pp. 209–253.

62. George Padmore, *Pan-Africanism or Communism* (New York: Doubleday and Co., 1971), p. 326.

63. Shula Marks and Stanley Trapido, "Lord Milner and the South African State," *History Workshop* 8 (1979), pp. 50–85.

64. Ronald Robinson and John Gallagher with Alice Denny, *Africa and the Victorians* (London: Macmillan and Co., 1961), p. 61.

65. Peter Delius, *The Land Belongs to Us: The Pedi Polity, the Boers, and the British in the Nineteenth Century Transvaal* (Berkeley: University of California Press, 1984), p. 1.

66. J. A. Hobson, *The War in South Africa* (London: Nisbet, 1900).

67. Robinson and Gallagher, *Victorians*, p. 63.

68. Marian Lacey, *Working for Boroko: The Origins of a Coercive Labour System in South Africa* (Johannesburg: Ravan Press: 1981), p. 6.

69. Shula Marks, "Class, Ideology, and the Bambatha Rebellion," in Donald Crummey, ed., *Banditry, Rebellion, and Social Protest in Africa* (London: James Currey, Ltd., 1986), pp. 351–372.

70. Gwendolen Carter, *The Politics of Inequality: South Africa since 1948* (New York: Frederick A. Praeger, 1958), p. 14.

71. Gwendolen Carter, Thomas Karis, and Newell Stultz, *South Africa's Transkei* (Evanston, Ill.: Northwestern University Press, 1967), p. 53.

72. Charles Simkins, "Agricultural Production in the African Reserves of South Africa, 1918–1969," *Journal of Southern African Studies* 7, 2 (April 1981), pp. 256–283.

73. Carter, Karis, and Stultz, *Transkei*, p. 53.

74. R. M. Godsel, "The Regulation of Labour," in Robert Schrire, ed., *South Africa, Public Policy Perspectives* (Cape Town: Juta, 1982), p. 231.

75. Saul Dubow, *Racial Segregation and the Origins of Apartheid in South Africa, 1919–36* (New York: St. Martin's Press, 1989), pp. 133–134.

76. T. R. H. Davenport, "Some Reflections on the History of Land Tenure in South Africa, Seen in the Light of Attempts by the State to Impose Political and Economic Control," *Acta Juridica* (1985), p. 61.

77. Walshe, *The Rise of African Nationalism,* pp. 55–56.

78. Colin Bundy, *The Rise and Fall of the South African Peasantry* (Berkeley: University of California Press, 1979), p. 32.

79. David Welsh, "The Political Economy of Afrikaner Nationalism," in Adrian Leftwich, ed., *South Africa: Economic Growth and Political Change* (New York: St. Martin's Press, 1974), p. 251.

80. Dan O'Meara, "Analysing Afrikaner Nationalism: The 'Christian-National' Assault on White Trade Unionism in South Africa, 1934–1948," *African Affairs* 77, 306 (January 1978), pp. 45–72.

81. Legassick, "Gold, Agriculture . . . ," p. 187.

82. T. H. Marshall and Tom Bottomore, *Citizenship and Social Class* (1952; London and Concord, Mass.: Pluto Press, 1992), p. 28.

83. De Kiewiet, *A History of South Africa,* p. 225.

84. Shula Marks, "Natal, the Zulu Royal Family, and the Ideology of Segregation," *Journal of Southern African Studies* 4, 2 (April 1978), pp. 172–194.

85. Nelson Mandela, *Long Walk to Freedom* (Boston: Little, Brown and Co., 1994), pp. 55–58.

86. Alfred Meusel, "Revolution and Counter-Revolution," in *Encyclopedia of the Social Sciences* (New York: Macmillan, 1942), p. 373.

87. Hermann Giliomee, "The Changing Political Functions of the Black Homelands," in Hermann Giliomee and Lawrence Schlemmer, eds., *Up against the Fences: Poverty, Passes, and Privilege in South Africa* (New York: St. Martin's Press, 1985), pp. 42–48.

88. Morris Szeftel, "The Transkei: Conflict Externalization and Black Exclusivism," in University of London, Institute of Commonwealth Studies, *Collected Seminar Papers on the Societies of Southern Africa in the 19th and 20th Centuries,* vol. 3 (October 1971–June 1972), pp. 155–173.

89. Under Section 10 of the Urban Areas Act (1923), Africans, who through continuous residence and/or employment could establish a legal claim to residence, were allowed to live in the urban townships. All other Africans were, supposedly, citizens of one of the "homelands."

90. Bill Freund, "Forced Resettlement and the Political Economy of South Africa," *Review of African Political Economy* 29 (July 1984), p. 50.

91. Wilmot James, "The South African State in Transition" (paper prepared for the South African Politics Section of the African Studies Association Annual Conference held in Boston, Massachusetts, December 6–10, 1983), p. 15.

92. Mary Benson, *The African Patriots* (London: Faber and Faber, 1963), pp. 17 and 332.

93. W. M. MacMillan, *Complex South Africa* (London: Faber and Faber, 1930), p. 112.

94. Charles Bloomberg, *Christian-Nationalism and the Rise of the Afrikaner*

Broederbond in South Africa, 1918–1948, ed. Saul Dubow (Bloomington: Indiana University Press, 1989), p. 1; also on the subject of Afrikaner ideology see Leonard Thompson, *The Political Mythology of Apartheid* (New Haven: Yale University Press, 1985).

95. Leo Kuper, "African Nationalism in South Africa," in Monica Wilson and Leonard Thompson, eds., *The Oxford History of South Africa* (Oxford: Oxford University Press, 1969), 2 vols., vol. 2, p. 425.

96. Benson, *African Patriots*, p. 42.

97. Ibid., p. 43.

98. S. Bangani Ngcobo, "African Elites in South Africa," *International Social Science Bulletin* (New York: UNESCO, 1956) 8, 3, p. 432; also see Norman Etherington, *Preachers, Peasants, and Politics in South East Africa, 1835–80: African Christian Communities in Natal, Pondoland, and Zululand* (London: Royal Historical Society, 1978).

99. Marks, "Zulu Royal Family," p. 19.

100. Neville Hogan, "The Posthumous Vindication of Zachariah Gqishela: Reflections on the Politics of Dependence at the Cape in the Nineteenth Century," in Marks and Atmore, eds., *Economy and Society*, pp. 226–227; for a profile of John Tengo Jabavu see L. D. Ngcongco, "John Tengo Jabavu, 1859–1921," in Christopher Saunders, ed., *Black Leaders in Southern African History* (London: Heinemann Educational, 1979), pp. 142–156.

101. Andre Odendaal, *Vukani Bantu: The Beginnings of Black Protest Politics in South Africa to 1912* (Cape Town: David Philip, 1984), p. 8.

102. Quoted in Leo Kuper, *An African Bourgeoisie* (New Haven: Yale University Press, 1965), p. 194.

103. Robert W. July, *The Origins of Modern African Thought: Its Development in West Africa during the Nineteenth and Twentieth Centuries* (New York and Washington, D.C.: Frederick A. Praeger, 1967), p. 209.

104. Jordan Ngubane, *An African Explains Apartheid* (London: Pall Mall Press, 1963), p. 84.

105. R. V. Selope Thema, "How Congress Began," in Motholi Mutloastse, ed., *Reconstruction* (Johannesburg: Ravan Press, 1981), p. 108.

106. Jordan Ngubane, *Ushaba: The Hurtle to Blood River* (Washington, D.C.: Three Continents Press, 1974), p. 160.

107. Ngubane, *An African Explains*, p. 71.

108. Ibid., p. 74.

109. Shula Marks, "The Tradition of Non-Racism in South Africa" (paper presented at a conference on "Democracy, Popular Precedents, Practice, Culture" sponsored by the History Workshop of the University of the Witwatersrand, Johannesburg, July 13–15, 1994), pp. 1–22.

110. Kuper, "African Nationalism," p. 453.

111. Plaatje, *Native Life*; B. M. Kies, "The Contribution of Non-European People to World Civilization," in Maurice Hommel, ed., *The Contribution of*

Non-European People to World Civilization (1953; Johannesburg: Skotaville Publishers, 1989), pp. 1–47.

112. Kies, "Contribution."

113. Germaine A. Hoston, *Marxism and the Crisis of Development in Prewar Japan* (N.J.: Princeton University Press, 1986), p. ix.

3. LIBERALISM, POPULISM, AND SOCIALISM

1. This statement appeared in a seminal article written by H. V. Hodson which provided impetus for the founding of the British Institute of Race Relations in 1950. See Chris Mullard, *Race, Power, and Resistance* (London: Routledge and Kegan Paul, 1985), p. 13.

2. Quoted in Peter Walshe, *The Rise of African Nationalism in South Africa: The African National Congress, 1912–1952* (London: C. Hurst and Co., 1970), p. 97.

3. Robert W. July, *The Origins of Modern African Thought: Its Development in West Africa during the Nineteenth and Twentieth Centuries* (New York and Washington, D.C.: Frederick A. Praeger, 1967), p. 376.

4. Neville Hogan, "The Posthumous Vindication of Zachariah Gqishela: Reflections on the Politics of Dependence at the Cape in the Nineteenth Century," in S. Marks and A. Atmore, eds., *Economy and Society in Pre-Industrial South Africa* (London: Longman, 1980), pp. 276–277.

5. Walshe, *Rise of African Nationalism,* p. 25.

6. Jordan Ngubane, *An African Explains Apartheid* (New York: Frederick A. Praeger, 1963), p. 73.

7. Saul Dubow, *Racial Segregation and the Origins of Apartheid in South Africa, 1919–36* (New York: St. Martins Press, 1989) provides a comprehensive discussion of the extensive literature on segregation; for an early discussion of African-American influence see R. Hunt Davis Jr., "The Black American Component in Southern Africa: Responses to Colonialism in South Africa, ca. 1890–1914," *Journal of Southern African Affairs* 3, 1 (January 1978), pp. 65–84, and Robert H. Hill and Gregory A. Pirio, "'Africa for the Africans': The Garvey Movement in South Africa, 1920–1940," in Shula Marks and Stanley Trapido, eds., *The Politics of Race, Class, and Nationalism in Twentieth Century South Africa* (New York: Longman, 1987), pp. 209–253.

8. Leo Kuper, "African Nationalism in South Africa, 1910–1964," in Monica Wilson and Leonard Thompson, eds., *The Oxford History of South Africa* (Oxford: Oxford University Press, 1917), 2 vols., vol. 2, p. 433.

9. Although he did not use this terminology, Ngubane identified a similar dichotomy in black church history; see *An African Explains Apartheid,* p. 74.

10. Ibid., p. 193; also see I. B. Tabata, "Why Compromise?" in his *The Awakening of a People* (London: Spokesman Books, 1974), pp. 24–33.

11. For a recent discussion of the indigenous meanings of liberalism,

see C. J. Driver, "Between the Hammer and the Anvil: The Quandary of Liberalism in South Africa," in R. Hunt Davis Jr., ed., *Apartheid Unravels* (Gainesville: University of Florida Press, 1991), pp. 58–76.

12. Tabata, *Awakening of a People*, p. 85.

13. I. B. Tabata, "On the Organization of the African People: Extracts from a Letter to a Friend (Nelson Mandela)," June 16, 1948, p. 2. Beineke Rare Manuscripts Collection, Yale University.

14. C. J. Driver, *Patrick Duncan: South African and Pan-African* (London: Heinemann, 1980), p. 244, reports that several PAC members were taken with the name "Azania," which appeared in Evelyn Waugh's 1932 novel *Black Mischief*. They wrote to Waugh to inquire about the name and were incorrectly informed by him that "Azania" was the name of an ancient African kingdom. Based on this misinformation, they pressed the PAC to officially adopt the name as an alternate designation for South Africa.

15. "Kanyisa" (Jordan Ngubane), "Congress at the Crossroads," *Inkundla ya Bantu* (March 13, 1947).

16. Thomas Karis and Gwendolen Carter, eds., *From Protest to Challenge: A Documentary History of African Politics in South Africa, 1882–1979*, 5 vols., vol. 4 (Stanford, Calif.: Hoover Institution Press, 1977), pp. 114–115.

17. Gail Gerhart, *Black Power in South Africa: The Evolution of an Ideology* (Berkeley: University of California Press, 1979), p. 74.

18. Robert R. Edgar and Luyanda Ka Msumza, eds., *Freedom in Our Lifetime: The Collected Writings of Anton Muziwakhe Lembede* (Athens: Ohio University Press, 1996), p. 21.

19. Walshe, *Rise of African Nationalism*, p. 151.

20. See *The Congress Youth League Manifesto* (Document 48), in Karis and Carter, eds., *From Protest to Challenge*, vol. 2, p. 301.

21. Tom Lodge, *Black Politics in South Africa since 1945* (London: Longman, 1983), p. 36.

22. A. M. Lembede, "African Trade Unions" (New Haven: Yale University, The Gail Gerhart Collection, Beineke Rare Manuscripts Library, 1947); see also Edgar and Msumza, eds., *Freedom in Our Lifetime*.

23. Archie Mafeje, "The Gagged and Ham-Strung Movement (the ANC)" (unpublished paper), n.d., p. 16.

24. Lodge, *Black Politics*, p. 80.

25. Frantz Fanon, *The Wretched of the Earth* (New York: Grove Press, 1963), p. 32.

26. See Walshe, *Rise of African Nationalism*, pp. 354–361; Gerhart, *Black Power*, pp. 45–84.

27. Neville Alexander, "Aspects of Non-Collaboration in the Western Cape, 1943–1963," *Social Dynamics* 12, 1 (1986), p. 9.

28. Ernesto Laclau, *Politics and Ideology in Marxist Theory* (London: New Left Books, 1977), p. 12.

29. For an elaboration of Unity Movement Marxism as a theory of revolution, see Karrim Essack, *Reform or Revolution in South Africa* (Dar es Salaam, Tanzania: Thakers, 1982).

30. Sheridan Johns, "The Birth of the Communist Party of South Africa," *International Journal of African Historical Studies* 9, 3 (1976), and R. E. and H. J. Simons, *Class and Colour in South Africa, 1850–1950* (New York: Penguin Press, 1968); also see Johns, "Marxism-Leninism in a Multi-Racial Environment: The Origins and Early History of the Communist Party of South Africa, 1914–1932" (unpublished Ph.D. dissertation, Harvard University, 1965); much of the material in this dissertation has been recently published in *Raising the Red Flag: The International Socialist League and the Communist Party of South Africa, 1914–1932* (Bellville, South Africa: Mayibue Books, 1995).

31. R. W. Johnson, *How Long Will South Africa Survive?* (London: Oxford University Press, 1977), p. 21.

32. Philip Bonner, "The Transvaal Native Congress 1917–1920: The Radicalisation of the Black Petty Bourgeoisie on the Rand," in S. Marks and R. Rathbone, eds., *Industrialisation and Social Change in South Africa: African Class Formation, Culture and Consciousness, 1870–1930* (New York: Longman, 1982), p. 271.

33. Quoted in Motsoko Pheko, *Apartheid: The Story of a Dispossessed People* (London: Marram Books, 1972), p. 126.

34. Quoted in David Levering Lewis, *W. E. B. DuBois: Biography of a Race, 1868–1919* (New York: Henry Holt and Co., 1993), p. 421.

35. Mark Naison, *Communists in Harlem during the Depression* (Urbana: University of Illinois Press, 1983), and Harold Cruse, *The Crisis of the Negro Intellectual* (New York: William Morrow, 1967).

36. George Padmore, *The Life and Struggles of Negro Toilers* (1931; Hollywood, Calif..: Sun Dance Press, 1971), p. 125; on the life of Padmore see James R. Hooker, *Black Revolutionary: George Padmore's Path from Communism to Pan-Africanism* (New York: Praeger Publishers, 1967).

37. Philip Bonner, "The Decline of the ICU: A Case of Self-Destruction," *South African Labour Bulletin* 1, 6 (Sept.–Oct. 1974), pp. 38–43; also see Sheridan W. Johns III, "Trade Union, Pressure Group, or Mass Movement? The Industrial and Commercial Workers' Union of Africa," Robert I. Rotberg and Ali Mazrui, eds., *Protest in Black Africa* (New York: Oxford University Press, 1970), pp. 695–754.

38. George Padmore, *Pan-Africanism or Communism* (New York: Doubleday and Co., 1972), p. 326.

39. Lodge, *Black Politics*, p. 8.

40. Peter Walshe, *Black Nationalism in South Africa: A Short History* (Johannesburg: Ravan Press, 1973), p. 22; also see his *Rise of African Nationalism*, p. 158.

41. Robert Hill, "General Introduction," in Robert Hill, ed., *Marcus*

Garvey and Universal Negro Improvement Association Papers, 9 vols., vol. 1 (Berkeley: University of California Press, 1983), p. lxx.

42. Robert Hill and Barbara Blair, eds., *Marcus Garvey: Life and Lessons* (Berkeley, Los Angeles, and London: University of California Press, 1987), pp. 296–299.

43. Padmore, *Pan-Africanism or Communism,* p. 7.

44. Hill, ed., *Marcus Garvey and Universal Negro Improvement Association Papers,* vol. 1, p. 304.

45. Sheridan Johns, "The Comintern, South Africa and the Black Diaspora," *Review of Politics* 37, 2 (April 1975), p. 210.

46. Edward T. Wilson, *Russia and Black Africa before World War II* (New York: Holmes and Meier, 1974), p. 31.

47. Ibid., p. 185; also see, Johns, "Comintern," p. 209.

48. John Gomas shared this recollection with me in a personal discussion in Cape Town in May 1977.

49. Colin Legum, *Pan Africanism: A Short Political Guide* (New York: Frederick A. Praeger, 1963), pp. 105–106.

50. Martin Legassick, *Class and Nationalism in South Africa* (New York: Syracuse University, Eastern African Studies Program, 1973), p. 23.

51. Albert Nzula, I. I. Potekhin, and A. Z. Zusmanovich, *Forced Labour in Colonial Africa,* trans. Hugh Jenkins (London: Zed Press, 1979), p. 167.

52. South African Communist Party, ed., *South African Communists Speak: Documents from the History of the South African Communist Party, 1915–1980* (London: Inkululeko, 1985), pp. 120–122.

53. Moses Kotane, "Extracts from 'Japan—Friend or Foe?'" in South African Communist Party, ed., *South African Communists Speak,* p. 168.

54. Paul B. Rich, *White Power and Liberal Conscience: Racial Segregation and South African Liberalism, 1921–1960* (Manchester: Manchester University Press, 1984), p. 86.

55. Nelson Mandela, *Long Walk to Freedom* (Boston: Little, Brown and Co., 1994), pp. 100–120.

56. Alex Callinicos, "Marxism and Revolution in South Africa," *International Socialism* 2, 31 (Spring 1986), p. 46.

57. George M. Fredrickson, *Black Liberation: Comparative History of Black Ideologies in the United States and South Africa* (New York and Oxford: Oxford University Press, 1995), p. 207.

58. Bojana V. Jordan, *We Will Be Heard: A South African Exile Remembers* (Boston: Quinlan Press, 1986), chapter 7.

59. R. E. van der Ross, *The Rise and Decline of Apartheid* (Cape Town: Tafelberg Publishers, 1986), p. 174.

60. Gavin Lewis, *Between the Wall and the Wire: A History of South African "Coloured" Politics* (Cape Town and Johannesburg: David Philip, 1987), p. 215.

61. Tom Lodge, "The Parents' School Boycott: Eastern Cape and East

Rand, 1955," in Peter Kallaway, ed., *Apartheid and Education: The Education of Black South Africans* (Johannesburg: Ravan Press, 1984), pp. 270–274.

62. Van der Ross, *Apartheid,* p. 211.

63. See Tsotsi's 1958 Presidential Address given to the AAC's Annual Conference (December 14–16, 1958), in Karis and Carter, eds., *From Protest to Challenge,* vol. 3, p. 493.

64. For example, James Leatt, Theo Kneifel, and Klaus Nurnberger, *Contending Ideologies in South Africa* (Cape Town: David Philip, 1986), p. 145; for an in-depth discussion of the relationship between the communist and nationalist movements, see Stephen Ellis and Tsepo Sechaba, *Comrades against Apartheid: The ANC and the South African Communist Party in Exile* (Bloomington: Indiana University Press, and London: James Currey, 1992).

65. Mafeje, "Gagged and Ham-Strung," p. 8.

66. For example, see Edmond J. Keller and Donald Rothchild, eds., *Afro-Marxist Regimes: Ideology and Public Policy* (Boulder, Colo.: Lynne Rienner Publishers, 1987).

67. Joe Slovo, "The Theory of the South African Revolution" (paper presented at a Conference on the "Socio-Economic Trends and Policies in Southern Africa," Dar es Salaam, November 29–December 7, 1975), p. 2.

4. A NEW LEFT BATTLES APARTHEID

1. Eric Hobsbawm, "Intellectuals and the Class Struggle," in his *Revolutionaries, Contemporary Essays* (New York: New American Library, 1973), p. 247.

2. Craig Charney, "Thoughts on Revolution," *Times Higher Education Supplement* (June 17, 1983), p. 10.

3. Steven Philip Kramer, *Socialism in Western Europe: The Experience of a Generation* (Boulder, Colo.: Westview Press, 1984), pp. xii–xiii. Kramer offers a succinct description of Mannheim's concept of generation; also see Karl Mannheim, "What Is a Social Generation," in Anthony Esler, ed., *Conflict of Generations in Modern History* (Lexington, Mass.: D. C. Heath, 1974), and for the original version see Karl Mannheim, *Essays on the Sociology of Knowledge,* Paul Kecskemeti, ed. and trans. (London: Routledge and Kegan Paul, 1953).

4. Pan Africanist Congress, *The National Mandate in Azania* (PAC Publication, n.d., c. 1981).

5. Herbert Gintis, "The New Working Class and Revolutionary Youth," *Socialist Revolution* (May–June 1970), p. 21.

6. See Heribert Adam, *Modernizing Racial Domination: South Africa's Political Dynamics* (Berkeley and Los Angeles: University of California Press, 1971).

7. Linda Chisholm, "Redefining Skills: Black Education in South Africa in the 1980's," in Peter Kallaway, ed., *Apartheid and Education: The Education of Black South Africans* (Johannesburg: Ravan Press, 1984), pp. 387–410.

8. Sam C. Nolutshungu, *Changing South Africa: Political Considerations* (New York: Holmes and Meier, 1982), p. 119.

9. Wilmot James, "The South African State in Transition" (paper presented at the African Studies Association Annual Conference, December 6–10, 1983), p. 9.

10. John D. Brewer, "Black Protest in South Africa's Crisis: A Comment on Legassick," *African Affairs* 85, 339 (April 1986), p. 287.

11. Quoted in David Smock, *Black Education in South Africa: The Current Situation* (South African Education Program, Institute of International Education, January 1983), p. 23.

12. Craig Charney, "Thinking of Revolution: The New South African Intelligentsia," *Monthly Review* 38 (December 1986), p. 18.

13. Nolutshungu, *Changing South Africa,* pp. 82–91.

14. Barbara and John Ehrenreich, "The Professional-Managerial Class," in Pat Walker, ed., *Between Labor and Capital* (Boston: South End Press, 1979), pp. 26–34.

15. Alvin W. Gouldner, *The Future of Intellectuals and the Rise of the New Class* (New York: Seabury Press, 1979).

16. Erik Olin Wright, "Intellectuals and the Class Structure of Capitalist Society," in Walker, ed., *Between Labor and Capital,* pp. 191–193.

17. Quoted in Gouldner, *The Rise of the New Class,* p. 33.

18. Edward Shils, "Dreams of Plenitude, Nightmares of Scarcity," in Seymour Martin Lipset and Philip G. Altbach, eds., *Student Revolt* (Boston: Houghton Mifflin, 1969), p. 1.

19. Lewis Feuer, "The Conflict of Generations," in Gilbert Abcarian, ed., *American Political Radicalism* (Waltham, Mass.: Xerox College Publishing, 1971), p. 45.

20. Cyril Levitt, "The New Left, the New Class and Socialism," *Higher Education* 8, 6 (November 1979), p. 641.

21. Arthur Hirsh, *The French New Left: An Intellectual History from Sartre to Gorz* (Boston: South End Press, 1981), p. 6.

22. National Union of South African Students, *Report of President and Vice-President Department* (44th Student Assembly, July 1968), Appendix M, p. 3.

23. Martin Legassick and John Shingler, "South Africa," in Donald K. Emerson, ed., *Students and Politics in Developing Nations* (New York: Praeger Publishers, 1968), p. 103.

24. Leo Marquard, *The Peoples and Policies of South Africa* (London: Oxford University Press, 1969), 4th ed., p. 207.

25. Margo Russell, "Intellectuals and Academic Apartheid, 1950–1955," in Pierre Van den Berghe, ed., *The Liberal Dilemma in South Africa* (New York: St. Martin's Press, 1979), p. 136.

26. T. B. Davie, *Education and Race Relations in South Africa: The Interaction of Colonial Policies and Race Relations in South Africa* (Johannesburg: South African Institute of Race Relations, 1955), p. 1.

27. Alexander Hepple, *Verwoerd* (London: Penguin Books, 1967), p. 212.

28. Thomas Karis and Gwendolen M. Carter, *From Protest to Challenge: A Documentary History of African Politics in South Africa, 1882–1990* (Stanford, Calif.: Hoover Institution Press, 1973), 5 vols., vol. 2, p. 3.

29. Hepple, *Verwoerd*, p. 218.

30. John Samuel, "Background Paper on the State of Education in South Africa" (paper presented at the Ford Foundation Conference on Education in South Africa, 1986), p. 5. John Samuel was for many years the Director of the South African Council of Higher Education (SACHED).

31. Excerpt from the *Christian National Education Manifesto* (1948).

32. Marquard, *Peoples and Policies of South Africa*, p. 207.

33. Quoted in Kogila Adam, "Dialectic of Higher Education for the Colonized: The Case of Non-White Universities in South Africa," in Heribert Adam, ed., *South Africa: Sociological Perspectives* (London: Oxford University Press, 1971), p. 199.

34. John A. Marcum, *Education, Race, and Social Change in South Africa* (Berkeley: University of California Press, 1982), p. 2.

35. Neville Rubin, *History of the Relations between NUSAS, the Afrikaanse Studentebond and Afrikaans University Centres* (Published by National Union of South African Students, 1959), p. 3.

36. Legassick and Shingler, "South Africa," p. 122.

37. The South African Institute of Race Relations, *Survey of Race Relations in South Africa* (Johannesburg: South African Institute of Race Relations, 1966), p. 7.

38. Jordan Ngubane, *An African Explains Apartheid* (London: Pall Mall Press, 1963), pp. 57–58.

39. Davie, *Education and Race*, p. 17.

40. Bruce Murray, "The 'Democratic' Left at Wits 1943–1948: The Federation of Progressive Students and Student Politics" (paper delivered at the History Workshop conference on Democracy—Popular Precedents, Practice, Culture at the University of the Witwatersrand, Johannesburg, July 13–15, 1994).

41. Shula Marks, "Ruth First: A Tribute," *Journal of Southern African Studies* 10, 1 (October 1983), pp. 123–124.

42. Martin Legassick, *The National Union of South African Students* (Los Angeles: African Studies Center, University of California, 1967), p. 14.

43. Ongokopotse Ramothiki Tiro, "Bantu Education," in G. M. Nkondo, ed., *The Turfloop Testimony* (Johannesburg: Ravan Press, 1976), Appendix.

44. The South African Institute of Race Relations, *Survey of Race Relations in South Africa* (Johannesburg: South African Institute of Race Relations, 1980), p. 544.

45. Ibid.

46. Nkondo, *Turfloop Testimony*, p. 5.

47. Z. K. Matthews, "The African Awakening and the Universities" (presentation given as the Third T. B. Davie Memorial Lecture, University of Cape Town, August 13, 1961, and reproduced by the South African Institute of Race Relations).

48. Rubin, *NUSAS, the Afrikaanse Studentebond . . .*, pp. 10–12.

49. Quoted in Legassick, *NUSAS*, p. 45.

50. *Year Book of International Organizations 1983–84* (New York: K. G. Sauer, Verlag, 1984), p. B2788.

51. Philip G. Altbach and Norman Uphoff, *The Student Internationals* (Metuchen, N.J.: Scarecrow Press, 1973), p. 17.

52. *Entrenched Clauses and Correlated Resolutions of the National Union of South African Students* (45th Student Assembly, August 1969), p. 27.

53. Legassick, *NUSAS*, p. 18.

54. NUSAS, *Entrenched Clauses* (1969), p. 24.

55. Edwin S. Munger, "The First Pan African Student Conference: A Letter from Edwin S. Munger," *African Field Reports, 1952–1961* (Cape Town: C. Struik, 1961), p. 240. These are reports of the American Universities Field Staff.

56. Ibid., p. 241.

57. Legassick and Shingler, "South Africa," p. 122.

58. Adam, "Dialectic of Higher Education," p. 202.

59. T. V. Bear, "Background to Student Activities at the University College of Fort Hare," in Hendrik W. Van der Merwe and David Welsh, eds., *Student Perspectives on South Africa* (Cape Town: David Philip, 1972), p. 170.

60. NUSAS, *Entrenched Clauses* (1969), p. 25.

61. Ibid.

62. NUSAS, *Report of President and Vice-President Department* (44th Assembly 1968), Appendix M, p. 3.

63. Legassick, *NUSAS*, p. 43.

64. Ibid.; also see Gail Gerhart, "The South African Student Organization, 1968–1975" (paper presented at the Annual Conference of the African Studies Association, San Francisco, October 29–November 1, 1975), p. 5.

65. Gerhart, "SASO," p. 6.

66. Legassick, *NUSAS*, p. 44.

67. Baruch Hirson, *Year of Fire, Year of Ash: The Soweto Rebellion, Roots of a Revolution?* (London: Zed Press, 1979), p. 69.

68. Steve Biko, "Letter to Students' Representatives Council," in his *I Write What I Like: A Selection of His Writings* (New York: Harper and Row, 1978), p. 10; and Nolutshungu, *Changing South Africa*, p. 168.

69. NUSAS, *Report of President and Vice-President Department* (44th Assembly 1968), p. 58.

70. Ibid., Appendix P.

71. B. A. Khoapa, ed., *Black Review,* 1972 (Durban: Black Community Programmes, 1973), p. 186.

72. NUSAS, *Report of President and Vice-President Department* (49th Student Assembly, July 1972), n.p.

73. Legassick, NUSAS, p. 43.

74. NUSAS, "Press Release," included in *Report of President and Vice-President Department* (45th Student Assembly, August 1969), Appendix B.

75. Bear, "Background," p. 163.

76. J. A. Strong, "Political Socialization: A Study of Southern African Elites" (Ph.D. dissertation, Syracuse University, 1968), pp. 55–69.

77. Nolutshungu, *Changing South Africa,* p. 167.

78. NUSAS, *Half-Yearly Executive Meeting Report* (45th Student Assembly, 1969).

79. Hirson, *Year of Fire,* p. 65.

80. Geoff Budlender, "Report on the Roma Conference—June 1973," NUSAS, *Minutes of the 50th Student Assembly* (July 15, 1973); quote taken from Article II of *The Southern African Student Movement Draft Constitution,* reproduced as an appendix to Budlender's report.

81. Hirson, *Year of Fire,* p. 114.

82. Nolutshungu, *Changing South Africa,* pp. 188–189.

83. Fozia Fisher, "Class Consciousness among Colonized Workers in South Africa," in T. Adler, ed., *Perspectives on South Africa* (Johannesburg: University of the Witwatersrand, 1977), p. 331.

84. Nolutshungu, *Changing South Africa,* p. 139.

85. Stephen M. Davis, *Apartheid's Rebels: Inside South Africa's Hidden War* (New Haven: Yale University Press, 1987), p. 64.

86. Lawrence Schlemmer, "The Stirring Giant: Observations on the Inkatha and Other Black Political Movements in South Africa," in Robert Price and Carl Rosberg, eds., *The Apartheid Regime* (Berkeley: Institute of International Studies, 1980), p. 118.

87. Chief Gatsha Buthelezi, "Reply to 'Student Leader Speaks to the World,'" n.d. Buthelezi was responding to an interview Mashinini gave to the *World*'s editor, Percy Qoboza, on August 10, 1976.

5. THE BLACK REPUBLICAN SYNTHESIS

1. R. W. Johnson, *How Long Will South Africa Survive?* (New York: Oxford University Press, 1978), p. 23.

2. Shula Marks, *The Ambiguities of Dependence in South Africa: Class, Nationalism, and the State in Twentieth-Century Natal* (Baltimore and London: John Hopkins University Press, 1986), p. 110.

3. Richard L. Sklar, "The Colonial Imprint on African Political Thought," in Gwendolen Carter and Patrick O'Meara, eds., *African Independence: The First Twenty-five Years* (Bloomington: Indiana University Press, 1985), p. 9.

4. Although this has been the long-time position of the ANC-SACP, recently Mahmood Mamdani of Cape Town University has challenged this exceptionalist formulation, contending instead that "South Africa, is actually the generic form of the colonial state in Africa"; see his *Citizen and Subject: Contemporary Africa and the Legacy of Late Colonialism* (Princeton, N.J.: Princeton University Press, 1996), p. 8.

5. Neville Alexander, *Sow the Wind: Contemporary Speeches* (Johannesburg: Skotaville Publishers, 1985), p. 36.

6. Baruch Hirson, *Year of Fire, Year of Ash: The Soweto Rebellion, Roots of a Revolution?* (London: Zed Press, 1979), pp. 113–119.

7. Craig Calhoun, *The Question of Class Struggle: Social Foundations of Popular Radicalism during the Industrial Revolution* (Chicago: University of Chicago Press, 1982), p. 98.

8. For a remarkably insightful analysis of the interaction of discourses of power and subordination, see James C. Scott, *Domination and the Arts of Resistance: Hidden Transcripts* (New Haven: Yale University Press, 1990).

9. Neville Alexander (No Sizwe), *One Azania, One Nation: The National Question in South Africa* (London: Zed Press, 1979), p. 121. As a good indication of the depth of Old Left attitudes, I. B. Tabata, the major theoretician of the Unity Movement, criticizes Alexander for not being critical enough of the BCM; see his *Apartheid: Cosmetics Exposed* (Cape Town: Prometheus Publications, 1985), pp. 43–48.

10. Archie Mafeje, "Soweto and Its Aftermath," *Review of African Political Economy*, no. 11 (January–April 1978), p. 22.

11. Eddie Webster, "Competing Paradigms: Towards a Critical Sociology in Southern Africa," *Social Dynamics* 11, 1 (1985), p. 45.

12. South African Institute of Race Relations, *Survey of Race Relations in South Africa* (Johannesburg: South African Institute of Race Relations, 1972), p. 392.

13. See his *Lessons of Struggle: South African Internal Opposition, 1960–1990* (New York and Oxford: Oxford University Press, 1992), especially chapter 3.

14. Toussaint, "'Fallen among Liberals': An Ideology of Black Consciousness," *African Communist* 78 (1979), pp. 18–30.

15. Ibid.

16. Quoted in Roland Stanbridge, "Contemporary African Political Organizations and Movements," in Robert M. Price and Carl G. Rosberg, eds., *The Apartheid Regime* (Berkeley: Institute of International Studies, 1980), p. 87.

17. Dennis Davis and Robert Fine, "Political Strategies and the State: Some Historical Observations," *Journal of Southern African Studies* 12, 1 (October 1985), p. 39.

18. Steve Biko, *I Write What I Like: A Selection of His Writings*, edited with

a Personal Memoir by Aelred Stubbs, C. R. (San Francisco: Harper and Row, 1978), pp. 33–39.

19. Millard Arnold, ed., *Steve Biko: Black Consciousness in South Africa* (New York: Random House, 1978), p. 218.

20. Aelred Stubbs, "Martyr of Hope: A Personal Memoir," in Biko, *I Write What I Like,* p. 182.

21. Biko, "Our Strategy of Struggle," in *I Write What I Like,* p. 149.

22. See Donald Woods, *Biko* (New York: Atheneum Press, 1981; London: Paddington Press, 1978).

23. Biko, *I Write What I Like,* p. 37.

24. Quoted in Irvin Louis Horowitz, *Radicalism and the Revolt against Reason: The Social Theories of Georges Sorel* (London: Routledge and Kegan Paul, 1961), p. 81.

25. Jordan K. Ngubane, *Conflict of Minds* (New York: Books in Focus, 1979).

26. Biko, *I Write What I Like,* p. 29.

27. Nyameko (Barney) Pityana, "Afro-American Influences on the Black Consciousness Movement" (paper presented at a conference sponsored by the African Studies Center at Howard University, Washington, D.C., 1979), p. 3.

28. Biko, *I Write What I Like,* pp. 69–70.

29. Dick Howard and Karl E. Klare, *The Unknown Dimension: European Marxism since Lenin* (New York: Basic Books, 1972); see the introductory chapter by Klare, "The Critique of Everyday Life, the New Left and the Unrecognizable Marxism," and the chapter by Howard, "The Historical Context."

30. Claybourne Carson, *In Struggle: SNCC and the Black Awakening of the 1960's* (Cambridge, Mass.: Harvard University Press, 1981), p. 175.

31. Locksley Edmondson, "The Internationalization of Black Power: Historical and Contemporary Perspectives," *Mawazo* 1, 4 (December 1968), pp. 16–30.

32. E. Victor Wolfenstein, *The Victims of Democracy: Malcolm X and the Black Revolution* (Los Angeles: University of California Press, 1981), p. 23.

33. Klare, *Unknown Dimension,* p. 21fn. Klare contends that the struggles of blacks in the United States influenced the European left regarding the importance of minority struggles.

34. Carson, *In Struggle,* p. 94.

35. Gail M. Gerhart, *Black Power in South Africa: The Evolution of an Ideology* (Los Angeles: University of California Press, 1978), p. 275.

36. Heribert Adam, "The Rise of Black Consciousness in South Africa," *Race* 15, 2 (October 1973), p. 150.

37. Carson, *In Struggle,* p. 9.

38. Ibid., pp. 105–106; see Arnold, *Steve Biko,* for Biko's discussion of communists.

39. Sam C. Nolutshungu, *Changing South Africa: Political Considerations* (New York: Holmes and Meier, 1982), p. 178.

40. Gail Gerhart, "The South African Student Organization, 1968–1975" (paper presented at the Annual Conference of the African Studies Association, San Francisco, October 29–November 1, 1975), p. 21.

41. Michael Rogin, "In Defense of the New Left," *Democracy* (Fall 1983), pp. 106–116.

42. Harold Jacobs and James Petras, "Populist Students and Corporate Society," *International Socialist* 4, 19 (February 1967), p. 144.

43. Carson, *In Struggle,* p. 46.

44. Ongokopotse Ramothiki Tiro, "Bantu Education," in G. M. Nkondo, ed., *The Turfloop Testimony* (Johannesburg: Ravan Press, 1976), p. 92.

45. Biko, *I Write What I Like,* pp. 69–70.

46. Mafika Pascal Gwala, "Towards the Practical Manifestation of Black Consciousness," in *Black Renaissance* (paper presented at the Black Renaissance Convention, December 1974), p. 29.

47. Ibid., p. 31.

48. See C. B. Macpherson, "Revolution and Ideology in the Late Twentieth Century," in his *Democratic Theory: Essays in Retrieval* (London: Oxford University Press, 1973), pp. 157–169.

49. See Biko, *I Write What I Like,* and for the full transcription of his famous court testimony, see Arnold, *Steve Biko.*

50. Russell Hanson, *The American Imagination: Conversations with Our Past* (Princeton, N.J.: Princeton University Press, 1985), p. 24.

51. Anthony Giddens, *Profiles and Critiques in Social Theory* (Berkeley: University of California Press, 1982), p. 100.

52. Biko, "Our Strategy of Struggle," in *I Write What I Like,* pp. 143–151.

53. I am indebted to Wendy Sarvasy for this conception of the relationship between prefigurative politics and permanent revolution.

54. Harold Cruse, *Crisis of the Negro Intellectual* (New York: William Morrow, 1968), pp. 118–119.

55. See "After the Uprising: Division and Realignment, 1977–1979," in his *Lessons of Struggle,* pp. 75–106.

6. AN ENDURING DUALITY

1. Francis Fukuyama, "The Next South Africa," *South Africa International* 22, 2 (October 1991), pp. 71–81.

2. Yoav Peled, "Ethnic Democracy and the Legal Construction of Citizenship: Arab Citizen of the Jewish State," *American Political Science Review* 86, 2 (June 1992), p. 433.

3. Ghita Ionescu and Ernest Gellner, eds., *Populism: Its Meaning and National Characteristics* (London: Macmillan Co., 1969).

4. See C. B. Macpherson, *The Real World of Democracy* (New York and Oxford: Oxford University Press, 1966), where populism, as well as liberalism and socialism, are identified as main sources of modern democratic thought.

5. Alan Scott, *Ideology and the New Social Movements* (London: Unwin Hyman, 1990), p. 24.

6. For an important distinction between racist social movements and movements of racial liberation, see Eugene Victor Wolfenstein, "Race, Racism, and Racial Liberation," *Western Political Quarterly* 30, 1 (March 1977), pp. 163–182.

7. See my "Racial Proletarianization and Some Contemporary Dimensions of Black Consciousness Thought," in R. Hunt Davis Jr., ed., *Apartheid Unravels* (Gainesville: University of Florida Press, Center for African Studies, 1991), pp. 77–99. On an historic attempt to fuse socialism and black nationalism under communist auspices, see Sheridan Johns, "The Comintern, South Africa, and the Black Diaspora," *The Review of Politics* 37, 2 (April 1975), pp. 200–234.

8. For a discussion of ANC economic policy, see Patrick Bond, "Neoliberalism Comes to South Africa," *Multinational Monitor* 17, 8 (May 1996), pp. 8–19.

9. "Capitalism at Work for the People," *The Electronic Mail and Guardian* (September 26, 1997), p. 1.

10. For a critique of these tendencies as misconceptions of the issues faced by the popular democratic movement, see John Saul, "South Africa: The Question of Strategy," *New Left Review* 160 (November/December 1986), pp. 3–21.

11. See, for example, "The Azanian Manifesto," in Anthony W. Marx, *The Lessons of Struggle: South African Internal Opposition, 1960–1990* (New York and Oxford: Oxford University Press, 1992), Appendix B, pp. 278–280.

12. Ernesto Laclau, "Towards a Theory of Populism," in his *Politics and Ideology in Marxist Theory: Capitalism, Fascism, Populism* (London: Verso, 1977), p. 174.

13. Umberto Eco, "Ur-Fascism," *New York Review of Books* 42, 11 (June 22, 1995), p. 4.

14. See, for example, the special issue of the *Journal of Southern African Studies* 20, 3 (September 1994)—guest edited by Saul Dubow, John Sharp, and Edwin Wilmsen—which is devoted to ethnicity and identity in southern Africa.

15. On this point see Gerhard Mare, *Ethnicity and Politics in South Africa* (London and New Jersey: Zed Books, 1993), pp. 58–62.

16. I draw this definition from Kenneth Anderson's review of the work of Christopher Lasch; see "Heartless World Revisited: Christopher Lasch's Parting Polemic against the New Class," *Times Literary Supplement* 4825 (September 22, 1995), p. 4.

17. Christopher Lowe, "Buthelezi, Inkatha, and the Problem of Ethnic Nationalism in South Africa," in Joshua Brown, Patrick Manning, Karin Shapiro, and Jon Wiener, eds., *History from South Africa: Alternative Visions and Practices* (Philadelphia: Temple University Press, 1991), p. 203.

18. For an important discussion of the populist implications of Buthelezi's reform strategy, see ibid., pp. 194–208. For an elaboration of the idea of capitalism as a social movement, see Richard L. Sklar, "Beyond Capitalism and Socialism in Africa," *Journal of Modern African Studies* 26, 1 (March 1988), pp. 1–21, citing as the primary source for this idea Martin J. Sklar, *The Corporate Reconstruction of American Capitalism, 1890–1916* (Cambridge: Cambridge University Press, 1988).

19. Richard L. Sklar, "The African Frontier for Political Science," in Robert Bates, V. Y. Mudimbe, and Jean O'Barr, eds., *Africa and the Disciplines* (Chicago and London: University of Chicago Press, 1993), p. 87.

20. Rob Amato, *Understanding the New Constitution: Everyone's Guide to the Development and Implications of the New South African Constitution* (Cape Town: Struik Publishers, 1994), p. 79.

21. For a discussion of the role of chieftaincy in a democratic South Africa, see Khanya B. Motshabi and Shreen G. Volks, "Towards Democratic Chieftaincy: Principles and Procedures," *Acta Juridica* (1991), pp. 104–115. Also, see Rich Mkhondo, "Chiefs Fight for Role in Democratic South Africa" (Reuters News Reports via NewsNet [RNO1W], October 26, 1995).

22. Nelson Mandela, *Long Walk to Freedom* (Boston: Little, Brown and Co., 1994).

23. *The Constitution of the Republic of South Africa Bill* [B 212B-93 (GA)], chapter 4, Section 43b, p. 26.

24. Bill Keller, "The Anti-Mandela," *The New York Times Magazine* (May 14, 1995), pp. 24–29.

25. For a reconsideration of traditional authority by authors who take the claims of postmodernists seriously, see Paul Heelas, Scott Lash, and Paul Morris, eds., *Detraditionalization* (Cambridge, Mass.: Blackwell Publishers, 1996).

26. Weber's comment is cited in J. Donald Moon, *Constructing Community: Moral Pluralism and Tragic Conflicts* (Princeton: Princeton University Press, 1993), p. 66.

27. On the notion of "hyper-masculinity," see Judith Grant, "Bringing the Noise: Hyper-Masculinity and the Power of Pose in Heavy Metal and Cross-over Rap," *The Journal of Social Philosophy* 27, 2 (Fall 1996), pp. 5–30. In addition, for a discussion of hyper-masculinity and black liberation, see E.

Victor Wolfenstein, "Reflections on Malcolm X and Black Feminism" (paper delivered at the 1996 annual meeting of the Western Political Science Association, Portland, Oregon, March 14–16).

28. I take this observation from Mitchell Cohen's review of Will Kymlicka, *Multicultural Citizenship: A Liberal Theory of Minority Rights* (Oxford: Clarendon Press, 1996), entitled "How Do We Make Citizens?" *Times Literary Supplement* 4847 (February 23, 1996), p. 26.

29. Michael J. Sandel, "America's Search for a New Public Philosophy," *The Atlantic Monthly* 277, 3 (March 1996), pp. 57–74.

30. Richard L. Sklar, "The African Frontier," pp. 86–87.

31. Peter Ekeh, "Colonialism and the Two Publics: A Theoretical Statement," *Comparative Studies in Society and History* 17, 1 (January 1975), pp. 91–112; for a recent exploration of citizenship and ethnic mobilization in Kenya, see Stephen N. Ndegwa, "Citizenship and Ethnicity: An Examination of Two Transition Movements in Kenyan Politics," *The American Political Science Review* 91, 3 (September 1997), 599–615.

32. This point is made more forcefully in a later version of Ekeh's "Colonialism and Two Publics." See his "Colonialism and the Development of Citizenship in Africa: A Study in Ideologies of Legitimation," in Onigu Otite, ed., *Themes in African Social and Political Thought* (Enugu, Nigeria: Fourth Dimension Publishers, 1978), pp. 302–334.

33. Thomas H. Marshall and Tom Bottomore, *Citizenship and Social Class* (1952; London: Pluto Press, 1992), pp. 17–27.

34. Martin Chanock, "The South African Native Administration Act of 1929: Reflections on a Pathological Case of Legal Pluralism," in Oliver Mendelsohn and Upendra Baxi, eds., *The Rights of Subordinated Peoples* (Oxford: Oxford University Press, 1994), p. 293.

35. Leo Kuper, *An African Bourgeoisie* (New Haven: Yale University Press, 1965), p. 379.

Bibliography

Adam, Heribert. "The Rise of Black Consciousness in South Africa." *Race* 15, 2 (October 1973): 149–165.

Adam, Heribert. *Modernizing Racial Domination: South Africa's Political Dynamics.* Berkeley and Los Angeles: University of California Press, 1971.

Adam, Kogila. "Dialectic of Higher Education for the Colonized: The Case of Non-White Universities in South Africa." In *South Africa: Sociological Perspectives,* edited by Heribert Adam. London: Oxford University Press, 1971.

Alexander, Neville. "Aspects of Non-collaboration in the Western Cape, 1943–1963." *Social Dynamics* 12, 1 (1986): 1–14.

Alexander, Neville [No Sizwe]. *One Azania, One Nation: The National Question in South Africa.* London: Zed Press, 1979.

Alexander, Neville. *Sow the Wind: Contemporary Speeches.* Johannesburg: Skotaville Publishers, 1985.

Altbach, Philip G., and Uphoff, Norman. *The Student Internationals.* Metuchen, N.J.: Scarecrow Press, 1973.

Amato, Rob. *Understanding the New Constitution: Everyone's Guide to the Development and Implications of the New South African Constitution.* Cape Town: Struik Publishers, 1994.

Anderson, Kenneth. "Heartless World Revisited: Christopher Lasch's Parting Polemic against the New Class." *Times Literary Supplement* no. 4825 (September 22, 1995): 3–4.

Arnold, Millard, ed. *Steve Biko: Black Consciousness in South Africa.* New York: Random House, 1978.

Bear, T. V. "Background to Student Activities at the University College of Fort Hare." In *Student Perspectives on South Africa,* edited by Hendrik W. Van der Merwe and David Welsh. Cape Town: David Philip, 1972.

Benson, Mary. *The African Patriots.* London: Faber and Faber, 1963.

Biko, Steve. *I Write What I Like: A Selection of His Writings.* Edited with a Personal Memoir by Aelred Stubbs. San Francisco: Harper and Row, 1978.

Bloomberg, Charles. *Christian-Nationalism and the Rise of the Afrikaner Broederbond in South Africa, 1918–1948.* Edited by Saul Dubow. Bloomington: Indiana University Press, 1989.

Bond, Patrick. "Neoliberalism Comes to South Africa." *Multinational Monitor* 17, no. 8 (May 1996): 8–19.

Bonner, Philip. "The Decline of the ICU: A Case of Self-Destruction." *South African Labour Bulletin* 1, 6 (September–October 1974): 38–43.

Bonner, Philip. "The Transvaal Native Congress 1917–1920: The Radicalisation of the Black Petty Bourgeoisie on the Rand." In *Industrialisation and Social Change in South Africa: African Class Formation, Culture and Consciousness, 1870–1930*, edited by S. Marks and R. Rathbone. New York: Longman, 1982.

Bozzoli, Belinda. *The Political Nature of a Ruling Class: Capital and Ideology in South Africa, 1890–1933.* London: Routledge and Kegan Paul, 1981.

Brewer, John D. "Black Protest in South Africa's Crisis: A Comment on Legassick." *African Affairs* #85, 339 (April 1986): 283–294.

Budlender, Geoff. "Report on the Roma Conference of June 1973." *Minutes of the 50th Student Assembly of the National Union of South African Students* (July 15, 1973); The Southern African Student Movement Draft Constitution reproduced as an appendix.

Bundy, Colin. *The Rise and Fall of the South African Peasantry.* Berkeley: University of California Press, 1979.

Buthelezi, Chief Gatsha. "Reply to 'Student Leader Speaks to the World.'" Buthelezi responds to an interview of Tsietsi Mashinini with the *World's* editor, Percy Qoboza, on August 10, 1976.

Calhoun, Craig. *The Question of Class Struggle: Social Foundations of Popular Radicalism during the Industrial Revolution.* Chicago: University of Chicago Press, 1982.

Callinicos, Alex. "Marxism and Revolution in South Africa." *International Socialism* 2, 31 (Spring 1986): 3–66.

Camaroff, Jean. *Body of Power, Spirit of Resistance: The Culture and History of a South African People.* Chicago and London: The University of Chicago Press, 1985.

Carson, Claybourne. *In Struggle: SNCC and the Black Awakening of the 1960's.* Cambridge, Mass.: Harvard University Press, 1981.

Carter, Gwendolen. *The Politics of Inequality: South Africa since 1948.* New York: Frederick A. Praeger, 1958.

Carter, Gwendolen; Karis, Thomas; and Stultz, Newell. *South Africa's Transkei.* Evanston, Ill.: Northwestern University Press, 1967.

Chanock, Martin. "The South African Native Administration Act of 1929: Reflections on a Pathological Case of Legal Pluralism." In *The Rights of Subordinated Peoples*, edited by Oliver Mendelsohn and Upendra Baxi. Oxford: Oxford University Press, 1994.

Charney, Craig. "Thinking of Revolution: The New South African Intelligentsia." *Monthly Review* 38 (December 1986): 10–19.

Charney, Craig. "Thoughts on Revolution." *Times Higher Education Supplement* (June 17, 1983): 10.

Chisholm, Linda. "Redefining Skills: Black Education in South Africa in the 1980's." In *Apartheid and Education: The Education of Black South Africans*, edited by Peter Kallaway. Johannesburg: Ravan Press, 1984.

Cohen, Mitchell. "How Do We Make Citizens? Review of Will Kymlicka, *Multicultural Citizenship, A Liberal Theory of Minority Rights.*" *Times Literary Supplement* no. 4847 (February 23, 1996): 26.

Cone, James H. *Martin and Malcolm and America: A Dream or a Nightmare.* Mary-knoll, N.Y.: Orbis, 1992.

Conference of Representatives of the University of Cape Town and University of the Witwatersrand. *The Open Universities in South Africa.* Johannesburg: Witwatersrand University Press, 1957.

Constitution of the Republic of South Africa Bill [B 212B -93 (GA)].

Cope, R. K. *Comrade Bill: The Life and Times of W. H. Andrews, Worker's Leader.* Cape Town: Stewart Printing Co., 1944(?).

Cox, Oliver C. *Caste, Class and Race.* 1948. Reprint, New York: Modern Reader Paperbacks, 1970.

Cruse, Harold. *Crisis of the Negro Intellectual.* New York: William Morrow and Co., 1967.

Dagger, Richard. *Civic Virtues: Rights, Citizenship and Republican Liberalism.* New York and Oxford: Oxford University Press, 1997.

Davenport, T. R. H. "Some Reflections on the History of Land Tenure in South Africa, Seen in the Light of Attempts by the State to Impose Political and Economic Control." *Acta Juridica* (1985): 53–76.

Davie, T. B. *Education and Race Relations in South Africa: The Interaction of Colonial Policies and Race Relations in South Africa.* Johannesburg: South African Institute of Race Relations, 1955.

Davis, Dennis, and Fine, Robert. "Political Strategies and the State: Some Historical Observations." *Journal of Southern African Studies* 12, 1 (October 1985): 25–48.

Davis, R. Hunt, Jr. "The Black American Component in Southern Africa: Responses to Colonialism in South Africa, ca. 1890–1914." *Journal of Southern African Affairs* 3, 1 (January 1978): 65–84.

Davis, R. Hunt, Jr., ed. *Apartheid Unravels.* Gainesville: University of Florida Press, 1991.

Davis, Stephen M. *Apartheid's Rebels: Inside South Africa's Hidden War.* New Haven: Yale University Press, 1987.

De Kiewiet, C. W. *A History of South Africa: Social and Economic.* London: Oxford University Press, 1957.

Delius, Peter. *The Land Belongs to Us: The Pedi Polity, the Boers, and the British in the Nineteenth Century Transvaal.* Berkeley: University of California Press, 1984.

Denoon, Donald. *Settler Capitalism: The Dynamics of Dependent Development in the Southern Hemisphere.* Oxford: Oxford University Press, 1983.

Driver, C. J. "Between the Hammer and the Anvil: The Quandary of Liberalism in South Africa." In *Apartheid Unravels,* edited by R. Hunt Davis, Jr. Gainesville: University of Florida Press, 1991.

Driver, C. J. *Patrick Duncan: South African and Pan-African.* London: Heinemann, 1980.

DuBois, W.E.B. *The Souls of Black Folk.* 1903. Reprint, New York: Bantam, 1989.

Dube, David. *The Rise of Azania, the Fall of South Africa.* Lusaka: Daystar Publications, 1983.

Dubow, Saul. *Racial Segregation and the Origins of Apartheid in South Africa, 1919–36.* New York: St. Martin's Press, 1989.

Dubow, Saul; Sharp, John; and Wilmsen, Edwin, eds. "Special Issue: Ethnicity and Identity in Southern Africa." *Journal of Southern African Studies* 20, 3 (September 1994).

Duly, Leslie Clement. "A Revisit with the Cape's Hottentot Ordinance of 1828." In *Studies in Economics and Economic History: Essays in Honour of Professor H. M. Robertson,* edited by Marcelle Kooy. Durham: Duke University Press, 1972.

Eco, Umberto. "Ur-Fascism." *The New York Review of Books* 42, 11 (June 22, 1995): 12–15.

Edgar, Robert. "Garveyism in Africa: Dr. Wellington and the American Movement in the Transkei." *Ufahamu* 6, 1 (1976): 31–57.

Edgar, Robert R., and Msumza, Luyanda Ka. *Freedom in Our Lifetime: The Collected Writings of Anton Muziwakhe Lembede.* Athens: Ohio University Press, 1996.

Edmondson, Locksley. "The Internationalization of Black Power: Historical and Contemporary Perspectives." *Mawazo* 1, 4 (December 1968): 16–30.

Ehrenreich, Barbara, and Ehrenreich, John. "The Professional-Managerial Class." In *Between Labor and Capital,* edited by Pat Walker. Boston: South End Press, 1979.

Ekeh, Peter. "Colonialism and the Development of Citizenship in Africa: A Study in Ideologies of Legitimization." In *Themes in African Social and Political Thought,* edited by Onigu Otite. Enugu, Nigeria: Fourth Dimension Publishers, 1978.

Ekeh, Peter. "Colonialism and the Two Publics: A Theoretical Statement." *Comparative Studies in Society and History* 17, 1 (January 1975): 91–112.

Ellis, Stephen, and Sechaba, Tsepo. *Comrades against Apartheid: The ANC and the South African Communist Party in Exile.* Bloomington: Indiana University Press, and London: James Currey, 1992.

Elphick, Richard. "The Khoisan to c. 1770." In *The Shaping of Southern African Society, 1652–1820,* edited by Richard Elphick and Hermann Giliomee. Cape Town: Longman Press, 1979.

Elphick, Richard. *Kraal and Castle: Khoikhoi and the Founding of White South Africa.* New Haven and London: Yale University Press, 1977.

Elphick, Richard, and Giliomee, Hermann. *The Shaping of Southern African Society, 1652–1820,* 1st ed. Cape Town: Longman Press, 1979.

Elphick, Richard, and Giliomee, Hermann. *The Shaping of Southern African Society, 1652–1820.* 2nd revised ed. Middletown, Conn.: Wesleyan University Press, 1988.

Essack, Karrim. *Reform or Revolution in South Africa.* Dar es Salaam, Tanzania: Thakers, 1982.

Etherington, Norman. *Preachers, Peasants, and Politics in South East Africa, 1835–80: African Christian Communities in Natal, Pondoland, and Zululand.* London: Royal Historical Society, 1978.

Fanon, Frantz. *The Wretched of the Earth.* New York: Grove Press, 1963.

Feuer, Lewis. "The Conflict of Generations." In *American Political Radicalism,* edited by Gilbert Abcarian. Waltham, Mass.: Xerox College Publishing, 1971.

Fisher, Fozia. "Class Consciousness among Colonized Workers in South Africa."

In *Perspectives on South Africa,* edited by T. Adler. Johannesburg: University of the Witwatersrand, 1977.

Fredrickson, George M. *Black Liberation: Comparative History of Black Ideologies in the United States and South Africa.* New York and Oxford: Oxford University Press, 1995.

Fredrickson, George M. *White Supremacy: A Comparative Study in American and South African History.* New York: Oxford University Press, 1981.

Freund, William Mark. "The Cape under the Transitional Governments, 1795–1814." In *The Shaping of South African Society, 1652–1840,* edited by Richard Elphick and Hermann Giliomee. 2nd revised ed. Middletown, Conn.: Wesleyan University Press, 1988.

Freund, William Mark. "Forced Resettlement and the Political Economy of South Africa." *Review of African Political Economy* no. 29 (July 1984): 49–63.

Freund, William Mark. "Society and Government in Dutch South Africa: The Cape and the Batavians, 1803–1806." Ph.D. dissertation, Yale University, 1971.

Fukuyama, Francis. "The Next South Africa." *South Africa International* 22, 2 (October 1991): 71–81.

Gerhart, Gail M. *Black Power in South Africa: The Evolution of an Ideology.* Los Angeles: University of California Press, 1978.

Gerhart, Gail. "The South African Student Organization, 1968–1975." Paper presented at the Annual Conference of the African Studies Association, San Francisco, October 29–November 1, 1975.

Giddens, Anthony. *Profiles and Critiques in Social Theory.* Berkeley: University of California Press, 1982.

Giliomee, Hermann. "The Changing Political Functions of the Black Homelands." In *Up against the Fences: Poverty, Passes, and Privilege in South Africa,* edited by Hermann Giliomee and Lawrence Schlemmer. New York: St. Martin's Press, 1985.

Gilroy, Paul. *The Black Atlantic: Modernity and Double Consciousness.* Cambridge, Mass.: Harvard University Press, 1993.

Gintis, Herbert. "The New Working Class and Revolutionary Youth." *Socialist Revolution* (May–June 1970): 13–43.

Godsel, R. M. "The Regulation of Labour." In *South Africa: Public Policy Perspectives,* edited by Robert Schrire. Cape Town: Juta, 1982.

Gouldner, Alvin W. *The Future of Intellectuals and the Rise of the New Class.* New York: Seabury Press, 1979.

Grant, Judith. "Bringing the Noise: Hyper-Masculinity and the Power of Pose in Heavy Metal and Cross-over Rap." *The Journal of Social Philosophy* 27, 2 (Fall 1996): 5–30.

Gwala, Mafika Pascal. "Towards the Practical Manifestation of Black Consciousness." In *Black Renaissance: Papers from the Black Renaissance Convention,* edited by Thoahlane Thoahlane. Johannesburg: Ravan Press, 1975.

Halisi, C. R. D. "Biko and Black Consciousness Philosophy: An Interpretation." In *Bounds of Possibility: The Legacy of Steve Biko and Black Consciousness,* edited by N. Barney Pityana, Mamphela Ramphele, Malusi Mpumlwana, and Lindy

Wilson. Cape Town: David Philip, and London and New Jersey: Zed Books, 1991.

Halisi, C. R. D. "From Liberation to Citizenship: Identity and Innovation in Black South African Political Thought." *Comparative Studies in Society and History* 39, no. 1 (January 1997): 61–85.

Halisi, C. R. D. "Racial Proletarianization and Some Contemporary Dimensions of Black Consciousness Thought." In *Apartheid Unravels,* edited by R. Hunt Davis, Jr. Gainesville: University of Florida Press, Center for African Studies, 1991.

Hanson, Russell. *The American Imagination: Conversations with Our Past.* Princeton, N.J.: Princeton University Press, 1985.

Heelas, Paul; Lash, Scott; and Morris, Paul, eds. *Detraditionalization.* Cambridge, Mass.: Blackwell Publishers, 1996.

Hepple, Alexander. *South Africa: A Political and Economic History.* London: Pall Mall Press, 1966.

Hepple, Alexander. *Verwoerd.* London: Penguin Books, 1967.

Hill, Robert. "General Introduction." In *Marcus Garvey and the Universal Negro Improvement Association Papers,* edited by Robert Hill. Vol. 9. Berkeley: University of California Press, 1983.

Hill, Robert H., and Pirio, Gregory A. "'Africa for the Africans': The Garvey Movement in South Africa, 1920–1940." In *The Politics of Race, Class, and Nationalism in Twentieth Century South Africa,* edited by Shula Marks and Stanley Trapido. New York: Longman, 1987.

Hill, Robert, and Blair, Barbara, eds. *Marcus Garvey: Life and Lessons.* Berkeley, Los Angeles, and London: University of California Press, 1987.

Hirsh, Arthur. *The French New Left: An Intellectual History from Sartre to Gorz.* Boston: South End Press, 1981.

Hirson, Baruch. *Year of Fire, Year of Ash: The Soweto Rebellion, Roots of A Revolution?* London: Zed Press, 1979.

Hobsbawm, Eric. *Revolutionaries: Contemporary Essays.* New York: New American Library, 1973.

Hobson, J. A. *The War in South Africa.* London: Nisbet, 1900.

Hogan, Neville. "The Posthumous Vindication of Zachariah Gqishela: Reflections on the Politics of Dependence at the Cape in the Nineteenth Century." In *Economy and Society in Pre-Industrial South Africa,* edited by S. Marks and A. Atmore. London: Longman, 1980.

Hooker, James R. *Black Revolutionary: George Padmore's Path from Communism to Pan-Africanism.* New York: Praeger Publishers, 1967.

Horowitz, Irving Louis. *Radicalism and the Revolt against Reason: The Social Theories of Georges Sorel.* London: Routledge and Kegan Paul, 1961.

Hoston, Germaine A. *Marxism and the Crisis of Development in Prewar Japan.* Princeton, N.J.: Princeton University Press, 1986.

Howard, Dick. "The Historical Context." In *The Unknown Dimension: European Marxism since Lenin,* edited by Dick Howard and Karl E. Klare. New York: Basic Books, 1972.

Institute of Christian National Education. *Christian National Education Manifesto.* 1948.

Ionescu, Ghita, and Gellner, Ernest, eds. *Populism: Its Meaning and National Characteristics.* London: Macmillan, 1969.

Isaac, Jeffrey C. "Republicanism vs. Liberalism? Reconsideration." *History of Political Thought* 9, 2 (Summer 1988): 349–377.

Jacobs, Harold, and Petras, James. "Populist Students and Corporate Society." *International Socialist* 4, 19 (February 1967): 144–172.

Jaffee, Hosea (Mnguni). *Three Hundred Years: A History of South Africa.* Cape Town: New Era Fellowship, 1952.

James, C. L. R. *A History of Pan-African Revolt.* Washington, D.C.: Drum and Spear Press, 1969.

James, Joy. *Transcending the Talented Tenth: Black Leaders and American Intellectuals.* New York: Routledge, 1997.

James, Wilmot Godfrey. "From Segregation to Apartheid: Miners and Peasants in the Making of a Racial Order, South Africa, 1930–1952." Ph.D. dissertation, University of Wisconsin, Madison, 1982.

James, Wilmot. "The Life Trajectories of a Working Class: South Africa, 1969–1981." Paper presented to the Africa Seminar, Center for African Studies, University of Cape Town, Cape Town, May 9, 1984.

James, Wilmot. "The South African State in Transition." Paper prepared for the South African Politics Section of the African Studies Association Annual Conference held in Boston, Massachusetts, December 6–10, 1983.

Janoski, Thomas. *Citizenship and Civil Society.* Cambridge: Cambridge University Press, 1998.

Johns, Sheridan W. "The Birth of the Communist Party of South Africa." *International Journal of African Historical Studies* 9, 3 (1976): 371–400.

Johns, Sheridan W. "The Comintern, South Africa, and the Black Diaspora." *The Review of Politics* 37, no. 2 (April 1975): 200–234.

Johns, Sheridan W. "Marxism-Leninism in a Multi-racial Environment: The Origins and Early History of the Communist Party of South Africa, 1914–1932." Unpublished Ph.D. dissertation, Harvard University, 1965.

Johns, Sheridan W. *Raising the Red Flag: The International Socialist League and the Communist Party of South Africa, 1914–1932.* Bellville, South Africa: Mayibue Books, 1995.

Johns, Sheridan W., III. "Trade Union, Pressure Group, or Mass Movement? The Industrial and Commercial Workers' Union of Africa." In *Protest in Black Africa,* edited by Robert I. Rotberg and Ali Mazrui. New York: Oxford University Press, 1970.

Johnson, R. W. *How Long Will South Africa Survive?* London: Oxford University Press, 1977.

Johnstone, Fredrick. *Race, Class and Gold: A Study of Class Relations and Racial Discrimination in South Africa.* London: Routledge and Kegan Paul, 1976.

Jordan, Bojana V. *We Will Be Heard, A South African Exile Remembers.* Boston: Quinlan Press, 1986.

July, Robert W. *The Origins of Modern African Thought: Its Development in West Africa during the Nineteenth and Twentieth Centuries.* New York and Washington: Frederick A. Praeger, 1967.

Karis, Thomas, and Carter, Gwendolen, eds. *From Protest to Challenge: A Documen-*

tary History of African Politics in South Africa, 1882–1979. Vol. 5. Stanford, California: Hoover Institution Press, 1977.

Keller, Bill. "The Anti-Mandela." *The New York Times Magazine* (May 14, 1995): 24–29.

Keller, Edmond J., and Rothchild, Donald, eds. *Afro-Marxist Regimes: Ideology and Public Policy.* Boulder, Colo.: Lynne Rienner Publishers, 1987.

Khoapa, B. A., ed. *Black Review, 1972.* Durban: Black Community Programmes, 1973.

Khopung, Ethel. *Apartheid: A Story of a Dispossessed People.* Dar es Salaam: Sharpeville Day Association Mbizana, 1972.

Kies, B. M. "The Contribution of Non-European People to World Civilization." In *The Contribution of Non-European People to World Civilization,* edited by Maurice Hommel. Johannesburg: Skotaville Publishers, 1989.

Klare, Karl E. "The Critique of Everyday Life, the New Left and the Unrecognizable Marxism." In *The Unknown Dimension: European Marxism since Lenin,* edited by Dick Howard and Karl E. Klare. New York: Basic Books, 1972.

Kotane, Moses. "Extracts from 'Japan—Friend or Foe?'" In *South African Communists Speak: Documents from the History of the South African Communist Party, 1915–1980,* edited by the South African Communist Party. London: Inkululeko Publications, 1981.

Kramer, Steven Philip. *Socialism in Western Europe: The Experience of a Generation.* Boulder, Colo.: Westview Press, 1984.

Kuper, Leo. *An African Bourgeoisie.* New Haven: Yale University Press, 1965.

Kuper, Leo. "African Nationalism in South Africa, 1910–1964." In *The Oxford History of South Africa,* edited by Monica Wilson and Leonard Thompson. Vol. 2. Oxford: Oxford University Press, 1969.

Kuper, Leo. *Race, Class, and Power: Ideology and Revolutionary Change in Plural Societies.* Chicago: Aldine Publishing Co., 1975.

Kymlicka, Will. *Multicultural Citizenship: A Liberal Theory of Minority Rights.* Oxford: Clarendon Press, 1995.

Lacey, Marian. *Working for Boroko: The Origins of a Coercive Labour System in South Africa.* Johannesburg: Ravan Press: 1981.

Laclau, Ernesto. *Politics and Ideology in Marxist Theory: Capitalism, Fascism, Populism.* London: New Left Books, 1977.

Leatt, James; Kneifel, Theo; and Nurnberger, Klaus. *Contending Ideologies in South Africa.* Cape Town: David Philip, 1986.

Legassick, Martin. *Class and Nationalism in South Africa.* New York: Syracuse University, Eastern African Studies Program, 1973.

Legassick, Martin. "Gold, Agriculture and Secondary Industry in South Africa, 1885–1970: From Periphery to Sub-Metropole as a Forced Labour System." In *The Roots of Rural Poverty in Central and Southern Africa,* edited by Robin Palmer and Neil Parsons. Berkeley: University of California Press, 1977.

Legassick, Martin. *The National Union of South African Students.* Los Angeles: African Studies Center, University of California, 1967.

Legassick, Martin. "The Northern Frontier to 1820: The Emergence of the Griqua People." In *The Shaping of Southern African Society, 1652–1820,* edited by Richard Elphick and Hermann Giliomee. Cape Town: Longman, 1979.

Legassick, Martin, and Shingler, John. "South Africa." In *Students and Politics in Developing Nations,* edited by Donald K. Emerson. New York: Praeger Publishers, 1968.

Legum, Colin. *Pan Africanism: A Short Political Guide.* New York: Frederick A. Praeger, 1963.

Lembede, A. M. *African Trade Unions.* The Gail Gerhart Collection, Beineke Rare Manuscripts Library, Yale University, 1947.

Levitt, Cyril. "The New Left, the New Class and Socialism." *Higher Education* 8, 6 (November 1979): 641–655.

Lewis, David Levering. *W. E. B. DuBois: Biography of a Race, 1868–1919.* New York: Henry Holt and Co., 1993.

Lewis, Gavin. *Between the Wall and the Wire: A History of South African "Coloured" Politics.* Cape Town and Johannesburg: David Philip, 1987.

Lodge, Tom. *Black Politics in South Africa since 1945.* London: Longman, 1983.

Lodge, Tom. "The Parents' School Boycott: Eastern Cape and East Rand, 1955." In *Apartheid and Education: The Education of Black South Africans,* edited by Peter Kallaway. Johannesburg: Ravan Press, 1984.

Lowe, Christopher. "Buthelezi, Inkatha, and the Problem of Ethnic Nationalism in South Africa." In *History from South Africa: Alternative Visions and Practices,* edited by Joshua Brown, Patrick Manning, Karin Shapiro, and Jon Wiener. Philadelphia: Temple University Press, 1991.

MacCrone, I. D. *Race Attitudes in South Africa.* Oxford: Oxford University Press, 1937.

MacMillan, W. M. *The Cape Coloured Question: A Historical Survey.* London: Faber and Gwyer, 1927.

MacMillan, W. M. *Complex South Africa.* London: Faber and Faber, 1930.

Macpherson, C. B. *Democratic Theory, Essays in Retrieval.* London: Oxford University Press, 1973.

Macpherson, C. B. *The Real World of Democracy.* New York and Oxford: Oxford University Press, 1966.

Mafeje, Archie. "The Gagged and Ham-Strung Movement (the ANC)." Unpublished paper, n.d.

Mafeje, Archie. "Soweto and Its Aftermath." *Review of African Political Economy* no. 11 (January–April 1978): 17–30.

Malherbe, V. C. "The Khoi Captains in the Third Frontier War." In *The Khoikhoi Rebellion in the Eastern Cape, 1799–1803,* edited by Susan Newton-King and V. C. Malherbe. Cape Town: Center for African Studies, University of Cape Town, 1981.

Mamdani, Mahmood. *Citizen and Subject: Contemporary Africa and the Legacy of Late Colonialism.* Princeton, N.J.: Princeton University Press, 1996.

Mandela, Nelson. *Long Walk to Freedom.* Boston: Little, Brown and Co., 1994.

Mannheim, Karl. *Essays on the Sociology of Knowledge.* Edited and translated by Paul Kecskemeti. London: Routledge and Kegan Paul, 1953.

Mannheim, Karl. "What Is a Social Generation." In *Conflict of Generations in Modern History,* edited by Anthony Esler. Lexington, Mass.: D.C. Heath, 1974.

Marais, J. S. *Maynier and the First Boer Republic.* Cape Town: Maskew Miller, 1944.

Marcum, John A. *Education, Race, and Social Change in South Africa*. Berkeley: University of California Press, 1982.

Mare, Gerhard. *Ethnicity and Politics in South Africa*. London and New Jersey: Zed Books, 1993.

Marks, Shula. "African and Afrikaner." *Journal of African History* 11, 3 (1970): 435–447.

Marks, Shula. *The Ambiguities of Dependence in South Africa: Class, Nationalism, and the State in Twentieth-Century Natal*. Baltimore and London: Johns Hopkins University Press, 1986.

Marks, Shula. "Class, Ideology, and the Bambatha Rebellion." In *Banditry, Rebellion, and Social Protest in Africa,* edited by Donald Crummey. London: James Currey, 1986.

Marks, Shula. "Khoisan Resistance to the Dutch in the Seventeenth and Eighteenth Centuries." *Journal of African History* 13, 1 (1972): 55–80.

Marks, Shula. "Natal, the Zulu Royal Family, and the Ideology of Segregation." *Journal of Southern African Studies* 4, 2 (April 1978): 172–194.

Marks, Shula. "Ruth First: A Tribute." *Journal of Southern African Studies* 10, 1 (October 1983): 123–124.

Marks, Shula. "The Tradition of Non-Racism in South Africa." Paper presented at a conference on "Democracy, Popular Precedents, Practice, Culture" sponsored by the History Workshop of the University of the Witwatersrand, Johannesburg, July 13–15, 1994.

Marks, Shula, and Atmore, Anthony, eds. *Economy and Society in Pre-industrial South Africa*. London: Longman, 1980.

Marks, Shula, and Rathbone, Richard, eds. *Industrialisation and Social Change in South Africa: African Class Formation, Culture and Consciousness, 1870–1930*. New York: Longman, 1982.

Marks, Shula, and Trapido, Stanley. "Lord Milner and the South African State." *History Workshop* 8 (1979): 50–85.

Marks, Shula, and Trapido, Stanley, eds. *The Politics of Race, Class, and Nationalism in Twentieth Century South Africa*. New York: Longman, 1987.

Marquard, Leo. *The Peoples and Policies of South Africa*. 4th ed. London: Oxford University Press, 1969.

Marshall, Thomas H., and Bottomore, Tom. *Citizenship and Social Class*. London and Concord, Mass.: Pluto Press, 1992.

Marx, Anthony W. *The Lessons of Struggle: South African Internal Opposition, 1960–1990*. New York and Oxford: Oxford University Press, 1992.

Matthews, Z. K. "The African Awakening and the Universities." Third T. B. Davie Memorial Lecture, University of Cape Town, August 13, 1961, reproduced by the South African Institute of Race Relations.

Meer, Fatima. "African Nationalism: Some Inhibiting Factors." In *South Africa: Sociological Perspectives,* edited by Heribert Adam. London: Oxford University Press, 1971.

Meer, Fatima. "Black Nationalism, Homeland Nationalism." In *Church and Nationalism in South Africa,* edited by Theo Sundermeier. Johannesburg: Ravan Press, 1975.

Meer, Fatima. "The Black Woman in South Africa." In *Black Renaissance: Papers from the Black Renaissance Convention,* December 1974, edited by Thoahlane Thoahlane. Johannesburg: Ravan Press, 1975.

Meusel, Alfred. "Revolution and Counter-Revolution." In *Encyclopedia of the Social Sciences,* pp. 367–375. New York: Macmillan, 1942.

Mingione, Enzo. *Fragmented Societies: A Sociology of Economic Life beyond the Market Paradigm.* Cambridge, Mass.: Basil Blackwell, 1991.

Mkhondo, Rich. "Chiefs Fight for Role in Democratic South Africa." Reuters News Reports via NewsNet [RNO1W], October 26, 1995.

Moon, J. Donald. *Constructing Community: Moral Pluralism and Tragic Conflicts.* Princeton, N.J.: Princeton University Press, 1993.

Motshabi, Khanya B., and Volks, Shreen G. "Towards Democratic Chieftaincy: Principles and Procedures." *Acta Juridica* (1991): 104–115.

Mullard, Chris. *Race, Power, and Resistance.* London: Routledge and Kegan Paul, 1985.

Munger, Edwin S. "The First Pan African Student Conference: A Letter from Edwin S. Munger." *African Field Reports,* 1952–1961. Cape Town: C. Struik, 1961.

Murray, Bruce. "The 'Democratic' Left at Wits, 1943–1948: The Federation of Progressive Students and Student Politics." Paper delivered at the History Workshop conference "Democracy—Popular Precedents, Practice, Culture" at the University of the Witwatersrand, Johannesburg, July 13–15, 1994.

Naison, Mark. *Communists in Harlem during the Depression.* Urbana: University of Illinois Press, 1983.

Nasson, Bill. "The Unity Movement Tradition: Its Legacy in Historical Consciousness." In *History From South Africa: Alternative Visions and Practices,* edited by Joshua Brown, et al. Philadelphia: Temple University Press, 1991.

National Union of South African Students. *Entrenched Clauses and Correlated Resolutions of the National Union of South African Students.* August 1969.

National Union of South African Students. *Half-Yearly Executive Meeting Report.* Cape Town, December 6, 1969.

National Union of South African Students. "Minutes." *Half-Yearly Executive Meeting Report.* Cape Town, December 6, 1969.

National Union of South African Students. *Minutes of the 50th Student Assembly,* July 15, 1973.

National Union of South African Students. "NUSAS Press Release" included in *The Report of President and Vice-President Department.* 45th Student Assembly, August 1969, Appendix B.

National Union of South African Students. "A Release to Overseas National Unions, International Organizations and Overseas Representatives Regarding the Archie Mafeje Issue." In *Report of the President and Vice-President Department.* 44th National Assembly, August 1968, Appendix A.

National Union of South African Students. *Report of President and Vice-President Department.* 44th National Assembly, July 1968, Appendix M.

National Union of South African Students. *Report of the President and Vice-President Department.* 49th Student Assembly, July 1972.

Ndegwa, Stephen N. "Citizenship and Ethnicity: An Examination of Two Transition Movements in Kenyan Politics." *American Political Science Review* 91, 3 (September 1997): 599–616.

Newman, James L. *The Peopling of Africa: A Geographic Interpretation.* New Haven, Conn.: Yale University Press, 1995.

Newton-King, Susan. "The Labour Market of the Cape Colony, 1807–28." In *Economy and Society in Pre-industrial South Africa,* edited by Shula Marks and Anthony Atmore. London: Longman Group, 1980.

Newton-King, Susan. "The Rebellion of the Khoi in Graaff-Reinet, 1799–1803." In *The Khoikhoi Rebellion in the Eastern Cape, 1799–1803,* edited by Susan Newton-King and V. C. Malherbe. Cape Town: Center for African Studies, University of Cape Town, 1981.

Ngcobo, S. Bangani. "African Elites in South Africa." *International Social Science Bulletin* 8, 3 (New York: UNESCO, 1956): 431–440.

Ngcongco, L. D. "John Tengo Jabavu, 1859–1921." In *Black Leaders in Southern African History,* edited by Christopher Saunders. London: Heinemann Educational, 1979.

Ngubane, Jordan. *An African Explains Apartheid.* London: Pall Mall Press, 1963.

Ngubane, Jordan K. *Conflict of Minds.* New York: Books in Focus, 1979.

Ngubane, Jordan (Kanyisa). "Congress at the Crossroads." *Inkundla ya Bantu* (March 13, 1947).

Ngubane, Jordan. *Ushaba: The Hurtle to Blood River.* Washington, D.C.: Three Continents Press, 1974.

Nolutshungu, Sam C. *Changing South Africa: Political Considerations.* New York: Africana, 1982.

Ntloedibe, Elias L. *Here Is a Tree: A Political Biography of Robert Mangaliso Sobukwe.* Gaborone, Botswana: Century-Turn Press, 1995.

Nzula, Albert; Potekhin, I. I.; and Zusmanovich, A. Z. *Forced Labour in Colonial Africa.* Translated by Hugh Jenkins. London: Zed Press, 1979.

Odendaal, Andre. *Vukani Bantu: The Beginnings of Black Protest Politics in South Africa to 1912.* Cape Town: David Philip, 1984.

O'Meara, Dan. "Analysing Afrikaner Nationalism: The Christian-National Assault on White Trade Unionism in South Africa, 1934–1948." *African Affairs* 77, 306 (January 1978): 45–72.

Padmore, George. *The Life and Struggles of Negro Toilers.* Hollywood, Calif.: Sun Dance Press, 1971.

Padmore, George. *Pan-Africanism or Communism.* New York: Doubleday and Co., 1971.

Pan Africanist Congress. *The National Mandate in Azania.* PAC Publication, c. 1981.

Patterson, Orlando. *Slavery as Social Death: A Comparative Study.* Cambridge, Mass.: Harvard University Press, 1982.

Peires, J. B. *The House of Phalo: A History of the Xhosa People in the Days of Their Independence.* Berkeley and Los Angeles: University of California Press, 1982.

Peled, Yoav. "Ethnic Democracy and the Legal Construction of Citizenship: Arab Citizen of the Jewish State." *The American Political Science Review* 86, 2 (June 1992): 432–443.

Pettit, Philip. *Republicanism: A Theory of Freedom and Government*. Oxford: Clarendon Press, 1997.

Pheko, Motsoko. *Apartheid: The Story of a Dispossessed People*. London: Marram
Books, 1984.

Pityana, Nyameko. "Afro-American Influences on the Black Consciousness Movement." Paper presented at a conference sponsored by the African Studies
Center at Howard University, Washington, D.C., 1979.

Plaatje, Solomon. *Native Life in South Africa*. London: P. S. King and Son, 1916.
Reprint, Athens: Ohio University Press, 1991.

Plaatje, Solomon. "A Retrospect." In *Sol Plaatje: Selected Writings*, edited by Brian
Willan. Johannesburg: Witwatersrand University Press, 1996.

Pocock, J. G. A. *The Machiavellian Moment*. Princeton, N.J.: Princeton University
Press, 1975.

Rich, Paul B. *White Power and Liberal Conscience: Racial Segregation and South African
Liberalism, 1921–1960*. Manchester: Manchester University Press, 1984.

Riesenberg, Peter. *Citizenship in the Western Tradition*. Chapel Hill and London:
University of North Carolina Press, 1992.

Robinson, Ronald, and Gallagher, John, with Denny, Alice. *Africa and the Victorians: The Official Mind of Imperialism*. London: Macmillan and Co., 1961.

Rogin, Michael. "In Defense of the New Left." *Democracy* (Fall 1983): 106–116.

Roux, Edward. *Time Longer Than Rope: A History of the Black Man's Struggle for
Liberation in South Africa*. 1948. Reprint, Madison: University of Wisconsin
Press, 1964.

Rubin, Neville. *History of the Relations between NUSAS, the Afrikaanse Studentebond
and Afrikaans University Centres*. Published by the National Union of South
African Students, 1959.

Russell, Margo. "Intellectuals and Academic Apartheid, 1950–1955." In *The
Liberal Dilemma in South Africa*, edited by Pierre Van den Berghe. New York:
St. Martin's Press, 1979.

Samuel, John. "Background Paper on the State of Education in South Africa."
Paper presented at the Ford Foundation Conference on Education in South
Africa, 1986.

Sandel, Mitchell J. "America's Search for a New Public Philosophy." *The Atlantic
Monthly* 277, 3 (March 1996): 57–74.

Saul, John. "South Africa: The Question of Strategy." *New Left Review* 160 (No-
vember/December 1986): 3–21.

Schlemmer, Lawrence. "The Stirring Giant: Observations on the Inkatha and
Other Black Political Movements in South Africa." In *The Apartheid Regime*,
edited by Robert Price and Carl Rosberg. Berkeley: Institute of International Studies, 1980.

Schutte, Gerrit. "Company and Colonists at the Cape, 1652–1795." In *The Shaping of South African Society, 1652–1840*, edited by Richard Elphick and Hermann Giliomee. 2nd revised ed. Middletown Conn.: Wesleyan University
Press, 1988.

Scott, Alan. *Ideology and the New Social Movements*. London: Unwin Hyman, 1990.

Scott, James C. *Domination and the Arts of Resistance: Hidden Transcripts*. New
Haven, Conn.: Yale University Press, 1990.

Selope-Thema, R. V. "How Congress Began." In *Reconstruction,* edited by Motholi Mutloastse. Johannesburg: Ravan Press, 1981.

Shils, Edward. "Dreams of Plentitude, Nightmares of Scarcity." In *Student Revolt,* edited by Seymour Martin Lipset and Philip G. Altbach. Boston: Houghton Mifflin, 1969.

Simkins, Charles. "Agricultural Production in the African Reserves of South Africa, 1918–1969." *Journal of Southern African Studies* 7, 2 (April 1981): 256–283.

Simons, H. J., and Simons, R. E. *Class and Colour in South Africa, 1850–1950.* New York: Penguin, 1968.

Sitas, Ari, and Bonnin, Debbie. "Lessons from the Sarmcol Strike." In *Popular Struggles in South Africa,* edited by William Cobbett and Robin Cohen. Trenton, N.J.: Africa World Press, 1988.

Sklar, Martin J. *The Corporate Reconstruction of American Capitalism, 1890–1916.* Cambridge: Cambridge University Press, 1988.

Sklar, Richard L. "The African Frontier for Political Science." In *Africa and the Disciplines,* edited by Robert Bates, V. Y. Mudimbe, and Jean O'Barr. Chicago and London: University of Chicago Press, 1993.

Sklar, Richard L. "Beyond Capitalism and Socialism in Africa." *Journal of Modern African Studies* 26, 1 (March 1988): 1–21.

Sklar, Richard L. "The Colonial Imprint on African Political Thought." In *African Independence: The First Twenty-five Years,* edited by Gwendolen Carter and Patrick O'Meara. Bloomington: Indiana University Press, 1985.

Slovo, Joe. "The Theory of the South African Revolution." Paper presented at a Conference on the "Socio-economic Trends and Policies in Southern Africa," Dar es Salaam, November 29–December 7, 1975.

Smock, David. *Black Education in South Africa: The Current Situation.* South African Education Program, Institute of International Education, January 1983.

South African Communist Party. *South African Communists Speak: Documents from the History of the South African Communist Party, 1915–1980.* London: Inkululeko, 1985.

South African Institute of Race Relations. *Survey of Race Relations in South Africa (1965).* Johannesburg: South African Institute of Race Relations, 1966.

South African Institute of Race Relations. *Survey of Race Relations in South Africa (1971).* Johannesburg: South African Institute of Race Relations, 1972.

South African Institute of Race Relations. *Survey of Race Relations in South Africa (1979).* Johannesburg: South African Institute of Race Relations, 1980.

Stanbridge, Roland. "Contemporary African Political Organizations and Movements." In *The Apartheid Regime,* edited by Robert M. Price and Carl G. Rosberg. Berkeley: Institute of International Studies, 1980.

Stoler, Ann Laura. *Race and the Education of Desire: Foucault's History of Sexuality and the Colonial Order of Things.* Durham and London: Duke University Press, 1995.

Strong, J. A. "Political Socialization: A Study of Southern African Elites." Ph.D. dissertation, Syracuse University, 1968.

Stubbs, Aelred, C. R. "Martyr of Hope: A Personal Memoir." In Steve Biko, *I Write What I Like: A Selection of His Writings,* edited by Aelred Stubbs. San Francisco: Harper and Row, 1978.

Switzer, Les. *Power and Resistance in an African Society: The Ciskei Xhosa and the Making of South Africa.* Madison: University of Wisconsin Press, 1993.

Szeftel, Morris. "The Transkei: Conflict Externalization and Black Exclusivism." In *Collected Seminar Papers on the Societies of Southern Africa in the 19th and 20th Centuries.* Vol. 3. University of London, Institute of Commonwealth Studies (October 1971–June 1972).

Tabata, I. B. *Apartheid: Cosmetics Exposed.* Cape Town: Prometheus Publications, 1985.

Tabata, I. B. *The Awakening of the People.* London: Spokesman Books, 1974.

Tabata, I. B. "On the Organization of the African People: Extracts from a Letter to a Friend (Nelson Mandela)." June 16, 1948. Beineke Rare Manuscripts Collection, Yale University.

Talmon, Yonina. "Millenarian Movements." *Archives Européennes de Sociologie* 7, 2 (1966): 159–200.

Thompson, Leonard. *The Political Mythology of Apartheid.* New Haven, Conn.: Yale University Press, 1985.

Tiro, Ongokopotse Ramothiki. "Bantu Education." In *The Turfloop Testimony,* edited by G. M. Nkondo. Johannesburg: Ravan Press, 1976.

Tonnies, Ferdinand. *Community and Society.* East Lansing: Michigan State University Press, 1957.

Toussaint. "'Fallen among Liberals': An Ideology of Black Consciousness." *African Communist,* no. 78 (1979): 18–30.

Trapido, Stanley. "'The Friends of the Natives': Merchants, Peasants, and the Political Ideological Structure of Liberalism in the Cape, 1854–1910." In *Economy and Society in Pre-industrial South Africa,* edited by Shula Marks and Anthony Atmore. London: Longman Group, 1980.

Tsotsi, W. M. *From Chattel to Wage Slavery: A New Approach to South African History.* Maseru: Print and Publishing Co., 1981.

Van der Ross, R. E. *The Rise and Decline of Apartheid.* Cape Town: Tafelberg Publishers, 1986.

Walshe, Peter. *Black Nationalism in South Africa: A Short History.* Johannesburg: Ravan Press, 1973.

Walshe, Peter. *The Rise of African Nationalism in South Africa: The African National Congress, 1912–1952.* Berkeley: University of California Press, 1971.

Webster, Eddie. "Competing Paradigms: Towards a Critical Sociology in Southern Africa." *Social Dynamics* 11, 1 (1985): 44–48.

Welsh, David. "The Political Economy of Afrikaner Nationalism." In *South Africa: Economic Growth and Political Change,* edited by Adrian Leftwich. New York: St. Martin's Press, 1974.

Whitaker, C. S. *The Politics of Tradition: Continuity and Change in Northern Nigeria, 1946–1966.* Princeton, N.J.: Princeton University Press, 1970.

Williams, William Appleman. *The Great Evasion.* New York: New Viewpoints, 1974.

Wilson, Edward T. *Russia and Black Africa before World War II.* New York: Holmes and Meier, 1974.

Wilson, Monica Hunter. *Reaction to Conquest: Effects of Contact with Europeans on the Pondo of South Africa.* 2nd ed. London and New York: Oxford University Press, 1961.

Wolfenstein, Eugene Victor. "Race, Racism, and Racial Liberation." *Western Political Quarterly* 30, 1 (March 1977): 163–182.

Wolfenstein, E. Victor. "Reflections on Malcolm X and Black Feminism." Paper prepared for the annual meeting of the Western Political Science Association, Seattle, March 14–16, 1996.

Wolfenstein, E. Victor. *The Victims of Democracy: Malcolm X and the Black Revolution.* Los Angeles: University of California Press, 1981.

Woods, Donald. *Biko.* London: Paddington Press, 1978. Revised ed., New York: Henry Holt, 1987.

Wright, Erik Olin. "Intellectuals and the Class Structure of Capitalist Society." In *Between Labor and Capital,* edited by Pat Walker. Boston: South End Press, 1979.

Year Book of International Organizations 1983–84. New York: K. G. Sauer Verlag, 1984.

Index

Index

C. R. D. HALISI is currently a commissioned scholar with the Project on the Public Influences of African-American Churches. He is also engaged in research on citizenship and political development in South Africa. He teaches Political Science and PanAfrican Studies at California State University, Los Angeles.

CPSIA information can be obtained
at www.ICGtesting.com
Printed in the USA
LVOW04*0000261215

467857LV00011B/85/P

9 780253 335890